The Reform of Public Services under New Labour

The Reform of Public Services under New Labour

Narratives of Consumerism

Catherine Needham
Department of Politics
Queen Mary, University of London, UK

© Catherine Needham 2007

First published 2007 by
PALGRAVE MACMILLAN
Houndmills, Basingstoke, Hampshire RG21 6XS and
175 Fifth Avenue, New York, N.Y. 10010
Companies and representatives throughout the world

PALGRAVE MACMILLAN is the global academic imprint of the Palgrave Macmillan division of St. Martin's Press, LLC and of Palgrave Macmillan Ltd. Macmillan® is a registered trademark in the United States, United Kingdom and other countries. Palgrave is a registered trademark in the European Union and other countries.

ISBN 13: 978–1–4039–9531–5   hardback
ISBN 10: 1–4039–9531–1   hardback

This book is printed on paper suitable for recycling and made from fully managed and sustained forest sources. Logging, pulping and manufacturing processes are expected to conform to the environmental regulations of the country of origin.

A catalogue record for this book is available from the British Library.

Library of Congress Cataloging-in-Publication Data
Needham, Catherine, 1974–
    The reform of public services under New Labour : narratives of
    consumerism / Catherine Needham.
        p. cm.
    Includes bibliographical references and index.
    ISBN 1–4039–9531–1 (alk. paper)
        1. Human services–Great Britain. 2. Human services–Great Britain–
    Decision making–Citizen participation. 3. Great Britain–Social policy.
    4. Consumption (Economics) I. Title.

    HV248.N284 2007
    361.6'80941–dc22   2007018271

10   9   8   7   6   5   4   3   2   1
16   15   14   13   12   11   10   09   08   07

Printed and bound in Great Britain by
Antony Rowe Ltd, Chippenham and Eastbourne

Contents

List of Tables and Boxes

Tables

Boxes

Acknowledgements

This book, like many, owes its completion to the support and encouragement of many people. Grateful thanks must go to all those who were interviewed for the research, who willingly gave their time and experience. Thanks are owed to the Nuffield Foundation, which funded the focus groups. For extremely helpful comments on drafts thanks go to Ilan Jacobs, Martin McIvor and Graeme Trayner. Judith Bara provided essential input on research methods.

Many of the ideas in the book were tried out in conferences, seminars and workshops and have improved immeasurably as a result. I would like to thank all those who provided comments and suggestions at these events.

Thanks go to Gillian Peele and David Miller. George Jones was extremely helpful too. Thanks must also go to the Economic and Social Research Council for providing financial support for the research that underpins this volume.

The biggest debt is to Blake Woodham without whose support the book would never have made it this far.

The book owes its strengths to all these people. They are not of course responsible for its weaknesses.

Parts of Chapters 6 and 10 are revisions of articles I published in, respectively, *Public Administration*, vol. 84 (2006), no. 4, 845–60 and *Renewal*, vol. 14 (2006), no. 2, 55–60, adapted by kind permission of the editors of those journals.

Catherine Needham

1
Introduction: Citizens and Consumers

At the doctor's surgery, the local school, the JobCentre Plus, public service users have complex and multiple needs. However, they are likely to share a desire for prompt, polite and responsive service, which meets their individual requirements and enables them to feel engaged in the service process. These common and apparently uncontroversial expectations are central to the controversy over New Labour's public service reforms in the United Kingdom (UK). All of the attitudes listed are linked to consumerism in public services – a force that can, according to rival interpretations, drive up service standards or corrode the collective status underlying citizenship. Supporters of the consumer-oriented approach express bewilderment that anyone, other than unapologetic paternalists or producerists, could resist its penetration into public services. Critics of consumerism see its common sense pretensions as a hegemonic project to erode the distinctive civic space of public services. Both sides agree that consumerism has played a minor role in public services in the past, but they profoundly disagree about the role it should play in the future.

It is the extreme reactions that consumerism provokes, and the efforts of its supporters and critics to unmask the agenda of the opposition, that makes it a fascinating lens through which to explore New Labour's approach to public services. Government ministers proclaim the importance of customer-oriented public services, whilst social democrats point to a heritage of a decommodified welfare state. Historians highlight the political consciousness of the progressive consumer in battles over food price and quality, free trade and anti-apartheid struggles, whilst civic republican theorists denounce the individualising logic of *homo economicus*. Through exploring the role of consumerism in public services, it is possible to understand New

1

Labour's project for the reform of the welfare state, and to contribute to an understanding of its interpretation of citizenship.

Citizenship and consumerism

The relationship between citizenship and consumerism has taken central place in the progressive battleground, as the Blair government promotes its version of a consumerised citizenship against the traditions of citizenship endorsed by many on the centre-left of politics. A distinctive feature of this fight is the way that the combatants speak past each other, disagreeing on the terms of engagement. At issue usually is not the meaning of citizenship, but what it means to be a consumer. For whilst there is broad consensus about the nature of a good citizen – participatory, community-oriented, altruistic, law-abiding – no such consensus is apparent on the consumer. Much of the confusion, claim and counter-claim surrounding New Labour's public service reforms concerns conflicting accounts of what it means to treat the citizen as a consumer.

For critics of New Labour, the government has deliberately sought to rework the welfare state around a notion of the citizen-as-consumer – importing the restless acquisitiveness and individualism of the consumer into a sphere where other, more self-denying and collective norms of citizenship should operate. Marquand, for example, questions, 'how to preserve the values of citizenship and service in the face of consumerist pressures' (2004, p. 123). According to an earlier work by this author, 'consumerism may be fostering privatised and resentful citizen-consumers whose expectations of government can never be met' (Needham, 2003, p. 33). Lawson calls on the left 'to promote citizenship voice over consumerised choice' (2005). Rose highlights the ways in which 'advanced liberal governmentality' remakes parents, patients, prisoners as contractualised consumers, '...linked into a society through acts of socially sanctioned consumption and responsible choice...' (Rose, 1999, pp. 164–6). In these accounts, a consumerist approach is corrosive of citizenship, making public service transactions mirror market analogues as closely as possible, leaving the consumer armed only with an exit power and the injunction *caveat emptor*. Such concerns are not new. They have their roots in much older republican and social democratic discussions about the extent to which the public realm should be protected from commodification.

Government ministers have rebutted such arguments, with John Reid taking particular exception to the 'simple bifurcation' that contrasts the citizen with the consumer (2005). When ministers make a case for public services becoming more consumer-oriented, however, they are not defending acquisitive individualism so much as equating consumerism with a different tradition: that of user agency, empowerment and anti-elitism. According to John Reid, 'Consumerism is but one expression of past successes in the Left's efforts to "liberate" the majority from constraints of class, gender and poverty. It advances the desire for autonomy that is central to the concept of democratic self-government' (Reid, 2005). Critics of consumerism in public services are denounced by Reid for their paternalism, their refusal to allow people to make choices in important spheres of their lives. Anti-consumerism is associated with an unsustainable nostalgia for an idealised welfare state. As former health minister Alan Milburn put it, 'We are in a consumer age whether people like it or not. What will destroy the public services is the idea that you can retain the ethos of the 1940s in the 21st century' (Waugh, 2003). Anti-consumerism is equated with producerism, a knee-jerk defence of the privileges of workers in which user needs are sidelined. In these attacks, government ministers are joined by organisations such as the National Consumer Council (NCC), which is deeply suspicious of anti-consumerist urges within public services. As NCC Deputy Chief Executive Philip Cullum put it in a speech:

> I believe that taking a consumer-centred approach is vital to the development of our public services. This isn't about turning the public sector into the private sector, or imposing market values onto public services. It is about treating people decently – giving everyone access to essential services, ensuring they are of as high a standard as possible, and delivering them in a way that reflects the reality of users' lives.
>
> Cullum, 2004

The citizen-good/consumer-bad approach has also been rejected by historians of consumerism, who embrace a richer vision of the consumer. In the work of Hilton (2003) and Trentmann (2004, 2006) there are calls for awareness of the historicity of the consumer. Trentmann points out 'Citizenship and consumerism are omnipresent categories rather than successive ideal types' (2004, p. 396). He draws attention to the 'contingent and cyclical nature of the relationship between citizenship and consumerism', and the 'spectrum of social movements that today speak out on a vast range of consumer interests, from nutrition to the environment, and from disadvantaged consumers to choice and media regulation' (2006, p. 52). Hilton reminds readers of the importance of consumerism as 'a form of empowerment for consumers too often overlooked in a set of economic and political relations dominated by the interests of workers and employers' (2003, p. 337).

Clarke has also argued for a less simplistic account than that offered by the abstractions of citizen-as-political and consumer-as-economic approach, calling for sensitivity to the *social*, the 'conflicted and contested terrain' where government and public interact (Clarke, forthcoming). He highlights the progressive forces pushing public service professionals towards greater user responsiveness, such as the role of social movements around race/ethnicity, gender, sexuality, age and disability in promoting diversity (Clarke, forthcoming).

Given these multiple and contrasting perspectives on what it means to be a consumer of public services, there is no way straightforwardly to read off consumerist attributes in New Labour's reforms. Nor can the consumer's relationship with the citizen be asserted as a matter of principle. To explore public services through the lens of consumerism requires clearer criteria than currently exist. It should not be assumed however, that the role of consumer is infinitely malleable, nor that it is the same as being a citizen. Across these definitions there are common strands to the consumer, which provide a way into studying the concept. At the most obvious, they have a shared emphasis on the use of goods and services. However, they also offer a distinctive ontology and epistemology. By developing a clearer understanding of what it means to be a consumer, it is possible to explore how far New Labour's reforms of public services have been consumerist in nature, and what implications this has for citizenship.

Exploring consumerist trends within public services links into broader debates within British politics, crucially centred on the future of the Labour Party following the departure of Tony Blair as Prime Minister. Gordon Brown secured his position as the key rival to Blair in part by refusing to endorse the consumerist and market-oriented approaches to public service delivery that were being pursued by Blair, Reid, Milburn and others. In a widely quoted speech to the Social Market Foundation in 2003, Brown acknowledged the problems of introducing markets into health and education and called for 'the courage to recognise where markets do not work' (Brown, 2003). He has been optimistic about the power of a public service ethos to deliver high quality services rather than relying on competition and user choice to discipline providers (Peston, 2006, p. 299). Thus through exploring the implication of markets, choice and consumerism in public services, it is possible to understand better not only the future of the welfare state but also the future direction of the Labour Party.

Narratives of public service delivery

This book develops this understanding by drawing on three narratives within New Labour discourses on public services. The first two are consumerist narratives, based firstly on rights and standardisation and secondly on choice and differentiation. By recognising the composite strands within consumerism it becomes easier to understand how one set of authors can talk about consumerism without using the same vocabulary or sets of assumptions as other authors. It also becomes possible to draw links between reform strands which superficially look unconnected – for example New Labour's demand for public service users to have more choice, but also to get more consistent services. By showing that these narratives of consumerism have a shared logic, and a common account of the citizen as consumer, it is possible to then go on to explore how far New Labour's reforms are characterised by consumerism. There is also a third narrative explored here, that of coproduction. The third narrative is oriented around empowerment, opportunity and responsibility. It captures elements of the New Labour project which appear to run counter to consumerist tendencies. However, in exploring the use of this narrative in New Labour discourses, its potential to be co-opted as a narrative of consumerism is revealed.

The analysis is rooted in a broader approach to change in the welfare state over the previous 30 years, which has been captured elsewhere in the term 'marketisation' (Crouch, 2003, 2007; Clarke, 2004; Whitfield, 2006; Finlayson, 2007). The argument made here is that consumerist approaches have been an important sub-set of marketisation reforms, helping to explain the distinctive terrain of public service reform under New Labour, and shaping the very language through which political goals have been expressed.

The aim of the book is to focus not on *ad hoc* constructions of the public service user, but on stable and recurring patterns across different public services, at local and central government level and over time. Using content analysis of government texts and interviews with policy actors in central and local government, the book seeks to offer an understanding of how far the New Labour governments have developed a consumerist citizenship regime. Through exploring the usage of a series of keywords the book provides a comparison across public services, between levels of government and over time.

The focus is on central and local government in England since 1997. The research does not look systematically at the devolved governments in Scotland, Wales and Northern Ireland, recognising that these areas are developing their own distinctive patterns of public service reform (Jeffrey, 2004). The analysis shares the approach of governance scholars, in recognising the networks of partners involved with central and local government in the delivery of public services in England: executive agencies, non-departmental public bodies, private contractors and voluntary sector organisations (Rhodes, 1997; Bevir and Rhodes, 2003; Hill, 2005). However the focus is on policy actors within elected institutions – politicians and bureaucrats – as the most likely to be the lead partner in a partnership arrangement and to play a key role in shaping the citizenship regime.

The book does not have an explicit comparative focus, although it is clear that similar themes are evident in many other countries. Jenson and Phillips, for example, talk about changes to the citizen-state relationship in Canada, tracing a process of 'dismantling and reconstituting citizenship' in the late twentieth century, moving 'from equity towards marketisation' (2001, p. 71). These broader trends indicate that New Labour's approach is in part a manifestation of a larger trend. However, the examples of Scotland and Wales – the governments of both of which have expressed opposition to consumerised public services (Templeton, 2003; Hetherington, 2004) – indicate that pluralism is still possible – and that claims to 'a "reality" which is static, immutable or inexorably unfolding in a given direction' must be recognised as deliberate constructions by interested parties (Hay, 2004, p. 147).

Structure of the book

The next chapter of the book links the discussion of the citizen as consumer to other accounts of New Labour, explains what a narrative approach to political explanation involves and discusses a number of possible citizenship regimes. The chapter that follows focuses on the relationship between citizenship and consumerism, setting out what a consumerist citizenship regime would look like. It explores the contradictions inherent within consumerism, in which the consumer can be empowered and sovereign, or manipulated and alienated by constant pressures to consume. Definitions of terms – consumer, customer, consumerism – are also provided here.

The fourth chapter considers New Labour's approach in historical perspective to understand better the citizenship regime inherited in

1997. The chapter contrasts the Poor Law assumption that citizenship was incompatible with reliance on public services with the Beveridgean assumption that citizenship was intimately linked to public service use. The growing political salience of the user of public services from the 1960s is identified, linked to the individualism and anti-professional thrust of public choice theory and Thatcherite Conservatism, as well as new left calls for more inclusive and participatory services. The Citizen's Charter, launched by John Major in 1991, is identified as a key milestone given its emphasis on equipping the user with information and redress if services did not meet standards. However a consumerist citizenship regime was not fully developed by 1997, as public services were often responsive to their users only through channels of complaint.

Chapter 5 outlines the broad contours of New Labour's public service reforms, preparing the ground for the more detailed textual analysis that follows in subsequent chapters. Taking the new public management paradigm as a starting point the discussion traces the common themes of Conservative and New Labour public service reforms, based around cost-containment, decentralisation and risk transfer. It highlights the underlying logic of marketisation within these reforms and discusses consumerism as one aspect of a broader marketisation approach.

The sixth chapter draws on the speeches of Tony Blair, to explore the ways in which the Prime Minister uses language to refer to those who use and benefit from public services. Keywords are developed which can be the basis for exploring consumerism through content analysis. The chapter highlights the importance that Blair accords to certain keywords – particularly community and parent – in his speeches, and the relatively small amount of attention paid to the citizen, the client and the consumer. However, in the way that Blair frames public service reforms in terms of public expectations and the need to reject ideology in favour of the pragmatic use of a range of service providers, there are clear strands of a consumer orientation. In talking about public services, Blair particularly emphasises the standardisation narrative, saying less about differentiation and coproduction. However the balance shifts over time, with these two alternative narratives becoming more important in Labour's second and third terms.

It is important to trace how the macro-political emphasis on consumerism is translated into tangible policy initiatives. Drawing on textual analysis of command papers (white and green papers) published by central government departments, Chapter 7 explores how the language and approach of consumerism is being perceived and applied by Whitehall policy actors. The documents show that standardisation is again the main narrative used, although choice becomes more important over time. Within the coproduction narrative, engagement and empowerment are given little attention compared to opportunity and responsibility, and analysis of context highlights how much these documents rely on individualised and punitive versions of coproduction. As in Blair's speeches, community and parent are the most widely used keywords, and rising user expectations are used to justify new patterns of private sector involvement in the delivery of services.

Chapter 8 considers how far the central government agenda of consumerism has been applied at local level in England. Local government has a much more direct interface with citizens than central government, and delivers or oversees most key services. Drawing on document analysis conducted by the author in 18 local authorities and interviews with officers and councillors, the chapter discusses the significance of the customer within local government and changing patterns of service delivery which reflect this language. Using content analysis software, patterns of usage are identified, highlighting again the discursive importance of community and the standardisation narrative. Standardisation is more important at the local than the national level, and initiatives such as choice and personalisation appear underdeveloped. This may be because changing trends at the national level have yet to be established within local government, or it may be that local authorities do not feel they have got close enough to a consistent service to abandon the effort in favour of differentiation. The second most utilised narrative in local government is coproduction, with the same combination of opportunity and responsibility that was evident in the national documents.

The term customer is the second most widely used keyword in local government after community. The chapter goes on to discuss the findings of interviews in central and local government which reveal the ways that the term customer is used in their organisations. The pattern is largely one of support for the term, but no clear organisational consensus on what it means. Different policy actors apply varying concepts of the customer, some based on a strong notion of choice, other based on the rights of users, and a third set emphasising courtesy and respect. Local government officers are generally enthusiastic about the language of customer, whereas councillors are more wary of the tensions between being a customer and being a citizen.

In Chapter 9 the empirical focus shifts from government to the user of public services. Ministerial speeches and white papers emphasise that the consumerist approach is demand-led, driven by public expectations. The survey material on what public service users want from their services is ambiguous, however, and highly dependent on how questions are worded. To understand these tensions and paradoxes, and make better sense of public attitudes to public service use, the chapter reports findings from ten focus groups conducted by the author, in which detailed exploration is undertaken into what citizens feel about and want from public services. The focus groups explore how people experience being users of public services; how they reconcile their roles as customer and citizen; what they want from public services; and their attitudes towards the public and private sectors as service providers. The research showed that respondents were much more familiar with being a customer than being a citizen, but retained a sense of the distinctiveness of public services, and were resistant to choice and private sector provision as creating elitism and risk.

The final chapter brings together the evidence presented in the book, in support of the hypothesis that the New Labour government has developed a consumerist citizenship regime. Responsiveness to service users is identified as a necessary goal for public services but the incoherent and blunt instrument of consumerism is argued to be inadequate as a way of achieving it. Consumerism encourages users to see public services as a way to satisfy individual demands, an approach which clashes with users' own understanding of public services as well as the demands of equity and solidarity. Beyond limitations for the individual user, consumerism has nothing to say about the collective goals of public services, which include pooling risk, redistributing advantage, delivering fairness, and providing good terms and conditions for the workforce.

The chapter moves on to explore alternative methods of reforming public services. It calls on government to explicitly recognise that public services play a role beyond the utilitarian one of maximising individual satisfaction, and to encourage experimentation with new forms of involvement which recognise the service user as collective participant. The book ends with insights from the coproduction literature, arguing for a form of public service delivery that involves users, but steers clear of the self-service state.

2
Public Service Reform: Narratives and Regimes

To characterise public service reform under New Labour, it is necessary to provide an explanatory framework and a set of tools of analysis. The research seeks to understand how public service reforms are positioned in a series of texts – Blair speeches, command papers, local government corporate plans – which provide a partial but illuminating account of discursive and policy priorities under New Labour. With its interest in discourse, the research takes an interpretative approach, and considers how these texts construct particular narratives around public services. The language of narratives is increasingly used in politics: commentators from within and outside New Labour have talked of a need for the Party to define or update its narrative (Taylor, 2001; Miliband, 2006; Toynbee, 2006). Observers of David Cameron's Conservative Party explain its repositioning in terms of a search for a narrative (Vine, 2005; Cowell, 2006). The notions of story-telling and internal logics contained within a narrative are a useful way to understand political purpose and identity.

To compare different sorts of public service narratives, the concept of a citizenship regime is utilised. Regimes provide stability and institutionalisation to political projects. The citizenship regime concept allows exploration of the ways in which the citizen is positioned within public service reforms, enabling comparisons to be drawn between regimes based on liberal notions of citizenship and those utilising libertarian, civic republican and communitarian conceptions.

This chapter positions the research within existing accounts of New Labour and develops the narrative and regime tools which will be used in subsequent chapters. It also provides a definition of public services, outlining the historical and theoretical contingency of the public service set, and discussing differences between services provided by the state and the market.

Studying New Labour

This work sits alongside other accounts of the distinctive features of Blair's New Labour party. Multiple texts have attempted to draw out the key themes of this political project. Some of these have readily entered into the version of past and present offered by the Labour leadership (Mandelson and Liddle, 1996; Giddens, 1998; Gould, 1998), drawing on what Hay calls 'Labour's highly mythologised past', and presenting New Labour in contrast to a discredited 'old Labour' (Hay, 2003, p. 186). Others have offered a more sceptical model of New Labour (Driver and Martell, 1998; Freeden, 1999; Hay, 1999; Finlayson, 2003a; Fairclough, 2000; Levitas, 2005; Hall, 2003; Marquand, 2004; Bevir, 2005). New Labour's relationship to political traditions, including social democracy, new liberalism, neoliberalism and Thatcherism has been interpreted differently in each account. Whilst the approach taken here has relevance to these debates, its focus is rather on how traditions of citizenship have been developed within the welfare state, and how they have been reinterpreted by New Labour.

In seeking to understand public service policy under New Labour, the book seeks to follow the path taken by a range of authors in identifying common themes which transcend particular public service areas. Some authors have highlighted the managerial orientation of New Labour (Clarke, 2004, p. 41; Lister, 2003, p. 429; Hall, 2003, p. 21). For others the 'nodal point' uniting disparate activities within the New Labour project is work (Dwyer, 1998; Lister, 2002; Clarke and Newman, 2004). Levitas has probed the discourses of social exclusion constructed by New Labour (2005). Crouch focuses on the commercialisation of public services, emphasising privatisation, contracting out and the introduction of markets (2003). Whitfield similarly looks at service reforms through the lens of marketisation (2006). For many of these authors, consumerism is a subsidiary theme, illustrative of the managerialism, work-orientation or marketisation of New Labour, but rarely used as a powerful explanatory variable in its own right. Here it is used as the key element uniting disparate elements of New Labour's agenda: including rights, choice, opportunity and responsibility. However the place of consumerism within overarching themes of public service reform, crucially individualism and marketisation, requires attention and is returned to in subsequent chapters.

The book offers an interpretive account of New Labour, and as such follows the approach taken by Hay (1999, 2003), Bevir and Rhodes (2003, 2006) and Bevir (2005). In their account of interpreting British governance, Bevir and Rhodes explain, 'Interpretive approaches begin from the insight that to understand actions, practices and institutions, we need to grasp the relevant meanings, the beliefs and preferences of the people involved' (Bevir and Rhodes, 2003, p. 1). They use the notion of 'traditions' – or what Finlayson calls 'prior institutionalised systems of meaning' (2004, p. 154) – as the basis of understanding social discourses. 'Traditions are not fixed entities... [they] are contingent products of the ways in which people develop specific beliefs, preferences and actions (Bevir and Rhodes, 2003, pp. 33–4). Such an approach presumes a dialectical relationship between tradition and agency: 'Tradition has no existence apart from the beliefs and actions of individual agents, and yet individuals always reach beliefs and attempt actions against the background of tradition' (Bevir and Rhodes, 2004, p. 160).

Narratives play a key role in the interpretive approach. They 'explain actions by reference to the beliefs and preferences of the relevant individuals ... [and] encompass the maps, questions, languages and historical stories used to explain British government' (Bevir and Rhodes, 2003, p. 26). Narrative approaches involve the study of what has been elsewhere called discourse, rhetoric, language and communication. Fischer highlights the importance of discourse to understanding policy outcomes: 'Discourse...does more than reflect a social or political "reality"; it actually constitutes much of the reality that has to be explained' (Fischer, 2003, p. vii–viii). Similarly Clarke *et al* argue: 'Rhetoric – the articulation of identities, trajectories and projects – is never "mere rhetoric". It is part of the political processes of building, cementing and mobilising alliances – and demobilising actual or potential opposition' (2000, p. 11). Fairclough argues that language is particularly relevant in relation to government: '...much of the action of government *is* language' (2000, p. 157). Finlayson highlights the importance of communication: 'The mechanism by which ideas are operationalised is communication. It is only through communication that ideas are able to be manifested either as ideological programmes or policy prescriptions' (Finlayson, 2003a, p. 22). All of these authors use methodologies that involve interpreting the ways that policy actors use language and the power dynamics behind it. A preference for the term narrative here is deliberate, however. A narrative has more specificity than analysis of discourse (Morrell, 2006, p. 372). It involves story-telling and internal logics: 'We account for actions, practices and institutions by telling a story about how they came to be as they are and perhaps also about how they are preserved' (Bevir and Rhodes, 2003, p. 20).

Studying New Labour through a narrative approach is particularly relevant given that the party has consciously and explicitly characterised its own search for ideological direction in narrative terms. As discussed above, ministers and advisers have talked of the need for the party to have a clear narrative to offer to voters (Taylor, 2001; Miliband, 2005; Milburn, 2006). Others have critiqued New Labour in terms of its absence of a coherent or suitably progressive narrative (Toynbee, 2006; Gamble, 2007, p. 34).

The narrative-based, interpretive approach taken here has more specificity than the general language of narrative, although retaining its sense of story-telling and self-justification. The approach is positioned in contrast to positivism or modern empiricism (Bevir, 2005), and as such has been criticised by Dowding for its rejection of the notion of truth and evidence (Dowding, 2004). Bevir acknowledges that interpretivism assumes that the author offers 'a narrative that is just one among a field of possible narratives' (Bevir, 2005, p. 125). However, this is not to say that all interpretations are equally plausible, rather that definitive accounts will remain elusive. The tools of interpretivism are well suited to the study of consumerism in public services, because it relies on the different narratives that people construct about the roles and expectations of the public service user. Fischer's more general point about discourse-based approaches holds true here: 'Whereas empiricism treats language and meaning as an ornament of social behaviour, a discursive approach makes clear that discourse and social meaning are internal to the very social systems we seek to research' (2003, p. viii).

A range of methodologies can be used to understand New Labour's approach to public services. Given the interest here in the way that policy actors use terminology and construct narratives around public services the approach taken is one of textual analysis – exploring and comparing the use of language in a range of different texts. In seeking to deconstruct New Labour discourse, the approach follows that of Fairclough (2000), Finlayson (2003a), Lister (2000, 2003), Clarke (2004, forthcoming), Levitas (2005), among others. Much attention has been paid to New Labour's preference for certain words and phrases over others – social justice rather than equality; social exclusion rather than poverty; rights only where twinned with responsibilities or duties (Lister, 2000; Finlayson, 2003a; Levitas, 2005) – and its fondness for verb-free sentence structures (Fairclough, 2000).

Here, to allow systematic comparisons to be made between levels of government, between services and over time, quantitative analysis is undertaken, using a series of keywords. On the basis of the quantitative findings, more detailed qualitative work is done. The content analytic method allows sensitivity to change over time, exploring data from across the period since 1997, rather than requiring that New Labour be characterised as unitary and unchanging. Similarly the book seeks to understand the differences between services, rather than assuming that Labour's health policies and criminal justice policies have been driven by the same assumptions and expectations. Claims made elsewhere about differences between services – such as that a punitive approach to welfare has been combined with a commitment to preserve the universalism of health and education services (Bevir, 2005, p. 95) – can be explored systematically through the comparative methods used here.

Analysis of language cannot provide a comprehensive account of the motivations or underlying rationale of policy actors. Actors may deliberately use language to mask their intentions, or they may make trivial choices to opt for one word rather than another. Language is not an accurate guide to policy implementation. As Clarke warns, 'We are perhaps too ready to treat policy texts and political visions as if they translate immediately and unproblematically into practice' (2004, p. 30). The approach taken here relies on a claim that the way that policy actors explain and justify their approaches in public documents, the narratives they construct around policies, are a relevant dimension in characterising the regimes that the actors seek to create. The analysis is by necessity simplifying. The complex and contested nature of public service design, delivery and use is recognised here, although the tools of analysis cannot reflect all this complexity. As Finlayson reflects, '...making sense of New Labour ultimately requires making sense of everything else. A project of such scope is impossible' (2003a, p. 21).

This book is written from a perspective sympathetic to concerns about the decline of the public, and seeks to home in on one aspect of this process – the threat to a tradition of public services as an expression of citizenship – to subject it to systematic analysis and to probe if and why it might have occurred. As discussed above, there has been much recent analysis in the UK of the relationship between the individual and the collective as a result of public service reforms and the perceived inadequacy of the Blairite balance between the market and the state. The book sites narratives of public service reform within these broader debates, exposing the underlying assumptions and paradoxes of New Labour's approach. However the conclusion rejects a golden age theory of civically informed public services. Nor does it offer a vilification of consumerism, or seek to deny the importance of consumer movements in improving service provision. Rather it argues that narratives of consumerism are being utilised by policy actors to remake public services in a way that leaves no room for collectivist traditions of citizenship. Public services must retain and strengthen their link to such collective traditions or else they risk marginalisation by politicians who can offer individual consumers more alluring deals in the private sector.

Studying public services

The research must begin with a clear understanding of what is meant by public services. The term 'public services' has become the preferred language to refer to what has elsewhere, and in earlier times, been called welfare services or the welfare state. To talk of 'public services' is to refer to a bundle of goods and services, although defining the content and size of this bundle is problematic. Even the welfare state was, as Clarke *et al* point out, 'an imaginary entity rather than an organisational whole' (Clarke *et al*, 2000, p. 3).

The basket of services that are encompassed in the term 'public services' requires an awareness of historical and theoretical contingency. A service is public partly as a result of characteristics of the service itself, and partly because of the extent of state provision in a particular place in a given era. Attempts to define public services have therefore tended to be either theoretical or descriptive, considering the nature of goods or the range of services on offer in a given setting.

Theoretical accounts of public services usually begin with the theory of public goods, expounded most famously by Samuelson. He identified a set of goods which had the feature of being 'pure public goods', in that they are available to everyone and do not diminish with use (Samuelson, 1954): lighthouses, traffic lights, security and justice systems are examples of this sort of goods. Since the benefits of these services cannot be restricted to those willing to pay for them, public provision averts a collective action problem in which generally beneficial goods are underprovided (Olson, 1971).

Economists have built on Samuelson's work to identify other categories of good. For example, services such as public utilities and roads, are 'common pool goods', non-excludable but subject to depletion through usage (Ostrom *et al*, 1988, p. 87; Ostrom, 1989, p. 47; Savas, 1987, pp. 45–6). Another category of public services are excludable and rationed through a user charge, as 'toll goods' (Savas, 1987, p. 47; Ostrom, 1989, p. 47). Parking permits and swimming pools fit into this category.

A striking feature of these categories of good is that despite meeting one or more of the criteria of Samuelson's pure public goods, they encompass only some of the services which governments provide and which are conventionally called public goods or public services. Most of these services – health, education, housing, welfare transfers – are both excludable and subtractable, and can therefore be categorised as private, rather than public goods in Samuelson's sense. These goods are provided due to their positive externalities and for that reason may be referred to as 'merit goods' (Musgrave, 1959, p. 44; Musgrave and Musgrave, 1980, pp. 84–5). Examples of such goods in the UK are the universally accessible services such as health and education, and the means-tested services such as housing and cash transfers to needy individuals (Savas, 1987, p. 44).

These public services are best understood as a heterogeneous mixture of services with shifting boundaries rather than a closed and generally agreed set. Steele and Corrigan used focus group research to assess public and expert views of what counted as a 'public service', finding that people could not agree: 'the most striking theme was inconsistency' (Steele and Corrigan, 2001, p. 3). They concluded that some services – particularly the NHS and state education – were seen as 'highly public', whereas others – railways, electricity supply – were seen as 'slightly public' (2001, p. 5).

The distinctive features of public services may best be encompassed in a negative, as services allocated on the basis of non-market principles. Taking an ideal-type market to be a distribution mechanism based on competition between providers, where services are allocated to freely choosing consumers using a signalling process based on price, such a mechanism is rarely used in public service provision. Public services are likely to incorporate one or more of the following features: there is a single provider; users do not pay for the service at the point of use; eligibility for the service is not determined by ability to pay (nor by private criteria such as friendship or kinship); the benefits of the service accrue beyond the individual user; the service is delivered or regulated by the state; providers of the service are shielded from market risk.

However theoretical barriers between public services and market-based services are rarely preserved so purely in practice. The reshaping of public sectors in a range of countries from the late 1970s – often characterised as new public management-type reforms – sought to improve the efficiency of public services through making them more closely resemble markets. Fundamental shifts in the last 20 years have included the privatisation of public utilities, subject to government regulation, the separation of the purchaser and provider roles of the state, the contracting out of non-core services, and the creation of delivery agencies, devolved from the central executive departments. Thus in the UK there are now bodies that are privately funded but publicly accountable (the utilities such as water companies), others that are publicly funded but privately run (such as private prisons), and bodies that are publicly financed and managed but along market lines with a range of purchasers and providers (such as the National Health Service). ⍺

Whilst public administration theorists have endeavoured to categorise public services on the basis of funding streams and channels of accountability, the 'publicness' of a service often describes only a widely shared sense that a service is a matter for the collective rather than the individual. Here, public services will be taken to encompass those services funded in whole or part by the state, in which eligibility depends on legally mandated criteria rather than ability to pay, and for which government is held accountable by voters. They include education, health, welfare (including social housing), law and order and (to a lesser extent) public transport.

Whilst it is impossible to derive a full picture of what it means to be a citizen from an account of public services, the provision of such services is central to the relationship between citizens and the government. Public service use is likely to be the most salient and intense aspect of government-citizen interaction for the majority of people. All citizens rely on public sanitation and environmental services; most use state education and health; some utilise housing and benefit services. For this reason, an analysis of public service use can give an insight into a core area of public policy and can contribute to a better understanding of the government-citizen relationship. In particular, it can reveal the assumptions about citizen and government that underpin policy-making.

Public services play a vital role in securing the collective welfare, but they also provide a lens on broader questions of identity, belonging, entitlement and accountability. Public services in some traditions of citizenship have been part of an expression of community, and the realisation of shared values such as equality and dignity (Tawney, 1931; Titmuss, 1968). Ignatieff describes the postwar welfare state, defined by Beveridge and Keynes as 'a civic bargain': 'Civic solidarity was built upon the presumption that the more a citizen received from the state the more easily he would connect his private interest to the public...' (Ignatieff, 1995, p. 67). Indeed solidarity was explicit in the goals of the new welfare state. The 1944 *Social Insurance* white paper based the postwar welfare state on the following ambition:

> The scheme as a whole will embrace, not certain occupations and income groups, but the entire population. Concrete expression is thus given to the solidarity and unity of the nation, which in war have been its bulwarks against aggression and in peace will be its guarantees of success in the fight against individual want and mischance.
>
> Cited in DSS, 1998, p. 9

To argue that citizens are positioned as consumers in relation to public services is to claim that different traditions of citizenship are at work, specifically those shaped by the market rather than principles of solidarity. Tracing the narratives underlying the provision of public services by New Labour policy actors helps to explain what these actors believe it means to be a citizen, as well as the rationale underlying services such as health, education and welfare provision.

Citizenship regimes

Discussions of public service consumption fit into broader debates about the appropriate boundaries between the public and the private. Defining these terms and determining their relative jurisdictions has been inseparable from political theorising since the classical era. Whilst Aristotle and subsequent republican theorists sought to separate off a public domain of politics from the economic and domestic spheres, other theorists, including liberal, Marxist and feminist theorists, have called for different demarcations between public and private. The appropriate role of the member of the political community – the citizen – has been central to such discussions. To understand the relationship between the citizen and the consumer in the delivery of public services, it is first necessary to develop an understanding of the way that citizenship can be interpreted and applied by policy actors such that a distinctive citizenship regime emerges.

Conceiving of the government-citizen relationship as a regime helps to make sense of complexity and to extract different traditions of citizenship. A number of authors have used a variant of the regime concept to denote the structures of power, organisation and legitimation within a state (Esping-Andersen, 1990; Clarke and Newman, 1997, pp. 60–1; Jenson and Phillips, 2001, p. 72). A regime approach goes 'beyond the interplay of individuals to explore the underlying structures and logics of a specific mode of coordination' (Clarke and Newman, 1997, p. 61). There is in particular a well-developed American literature on urban regimes, developed initially in case studies by Stephen Elkin (1987) and Clarence Stone (1989) and widely utilised by comparative scholars with an interest in UK local government (Stoker and Mossberger, 1994; Stoker, 1995; Harding, 2000; J. Davies, 2001). Stone, in his study of Atlanta politics, defines a regime as, 'an informal yet relatively stable group *with access to institutional resources* that enable it to have a sustained role in making governing decisions' (Stone, 1989, p. 4, emphasis in the original).

Distinctive features of the regime approach have included: attention to social production (governments' power to act) rather than social control (the coercive role of government); and a focus on informal coalition building between the state and non-state sectors (Stone, 1989, p. 229; Stoker, 1995, p. 65). Stoker draws attention to the way that regimes can be characterised by the 'solution set' that they adopt (1995, p. 67). He utilises Jones and Batchelor's argument that urban regimes 'codify solutions and problem definitions into a solution-set that tends to dominate policy-making for a period of time' (Jones and Batchelor, 1993, p. 18 in Stoker, 1995, p. 67). Thus part of the process of understanding a regime lies in characterisation of its solution set. Here narratives play a role, providing the discursive frame within which policy actors promote particular solution sets.

Although urban regime theorists have warned of the dangers of stretching the regime concept beyond their tightly imposed conceptual boundaries (Stoker, 1995, p. 62), the regime approach has been used to characterise distinctive types of welfare state (Esping-Andersen, 1990) and government-citizen relationship (Jenson and Phillips, 2001). Jenson and Phillips use the regime concept as the basis for understanding how state and non-state structures work together to configure particular conceptions of citizenship. They see citizenship as a social construction which varies over time but at some historical moments has enough stability that one can talk of a 'citizenship regime' (Jenson and Phillips, 2001, p. 72). Adapting Esping-Andersen's (1990) discussion of welfare regimes, they argue:

> The concept of a citizenship regime denotes the institutional arrangements, rules and understandings that guide and shape concurrent policy decisions and expenditures of states, problem definitions by states and citizens, and claims-making by citizens.
>
> Jenson and Phillips, 2001, p. 72

Whilst they do not use the language of solution sets, Jenson and Phillips make the related point that the citizenship regime 'encodes representation of the proper and legitimate social relations among and within these categories, as well as the borders of "public" and "private"' (Jenson and Phillips, 2001, p. 72). They take a neo-institutional approach, noting that a regime approach requires 'discursive and practical coherence in a wide range of institutional connections between state and citizens, states' and citizens' responses to the economic and political conditions' (2001, p. 71).

However, this new institutional approach can ascribe too much explanatory power to the ability of institutions to fix the content of solution sets. It is more helpful to understand individuals working within citizenship regimes that shape their responses but need not constrain them. As Bevir argues, 'different people construct pressures, institutions and outcomes differently depending in part on the tradition against the background of which they so do' (Bevir, 2005, p. 52). Here the notion of 'situated agency' is preferred to new institutionalism (Bevir, 2005, p. 22), allowing individual policy actors the scope to interpret the solution set within the context of, but not fixed by, traditions of citizenship.

It is the interpretations made by national and local policy actors in speeches, policy documents and interviews that are the focus of empirical research here. Speeches and documents are analysed to identify the way that policy-makers use narratives to construct solution sets. This approach does by necessity simplify and exclude aspects of the interactions between government and citizens. The research design does not address the implementation of policy. The gap between policy and implementation has been widely studied (Pressman and Wildavsky, 1973; Lipsky, 1980; Sabatier, 1991, p. 259). As Bevir argues, 'we should not assume that the ideas governments express always correspond to their practice. Gaps arise between the two because politicians dissemble and because their actions typically have unintended consequences' (Bevir, 2005, p. 83). The approach taken here illustrates the ways in which policy actors talk and write about service delivery – and the ways that people experience service use – but its scope does not extend to providing insights into how policies are implemented at the 'street level'.

Types of citizenship regime

To understand the delivery of public services in a particular era, it is necessary to understand the traditions of citizenship within which narratives of service entitlement and access are positioned. Whilst taking seriously Bevir and Rhodes's earlier injunction not to treat traditions as 'fixed entities', it is possible to cluster together groups of ideas on citizenship based on 'the shared understandings and historical connections that allow us to link its exponents with one another' (Bevir and Rhodes, 2003, p. 33).

Theorists of citizenship have generally sought to move beyond bland definitions of citizenship based on 'state membership', a definition that 'leads nowhere as well as everywhere' (Parry, 1991, p. 168). As Habermas argues, 'Citizenship as membership in a state only assigns a particular person to a particular nation whose existence is recognised in terms of international law' (Habermas, 1995, p. 260). This descriptive reality does little to advance an understanding of citizenship. Theories of citizenship have as a result sought to specify the conditions under which people belong to the political community. They identify and categorise *homo politicus*, a member of the *polis*, and provide different accounts of the responsibilities of the state, the community and the individual. They also outline the appropriate relationship between *homo politicus* and other social and economic roles, providing a guide to the extent to which the political role of citizen should be shaped by social and economic status. To begin to understand the range of possible citizenship regimes and the regime in a particular state, it is necessary to consider the traditions of citizenship that exist and the relationships between them.

Citizenship theorists often distinguish, implicitly or explicitly, between citizenship as status and as practice. The former focuses on the criteria for membership of the community, the latter on the rights and duties accorded to members (Walzer, 1989, p. 216; Pocock, 1995, p. 34; Kymlicka and Norman, 1995, p. 284; Jenson & Phillips, 2001, pp. 74–5). As status, citizenship designates full and equal membership of the political community and guarantees a set of rights to the citizen. Controversies about status include the extent to which citizenship can be denied to those seeking to enter the community (Carens, 1995, p. 229; Kymlicka, 2001, p. 26), and whether or not the nation-state should demarcate the boundary of that community (Habermas, 1995, p. 256; Miller, 2000, ch. 5; Caney, 2001, p. 975). As practice, citizenship is concerned with how those designated as citizens behave and are treated, including the rights they enjoy and their obligations towards other citizens and the government (Walzer, 1989, p. 216; Prior *et al*, 1995, p. 5).

The status and practice of citizenship are not unrelated. A number of authors emphasise that the nature of membership may shape the terms on which people participate. Marshall (1992, pp. 40–1), Taylor (1989, p. 178) and Miller (2000, p. 81) follow earlier republicans in arguing that loyalty based on shared national identity or shared history must underpin active citizenship, particularly if citizens are expected to prioritise collective goals over individual interests. Others have argued for a universalistic, global citizenship, to reflect obligations that lie beyond the nation state (Caney, 2001).

It is citizenship as practice that is of most relevance here, since this aspect has most bearing on the government-citizen relationship once constituted. Limiting a discussion of citizenship theory to its practice still leaves an array of theoretical approaches. As Aristotle wrote, 'The nature of citizenship...is a question which is often disputed: there is no general agreement on a single definition (Aristotle, 1992, p. 93). In the 2000 years since Aristotle was writing, the proliferation of literature on what it means to be a citizen has not simplified the process of definition. In fact, the practice of citizenship is relevant to most political controversies. As Kymlicka and Norman argue, 'almost every problem in political philosophy involves relations among citizens or between citizens and the state' (1995, p. 284).

To negotiate a path through multiple definitions it is helpful to draw on families of citizenship theory. A distinction between liberal and civic republican approaches, based on their different visions of *homo politicus*, is a common feature of the literature on citizenship (Barber, 1984, p. 91; Constant, 1988; Walzer, 1989, p. 216; Taylor, 1989, pp. 178–9; Habermas, 1994, p. 25; Van Steenbergen, 1994, p. 1; Miller, 1995, p. 135). A third category of libertarian citizenship is used here, following Miller (1995), because it provides a distinctive account of what is required of *homo politicus*. Other theorists have included a similar category of citizenship under the heading 'neo-liberal' (Faulks, 1998, p. 145; Axtmann, 1996, p. 45). A fourth model of citizenship considered here is the communitarian model. Scholars disagree about whether communitarianism offers a distinct type of citizenship (Van Gunsteren, 1994, p. 45; Kymlicka, 2002, p. 298) or is a variant of civic republicanism (Taylor, 1989; Habermas, 1994, p. 25). The communitarian approach is considered here as a separate category because its requirements of government are distinct from those of civic republicanism. Exploring the four types of citizenship, it is possible to draw out different conceptions of the role of the citizen, and the interaction between the citizen and government. Key elements of the four theories are sketched here, whilst recognising that each is itself a tradition: 'a group of ideas widely shared by several individuals although no one idea was held by them all' (Bevir and Rhodes, 2003, p. 33).

The liberal tradition, with its roots in natural law and social contract theory, positions the state as guarantor of security and defender of rights (Mill, 1963, p. 435). Individuals join together as citizens 'to obtain benefits through common action that they could not secure individually' (Turner, 1994, p. 167). Thus, '[t]he action is collective, but the point of it remains individual' (Turner, 1994, p. 167). The goal of civic activity is to allow citizens to pursue their non-political ends, their own 'conception of the good', as Rawls puts it, protected by a well-developed system of rights (Rawls, 1993, p. 13). Citizenship as practice requires citizens to undertake just so much activity as is necessary to sustain just and democratic institutions, which may include voting, payment of taxes and a willingness to serve in the military (Marshall, 1992, p. 45). Citizens must have a shared agreement on the terms of debate to ensure that everyone accepts collective decisions as just and binding (Rawls, 1993, p. 16). To ensure an equal platform for participation and to foster civic solidarity, most liberals (following the so-called 'new', 'reform' or 'welfare' liberals of the late nineteenth and early twentieth centuries) have supported taxation and redistribution, or 'social rights' as T.H. Marshall called them (Marshall, 1992, p. 16).

Libertarianism, described by Freeden as an 'attenuated' variant of liberalism, rejects the presumption that participation and social rights are required to sustain the political community (Freeden, 1996, p. 276). Libertarians embrace a residual vision of political institutions as necessary insulation from the state of nature. Citizenship establishes civil and political rights and provides those goods such as security that cannot be efficiently provided by the market, but it imposes few obligations. Participation and taxation are to be at the minimum level required to maintain supply of a small range of public goods, including policing and border controls. Much more than this core compromises individual freedom (Hayek, 1944, p. 10; Nozick, 1974, p. 113). In a rejection of the 'new liberal' assumption that individual agency requires social rights to flourish, some libertarians, such as Spencer, see welfare as 'tampering with the natural social order' (Spencer, 1969 – cited in Freeden, 1996, p. 290). Others, such as Friedman, admit the need to provide some support to the worst off but argue for welfare payments in cash to minimise state interference in establishing 'desirable' outcomes (Friedman, 1962, p. 190).

The civic republican tradition, with roots stretching back to Aristotle (384–322 BC) and Rousseau (1712–1778), envisages a different dynamic between government and the governed. Active involvement in the political community (self-government) is seen as allowing citizens to transcend their private interests and become free. For Aristotle, 'man is by nature a political animal' (Aristotle, 1992, p. 59). For Rousseau, participation in making laws allows citizens to be both subject to laws and free, since they are bound by rules that they themselves make (Rousseau, 1973, p. 174). In literature from the republican tradition, including Aristotle (1992, pp. 415–16), Rousseau (1973, p. 265) and Arendt (1958, pp. 209–10), citizens, whilst avoiding penury, are warned to eschew the distractions and corruptions of economic life. In the civic republican view citizenship is 'a quality that can only be realised in public, i.e. in a collectivity joined for a common purpose' (Elster, 1997, p. 139). The public arena is a transformative one, in which individuals arrive at an understanding of the common good through deliberation rather than using political institutions to pursue pre-political preferences (Barber, 1984, p. 136). Rather than rights, the civic republican model prioritises virtue, assuming as Van Gunsteren puts it, 'that more is needed than simply abiding by the rules' (1994, p. 45). Whereas liberal and libertarian approaches seek to protect individuals through non-interference, for the civic republican, autonomy comes from self-government (Dagger, 1997, p. 38). As Aristotle puts it, the citizen 'must regard all citizens as belonging to the state, for each is a *part* of the state' (Aristotle, 1992, p. 452 – emphasis in the original).

Communitarian approaches to citizenship share the civic republican assumption that the collective confers identity and meaning on the individual, but have some distinctive features. Whereas civic republicans give primacy to the political community, communitarians recognise the diverse groups and associations that confer purpose on individual lives and require loyalty (Walzer, 1995, p. 162).

Communitarians see citizenship in instrumental terms – as the construction of a shared identity to advance the interests of subcommunities – rather than presuming that it is a good in itself (Beiner, 1995, p. 14). Whereas republicans emphasise politics as a transformative process, communitarians see political forums as opportunities to promote a politics of the common good' (Sandel, 1984, pp. 16–17; Taylor, 1986).

Each of these four traditions of citizenship presumes a different vision of *homo politicus*, political man. For the civic republican the citizen is active in public life; for the communitarian citizenship is one of a number of identities derived from group membership; for the liberal citizenship is the public complement to an active private role; for the libertarian human flourishing occurs away from the domain of citizenship. For the purposes of characterising a citizenship regime it is necessary to understand the link between citizenship theories and regimes and to extract the key difference in these theories.

There are two relevant fault lines within traditions of citizenship. The first relates to the responsibility that the state bears for the welfare of the citizen, and concerns the coalition of actors who should be involved in processes of social production. Potential coalition members include the state, for-profit companies, non-profit organisations and private individuals. The coalition of members who together undertake social production and shape the citizenship regime will vary depending on which theory of citizenship is being adopted. Libertarians accept that some social production is required, but reject state involvement outside a small set of public goods. Liberals are likely to favour a combination of state and non-state providers with state involvement ensuring a level playing field such that citizens can participate politically on equal terms. Classical republicans tended to leave welfare questions aside on the assumption that the political community should not be tainted by economic issues, although recent republican theorists have recognised the need for a welfare state 'to make sure that the market economy's natural tendencies would not be allowed to vitiate the ideal of a community of equal citizens' (Ignatieff, 1995, p. 60). Communitarians also do not prescribe a particular package of welfare, although some have been distrustful of large state bureaucracies, assuming that welfare provision can best be done within communities. Etzioni, the so-called 'political communitarian' (Frazer, 1999, p. 11), has called for a 'principle of subsidiarity', in which the welfare state is scaled back to a core and other tasks given to individuals, families and communities (1994).

A second fault line within a citizenship regime concerns its prescription of the relationship between collective and individual interests. Liberals have tended to give pre-eminence to the protection of individual autonomy, whilst also recognising the need for solidarity across the political community. Libertarians dispute the need for solidarity and venerate individual choice over collective planning. However they are also distrustful of allowing aggregated political choices to determine extensive welfare packages, favouring individual market provision over collective allocations (Seldon, 1977, quoted in Clarke *et al*, 1987, p. 142). Civic republicans and communitarians emphasise the importance of solidarity in the *polis* or the group, and de-emphasise the value of responding to individual choices.

In the development of administrative linkages between state and citizen, governments operate within these traditions of citizenship. Citizen regimes are unlikely to map exactly onto one particular tradition of citizenship, but will have recognisable strands of one or more of them in the structure of administrative systems. These theoretical and administrative strands weave together to form the citizenship regime: the organisational and normative underpinnings of policy actors' conception of the citizen. Actors' endorsement of a particular tradition of citizenship has implicit and explicit features. Policy actors – politicians and bureaucrats – implicitly signal their conception of citizenship through the design of administrative structures. Explicit references to citizens and to the government-citizen relationship indicate to people how they are expected to behave as citizens and what they can expect from government. Thus to understand the relationship between citizenship and consumerism it is necessary to explore the narratives that policy actors use to shape a distinctive solution set.

Conclusion

Recent debates on public services in the UK have focused on how to take account of consumerism, and relate it to the political role of the citizen. In particular, attention has focused on how to remake public services to reflect user preferences, given the potential for public services to express common citizenship as well as deliver customer satisfaction. To study the relationship between citizenship and consumerism in the context of public services it is useful to utilise the concept of a citizenship regime. Theories of citizenship and institutions of social production combine to create a citizenship regime: a stable and widely accepted set of principles and practices that guide government-citizen interactions, and are expressed in the solution set used by policy actors. The book uses the concept of a citizenship regime to explore the extent to which the government-citizen relationship in England under New Labour is consumerist in character.

Although the book aims to explain public service reform through the lens of consumerism, the analysis offered here recognises that governments are plural institutions: 'the state is not a monolith', nor are all its actions reducible to a single template (Lister, 2003, p. 438). The ambiguities and contradictions of New Labour's 'jackdaw politics' approach have been widely noted (Powell, 2000). Greenleaf describes political parties as 'living oxymorons' (2003, p. 28) and the gap between the Labour Party and its leadership both now and for much of the twentieth century highlights the limitations of claims to offer a unified account of New Labour's public service reform. The discussion here seeks to characterise not the entire party but to reconstruct the narratives that its leaders and other policy actors utilise in the context of public services.

3
A Consumerist Citizenship Regime

The contested nature of consumption, consumerism, the consumer and the customer runs through the debate in the UK around public service reform. To explore Labour's citizenship regime, it is necessary to clarify some of these ambiguities. This chapter considers the diverse definitions of the consumer and consumerism in order to develop the criteria of a consumerist citizenship regime. The section below begins by discussing the relationship between the citizen and the consumer, highlighting the tendency in literature to contrast one with the other. The chapter then focuses on definitions of the consumer, arguing that the multiple meanings of the term need to be made explicit if consumerisation is to be studied. It goes on to set out the criteria of consumerism and to discuss how to compare New Labour's public service reforms against a consumerist citizenship regime.

The citizen versus the consumer

At the centre of this book lies the question of what the relationship is, and should be, between the citizen and the consumer in the delivery of public services. This is by no means virgin terrain. Many commentators on UK public services particularly after the Conservatives came to power in 1979, discussed reform in terms of the citizen and the consumer. Frequently the roles were contrasted, with the traits of one being the converse of the other. Examples include the claim that the citizen belongs in the public sphere, the consumer in the private sphere (Harms and Kellner, 1998; Marquand, 2004, p. 135); that the citizen is collectivist in orientation, whereas the consumer is individualistic (Wright, 1990, p. 90; Gyford, 1991, p. 181; Burns *et al*, 1994, p. 45; Chandler, 1996a, p. 50; Stewart, 1997, p. 5; Lusk, 1997, p. 68; Cooper and Hawtin, 1997, p. 7; Cairncross *et al*, 1997, p. 28); that citizenship presumes a common culture whereas consumerism emphasises diversity (Turner, 1994, p. 154); that the citizen role requires active production and creativity whereas the consumer role involves passive receipt (Gyford, 1991, p. 169; Marquand, 2004, p. 128); that the citizen has rights and obligations, whereas the consumer has choice (Cairncross *et al*, 1997, p. 32); and that the citizen holds decision-makers accountable through political channels, whereas the consumer holds service providers accountable through the market or via performance indicators (Burns *et al*, 1994, p. 44; Prior *et al*, 1995, p. 66; Beetham, 1996, p. 36; Elcock, 1996, p. 34; Cairncross *et al*, 1997, p. 187; Sullivan, 2001, p. 6).

There is a sense in this literature not only of contrast but also of rivalry: the more one is a consumer the less one can be a citizen. As Bauman has argued, 'The consumer market as a whole may be seen as an institutionalised exit from politics; or as a highly rewarding attraction, meant to encourage prospective customers to leave in droves the drab unprepossessing world of political, bureaucratic regulation' (1998, pp. 82–3). Some neo-liberal theorists have fostered this rivalry, disputing the relevance of citizenship. Pirie, for example, argues, 'Citizen's rights are...distant, diffuse and ineffective. Consumer rights are direct, personal, individual and effective. They empower people and enable them to change things' (Pirie, 2001). As Friedman and Friedman put it, 'When you vote daily in the supermarket, you get precisely what you voted for, and so does everyone else. The ballot box produces conformity without unanimity; the marketplace, unanimity without conformity' (1980, pp. 65–6). Even those who reject the new right approach have pointed out the advantages that consumption has over citizenship:

> Within most markets, at least those for consumer goods, we can participate directly and specifically in many different decisions, whereas we participate as citizens in the polity only indirectly and in formal and awkwardly aggregated ways at rare intervals in time.
>
> Crouch, Eder and Tambini, 2001, p. 11

It is common therefore to conceive the relationship between the citizen and the consumer in competitive and dichotomous terms: citizen and consumer roles compete for attention. For most of these authors, citizen and consumer inhabit different spaces: citizens are political actors in the public realm, consumers are economic actors in the private sector. To argue that the citizenship regime has been consumerised, however, makes a different claim, namely that the public realm of citizenship has become the territory of the consumer. For some of the authors cited above, such a claim would mean that citizenship had been tainted, infected with traits that are inappropriate for and may indeed be damaging to citizenship. Yet there are others who argue that the relationships are not contradictory or rival, but rather complementary. To be a consumer is simply to be a user of goods and services, which is just as relevant a role in the public sector as the private. Consumer agency can be a medium for collective political action rather than the activity of the isolated individual (Hilton, 2003; Trentmann, 2004, 2006). Ethical consumption for example, has a long history of being used as a tool to advance political movements, from anti-slavery, through the Nestle boycott, to current fair trade campaigns.

These debates are heavily laden with normative assumptions around the role of consumption (alienating, expressive, liberating), and the content of citizenship (liberal, libertarian, civic republican, communitarian). Some of these versions of consumption have a civic dimension; some models of the citizen easily incorporate consumer action. As discussed in Chapter 2, liberal theorists are more comfortable with an expansive private economic role for the citizen than civic republican theories. Acknowledging this contingent relationship between citizenship and consumption is important because it helps to explain why debates about it are so muddled and contradictory. In order to be a useful lens through which to study public service reform, it is necessary to spend time defining what it means to be a consumer.

Understanding the consumer

Whilst definitions of the citizen are multiple and conflicting, they share a common root in the legal status of citizenship. Definitions of the consumer are less firmly rooted, stemming simply from the act of using goods and services. From here economists, lawyers and sociologists have departed down different paths. For the economist, the consumer is a market actor, the driver of demand in the supply and demand chain (Becker, 1978). For the lawyer, the consumer is one of the agents of contract, through which the legal system supports the market economy (Taylor, 1999). For the sociologist, the consumer is part of a social structure of consumption, which shapes status and identity (Veblen, 1970, p. 35; Bourdieu, 1984, p. 1; Baudrillard, 1988, ch. 3). When authors discuss the role of consumer and its relationship to the citizen they often invoke one of these three senses without acknowledging the root. These three consumers need to be looked at in turn.

The first approach sees the consumer as an economic agent, making choices in a marketplace. A number of authors have understood the consumer in this sense. As Pollitt puts it, 'To be a consumer is to hold a particular position in a network of market relations' (Pollitt, 1994, p. 12). According to Cairncross *et al*: 'A key aspect of the position of consumers is the ability to exercise choice' (Cairncross *et al*, 1997, p. 186). In this economic model, the consumer is usually an unencumbered agent: choice is constrained only through individual resources and product availability. As Elster argues, 'The consumer chooses between courses of action that differ only in the way that they affect him' (Elster, 1997, p. 132). Control of the choice set is through aggregate signalling, rather than concerted action. Consumers 'do not participate in decisions concerning the products they buy except in choosing whether or not to buy it' (Elcock, 1996, p. 31). Consumers here are assumed to be individualistic: 'Consumers are not that interested in taking account of the preferences of other consumers; rather they seek to maximise their own advantage' (Burns *et al*, 1994, 44). Producers and consumers are engaged in a bilateral relationship based on voluntary exchange only for the duration of the transaction.

The chief weapon of the consumer in this account is the power of exit, which acts as a discipline on producers, ensuring that goods and services are provided at a quality and price which suits the consumer (Hirschman, 1970). In relation to public services, an economic approach makes such services 'the reciprocation of the payment of taxes' (Walsh, 1994, p. 69). It is a 'thin' definition of the consumer in that it presumes that nothing need be known about the characteristics of the consumer, the motivation behind the choices or the context within which choices are made. It is enough that, as Clarke puts it '[C]onsumers know their wants, can make rational choices and expect producers to serve them' (2004, p. 39). They are 'abstracted from other social roles' and make calculations about price and quality without allowing '"dogma", "ideology" or other forms of unreason' to cloud their choices (Clarke, 2004, pp. 39–40).

For some authors, this economic notion of the consumer has been too abstract or simplistic, and needs to be accompanied by the recognition that the consumer role in the marketplace is in reality predicated on a set of rights. In this second, more legal, approach to the consumer, the state intervenes in the market to enforce contracts and protect consumers. The approach is a liberal model of the consumer in the sense that rights are required to protect the choices of the individual. This account of the supported consumer is promoted by consumer organisations, which recognise the need to supplement the market power of the consumer with additional protections. It is the one invoked by Prior *et al* when they argue that consumers have specific rights: 'to receive information on standards and performance of services, to have individual needs assessed, to assert choices and preferences, to complain and to receive redress' (Prior *et al*, 1995, p. 15). Empowerment in this model comes through the guarantees of standardisation of service, instead of or in addition to choice and exit (Aldridge, 2003, p. 139).

Beyond enumerated rights, consumers in this definition may have certain entitlements such as being treated with respect and consulted about services. Butcher uses consumerism in this sense, defining it as 'consultation, courteous and helpful staff, well-publicised and readily available complaints procedures' (Butcher, 1997, p. 60). Potter sees consumerism in local government as helping to bring about changes in attitudes:

> Consumerism can help authorities to advance from considering individual members of their public as passive clients and recipients of services – who get what they are given for which they must be thankful – to thinking of them as customers with legitimate rights and preferences as well as responsibilities.
>
> Potter, 1988, p. 157

A crucial element in this version of consumerism is accountability. Service providers are encouraged to feel accountable to their users (Elcock, 1996, p. 34). Like the economic model, the legal/liberal approach assumes that the consumer is (or should be) a rational, frugal and goal oriented agent (Aldridge, 2003, p. 143). This version of consumerism is recognisable in the contemporary consumer movement, and in twentieth century struggles for consumer protection (Hilton, 2003).

Missing from economic and liberal approaches to the citizen-consumer is what Levine calls the 'social determinants' of consumption (Levine, 1981, p. 277 – quoted in King, 1987, p. 37). An alternative approach, which gives us a 'thick' notion of consumer, is based on the sociological factors that shape consumption. Emphasis here is placed not only on the use value of commodities, but also on the cultural significance of consumption. Preferences are assumed to be shaped in the social context of consumption rather than being fixed and exogenous (Veblen, 1970, p. 35; Bourdieu, 1984, p. 2). Sociologists have dis-agreed about the extent to which consumers are able to shape the meanings attached to goods (Fiske, 1989, p. 26), or are passive, uncriti-cal consumers of commodities, vulnerable to manipulation (Marcuse, 1964; Baudrillard, 1988, p. 67). However they agree that goods have social meaning, bestowing status and expressing identity.

The consumer in this third approach may be caught up in what Campbell calls 'the processes of wanting and desiring', restlessly seeking to acquire new products in order to affirm her place in society (Campbell, 2004, p. 28). Since only the 'wanter' can be an 'expert', 'the authority for decision-making [is] located firmly within the self', even whilst desires are socially constructed (Campbell, 2004, p. 29). The emphasis on desire makes this kind of consumerism an approach rooted in 'feeling and emotion' rather than 'reason and calculation' (Campbell, 2004, p. 29). Given that wants are unlimited whereas income is not, '"frustration" is a permanent state for the consumer' (Campbell, 1989, p. 95). Bauman similarly sees consumers as 'impa-tient, impetuous and restive...in a state of suspicion and disaffection' (1998, p. 25).

Since preferences are culturally informed in the sociological model, consumer preferences may be shaped endogenously through consumer culture. The susceptibility of the consumer to manipulation by adver-tising was noted by Schumpeter who critiqued the assumption of con-sumer rationality: '[Consumers] are so amenable to the influence of advertising and other methods of persuasion that producers often seem to dictate to them instead of being directed by them' (Schumpeter, 1976, p. 257). These techniques allow the manipulation of existing preferences and even the creation of new ones. As Pollitt puts it:

> The consumer is a bundle of preferences waiting to be satisfied. Consumers are to be researched so that the service or product can be designed so as to best meet their wants – or so that new appetites can be stimulated and supplied.
>
> Pollitt, 1993, p. 125

Thus although consumerism gives primacy to the meeting of subjective user preferences, these preferences may be shaped by producers.

The relationships between the economic, liberal and sociological approaches can be understood in different ways. One option is to see them as different layers in a composite account of the consumer. Most parsimonious are the assumptions of microeconomics that the consumer is a utility maximiser exercising choice in a marketplace. A further layer is added by liberal approaches, which accept the market role of the consumer, and also assume that the consumer is a possessor of rights, crucially the right of contract, protecting economic choices. A final layer is added by sociological theories, which recognise the market role of the consumer, and their reliance on a set of rights, but also take into account the social context within which choices are made and rights exercised. This approach proceeds from a thin to a thick account of the consumer.

Alternatively it is possible to emphasise the rivalry between these approaches. The rational, unencumbered, economic consumer contrasts with the socially embedded consumer motivated by feeling and desire. The model of the restless, emotional consumer can be seen as the opposite of the frugal and rational liberal consumer, armed with a package of rights. Both liberal and economic approaches are preference-accommodating, whereas the social model has something to say about how preferences are shaped. The liberal version is a denial of economic claims that unregulated markets alone will supply the needs of consumers. Whereas the economic and sociological accounts celebrate differentiation the liberal model calls for standardisation and regulation.

Thus the consumer is a contested figure. Similar ambiguities attend other terminology related to the consumer. The terms consumption and consumerism both describe what it is that consumers are engaged in, but whereas some authors use the terms interchangeably, others emphasise the differences. Aldridge, for example, suggests that consumerism can be conceived as the dystopian alternative to consumption (2003, p. 82), characteristic of the 'mass society' critiqued by Horkheimer and Adorno (1973) and Marcuse (1964). Both Bauman and Miles have discussed the paradox of consumerism being a form of self-expression and enforced conformity (Bauman, 1988, pp. 50–1; Miles, 1998, p. 5). Connelly links consumerism to economic models of supply and demand (1993, p. 5), whereas other authors have linked consumerism to forms of political mobilisation (Gabriel and Lang, 1995; Hilton, 2003). Thus definitions of consumerism are just as contested as those of the consumer.

The extent to which the term consumer is synonymous with terms such as customer and client, which share an emphasis on the receipt of goods and services, is also unclear. Some authors emphasise similarities between the terms customer and consumer. Lusk points out: '[B]oth "customer" and "consumer" orientations in social provision are equally the result of a "commercial" construction of the user/provider relationship' (Lusk, 1997, p. 68). However customer is seen as having some distinctive features. The customer can be understood as a sub-category of consumer, involved in a specific transaction with a particular supplier (Lusk, 1997, p. 69; Aldridge, 2003, pp. 35–6; Williams, 1988, p. 79). Usually this is a cash transaction, in which the customer pays the market price for a good or service (Gyford, 1991, p. 181; Crouch, 2003, p. 14). In his *Keywords*, Raymond Williams describe the customer as 'a buyer or purchaser' (Williams, 1988, p. 79). Similarly Gyford distinguishes between the consumer and the customer in the following way:

> The term 'consumer' at least embraces the notion of receipt of service without prejudging the terms on which that receipt takes place: the use of the term 'customer' is largely an import from the language of private sector management and could be taken to imply an exchange relationship of payment for services.
>
> Gyford, 1991, p. 18

This definition of customer, relating to a transactional relationship based on payment for services, is harder to apply to public services than the more abstract consumer, given that access to most public services is not conditional on user payment. The role of client can be differentiated from that of both consumer and customer, implying as it does 'a professional dependency' relationship (Gyford, 1991, p. 168). Clients, in the public and private sectors, may be able to make demands on the professionals whose services they enjoy, either free or paid. But the exclusivity of knowledge possessed by professional service-providers makes it difficult for clients to exercise control within the relationship. Consumer and customer make no such assumptions about power asymmetries. Gower Davies draws out the difference between customers and clients: 'The *customer* is always right: he can choose, criticise and reject. The *client*, on the other hand, gives up these privileges and accepts the superior judgement of the professional' (Gower Davies, 1974, p. 220, quoted in Burns *et al*, 1994, p. 40).

The consumerist citizenship regime

The contradictions in the role of consumer – active/passive, choice-based/rights-based, individualised/culturally embedded – hamper an understanding of what it means for government to develop a consumerist citizenship regime. As Hood *et al* point out, '[T]here is no standard scale of consumerisation' (Hood *et al*, 1996, p. 43). It is possible, however, to identify some common themes running through all of these definitions, which can form the basis of exploring consumerism in public services. The use of goods and services is the explicit or implicit feature of being a consumer in all of the accounts discussed above. Thus a consumerist citizenship regime can be characterised as one in which the government engages with people in their role as service user rather than in some of the non-service conditional roles that individuals might play *vis-à-vis* government, such as citizen and taxpayer. Whereas a citizen grants political authority to governments to act as its agent in the provision of public services, and in that sense is involved in the production of public services, a consumer is primarily defined in contrast to the productive role. The taxpayer is distinctive for their role in funding public services, whereas consumers are distinctive for using them. Thus, being a consumer is not the same as being a citizen or a taxpayer.

Second, consumerism has an individualistic ontology. Without ignoring the social context of consumption, most authors locate the consumer in the tradition of methodological individualism (Gyford, 1991, p. 181; Burns *et al*, 1994, p. 45; Lusk, 1997, p. 68; Chandler, 1996a, p. 50; Stewart, 1997, p. 5; Bauman, 2001, p. 318; Baldock, 2003, p. 69; Finlayson, 2003a, p. 214; Clarke, 2004, p. 39). As Clarke puts it, '[C]onsumerism constructs the public interest as a series of specific and individualised encounters and interactions: each consumer consumes a particular bit of service' (2004, p. 39). Although consumers may have the capacity to work collectively to decide their priorities, a consumerist citizenship regime focuses primarily on the individual as the unit of analysis. Consumer agency – for example a consumer boycott – may be collectively orchestrated but it is operationalised at the point of transaction between individual consumer and producer. Whilst consumer movements have shifted between a focus on narrowly individualistic consumers and more radical, social democratic and collective visions, as Hilton explains, they continue to work towards the goal expressed by Consumers' Association founder Michael Young, that individuals 'be made to matter' (Young, 1949, p. 4, quoted in Hilton, 2003, p. 343).

Third, a consumerist solution set has a distinctive epistemology, oriented towards the subjective experience of service use. The perspective of the service user is given primacy over the bureaucrat, professional or auditor (Potter, 1988, p. 158; Clarke and Newman, 1997, p. 117). As Campbell puts it in a discussion of modern consumerism, 'the authority for decision-making [is] located firmly within the self' (Campbell, 2004, p. 29). Whilst consumers need not be selfish, they are assumed to know their interests. As a 'sovereign consumer', writes Hood, 'you are generally taken to be the best judge of your own interests' and 'all tastes are equally meritorious' (1986, pp. 171, 178). In the consumerist citizenship regime, the aim of public service delivery therefore is to accommodate user preferences. Although such preferences may appear manipulated, false and contrary, they are taken to be equally valid. The transformative potential of politics is dormant.

Fourth, the consumerist citizenship regime is consequentialist. A consumerist approach is primarily concerned with the quality of the goods and services rather than the structures or processes of delivery. Boundaries between public and private services, or state and market providers, become irrelevant in this account: unlike the citizen, the role of consumer is not distinctively public or private. Although consumers have sometimes used their purchasing power to signal disapproval of certain sorts of exploitative modes of production, as in Fairtrade purchases, they can be assumed to be interested primarily in the quality of service rather than in the production process.

Thus a consumerist citizenship regime has the following features:

1. It engages with people as service users rather than in non-service roles.
2. It is individualistic and aggregative rather than collective.
3. It is preference-accommodating rather than transformative, deferring to the preferences of service users.
4. It is consequentialist, prioritising individual utility maximisation over structural or ideological aspects of service delivery.

The regime has parallels with the individualistic ontology of liberalism, therefore, although has little to say about the political role of the citizen. Its agnosticism about how preferences are shaped – and the extent to which the individual is shaped by the collective – separates consumerism off from civil republican or communitarian traditions of citizenship. The emphasis on meeting the aggregated preferences of consumers differentiates consumerism from the libertarian tradition of citizenship, since it involves no principled commitment to a small state, or to private over public provision.

The consumerist citizenship regime therefore takes a distinctive position on public service delivery. Within this regime, it is not necessary to ignore or finesse all the variations in the consumer role raised earlier in the chapter. Rather, it is possible to identify narratives of consumerism that incorporate different features. Two in particular capture the key features of the consumer. Both are consumerist in the sense that they are designed to improve services for individual users and sideline other rationales, or limits on, service delivery.

The first is a *standardisation* narrative, where public services are as consistent as possible, with an emphasis on fairness and equity. Legal or procedural mechanisms are put in place to secure users' rights, and ensure that they have access to information and to services. In this narrative the consumer need not play an active role in shaping services; user agency may be weakly developed. Although there are dangers in using a theory of production to characterise consumption (Warde, 1994, p. 231), this first narrative is broadly consistent with the Fordist principles of production, based on mass availability of goods of uniform and predictable quality (Harvey, 1989; Murray, 1989; Warde, 1994, p. 232).

The second is a *differentiation* narrative, where services are tailored to *Choice* meet the individual needs of users: the citizen-consumer is the recipient of personalised and differentiated services. In this narrative, consumers must be active, although forms of activity may vary from making a choice of provider to communicating with a monopoly supplier to agree a personalised form of service. This version of consumerism assumes a 'reflexive individualism', in which people must assess and calculate the risks of their choices (Giddens, 1994). With its explicit rejection of uniformity and one-size-fits-all, this rhetoric has been characterised as post-Fordist (Murray, 1989; Jessop, 1994; Warde, 1994) or postmodern (Harvey, 1989), encompassing 'a shift from homogeneity to heterogeneity, from principles of size, uniformity and predictability to those of scope, diversity and flexibility' (Miles, 1998, p. 7). This second narrative of consumerism can be seen as layered on *layer* top of the first – once equality of access, information and rights have been achieved then it is possible to move towards differentiation and choice. Alternatively, there may be tensions between the narratives, particularly in the extent to which the emphasis on equity in the first narrative is consistent with the emphasis on choice in the second.

These characteristics of consumerism have *prima facie* validity in the literature on New Labour. Many authors have highlighted the individualism underlying the New Labour approach (Bevir, 2005, p. 71; Driver and Martell, 1999, p. 163; Finlayson, 2003a, p. 61; Rustin, 2004). From Giddens and others, New Labour is seen as taking the concept of 'reflexive modernity' (Giddens, 1991), a requirement that the individual 'conceive of himself or herself as the centre of action, as the planning officer with respect to his/her own biography, abilities, orientations, relationships and so on' (Beck, 1992, p. 135). As Bevir puts it, 'New Labour...feeds hefty doses of individualism, competition, and materialism into the traditional social democratic ideal of community' (2005, p. 71).

Within this account of the individualised New Labour project, the discursive importance of the consumer and the customer has been widely noted (Driver and Martell, 1999, p. 68; Hall, 2003; Finlayson, 2003a, p. 132; Lister, 2003; Needham, 2003, 2004; Greener, 2005; Marquand, 2004, pp. 118, 128, 135). As Lister puts it, 'when Blair tells us that "in all walks of life people act as consumers and not just citizens" the suspicion is that it is the consumer rather than the citizen who represents the ideal New Labour welfare subject' (Lister, 2003, p. 438). Hall, in a review of New Labour, talks of 'the reduction of the citizen to consumer, and the "privatisation of need"' (Hall, 2003, p. 23).

The tendency of New Labour to defer to rather than shape public preferences has also been discussed elsewhere (Blyth, 1997; Pattie, 2001; Hay, 1999; Norris, 2001). It is an approach that Hay describes as 'neo-Downsian': 'Labour consistently engaged in the politics of preference-accommodation rather than that of preference-shaping – adapting and revising its policies on the basis of a strategic assessment of the sensitivities and aspirations of the electorate as evidenced in previous elections...' (Hay, 1999, p. 135). New Labour's reliance on surveys and focus groups to shape its policy and positioning has been well recorded (Gould, 1998).

The consequentialism of New Labour's approach – 'what matters is what works' – also fits the consumer model. As Clarke puts it 'New Labour has placed both resource and discursive emphasis on "delivery", addressing the task of overcoming the organisational, occupational and cultural obstacles to "modernisation" in public services' (Clarke, 2004, p. 38). Bevir notes that New Labour is critical of New Right models of contracting out and quasi-markets because it 'maintained an unhealthy dichotomy between the public and private sectors... The Third Way is supposed in contrast, to develop networks that will enable public and private organisations truly to collaborate' (2005, p. 46). This apparent pragmatism has been criticised by commentators on New Labour. As Hall, puts it:

> You foreground the pragmatic practicalities of 'delivery' in order to silence these other awkward questions about principle and purpose you would prefer not to have to answer. What 'delivery' presumes is

that no-one any longer cares who owns, runs, controls or profits from, health-care, providing the possessively-individual consumer's personal need is satisfied.

2003, pp. 22–3

The result, according to Clarke is a 'dogmatic pragmatism' (Clarke, 1999, p. 85 in Lister, 2003, p. 428), or as Hall puts it a '"new common sense"' (Hall, 2003, p. 18).

The importance of standardisation, the first narrative, to New Labour's approach to public services has been discussed in the context of the target and audit culture created by New Labour (Kelly, 2003). As Hall put it, under New Labour, 'The means to improve services are manage-rialist – audit culture, managers empowered over professionals, un-informative league tables, moralistic "shaming"...' (Hall, 2003, p. 21). Bentley highlights the 'technocratic, over-centralised Fabianism' of New Labour's approach (2007, p. 95). Goss points to the government's ongoing reliance on targets and tight civil service control of the deliv-ery process, 'seeing government as a centralised machine resembling the giant private corporations of the 1960s' (2007, p. 108). Others have positioned New Labour firmly within post-Fordism and the need to deliver differentiated services, the second narrative (Hay, 1999, p. 29; Finlayson, 2003a, p. 122). In *The Blair Revolution*, Mandelson and Liddle describe New Labour's welfare state as 'universal in its reach but no longer uniform in what it offers' (1996, p. 143 – quoted in Bevir, 2005, p. 89). Some have argued that the target-based approach charac-terised New Labour's first term but has been replaced by a greater emphasis on differentiation in the second and third terms (Hindmoor, 2005).

To consider New Labour and consumerism it is important to explore the relationship between these narratives in the discourses that are used by key policy actors. However, it is also necessary to consider the aspects of New Labour that so cannot easily be accommodated within consumerism. Many authors on New Labour have highlighted the importance of community as a New Labour motif (Driver and Martell, 1999; Fairclough, 2000; Levitas, 2000; Lister, 2000; Bevir, 2005). Similarly citizen has been a term that analysts have flagged up as key to the New Labour project (Clarke, 2004, p. 39; Lister, 2003, p. 428). The taxpayer is also an important role for New Labour, oriented towards the pursuit of efficiency and economy (Clarke, 2004, p. 39–40). Fur-ther, in relation to New Labour, it has been widely observed that users are not only granted rights and choices in public services, they also have responsibilities (Clarke *et al*, 2000; Lister, 2000; Finlayson, 2003a; Clarke, 2004; Newman, 2006). Responsibility is seen as a corollary of, and in some cases a substitute for, rights (Bevir, 2005, p. 68). Driver and Martell note that Labour's approach to community 'is strongly laced with ideas of reciprocity: helping the poor and unemployed gain that stake in society is conditional on them doing something about their own condition' (1999, p. 118). Johnson, writing about the personal social services under New Labour, notes how community is invoked as part of an attempt to establish mutual aid and self-reliance in place of welfare dependence (Johnson, 2001, p. 185). People are encouraged to be responsible users of health services, for example, through healthy lifestyles (Shaw and Aldridge, 2003, p. 39; Clarke, 2004, p. 34; Greener, 2005). According to Hall, the New Labour project is a neo-Foucauldian one of 'governmentality', in which 'slowly but surely, everybody – even if kicking and screaming to the end – becomes his/her own kind of "manager"' (2003, p. 18. See also Barry *et al*, 1996).

New Labour's use of these non-consumerist discourses needs to be assessed alongside its use of consumerist narratives. In the language of community and responsibility there is evidence of a third narrative of public service, which draws on *coproduction* rather than consumerism, in which the responsible user plays a role in delivering service outcomes. The coproduction approach, 'views citizens not as the passive targets or beneficiaries of government programs but as a vital element in their ultimate success or failure' (Brudney, 1984, p. 466). Some authors have seen coproduction as a subset of consumer empowerment (Hupe, 1993; Hood *et al*, 1996, pp. 44–5). However, it is an approach that understands the production and consumption processes as organically linked rather than functionally separate (Clarke and Newman, 1997, pp. 111, 117). The assumption that the right to service delivery is conditional on users behaving responsibly may clash with the assumptions about user entitlement or choice that flow from consumerism. Thus in exploring New Labour's citizenship regime, the third public service narrative, that of coproduction, needs to be placed alongside the standardisation and differentiation narratives.

Conclusion

In the last 20 years much academic and political attention has focused on citizen and consumer roles and the extent to which the citizen can (and should) adopt the characteristics of the consumer. Yet, despite all this attention, little progress has been made in clarifying what it means to treat the citizen as a consumer and how far governments are doing so. Existing literature has been too narrow in scope or too partisan, failing to provide an adequately rigorous analysis across all the relevant variables. There is a need therefore for an account of a consumerist citizenship regime to use as the basis for empirical research. The model developed here aims to overcome some of the limitations in the existing literature. It provides a basis for testing the extent to which recent governments have treated citizens as consumers.

Some accounts of citizen and consumer see them as competitive roles. However it is possible not to oppose them but to collapse one into the other, such that a citizen takes on attributes of the consumer. Relating this theory to a citizenship regime, a consumerist variant develops in which government actors – bureaucrats and elected officials – construct an ideal model of the citizen, through policy and language, based on consumerist attributes. Here the solution set is characterised by individualised forms of responsiveness driven by a rationale of consumer demand in a market environment, and ambivalence about public and private boundaries.

A range of data sources can be used to test these predictions. Drawing on a variety of sources – Blair's speeches, white and green papers, local authority corporate plans, interviews and focus groups – it is possible to probe the way that policy actors construct different narratives of service use. It is necessary also to test for non-consumerism in New Labour's public service discourses, through exploring the use of terms such as community and citizen, and being alert to coproductive as well as consumerist narratives.

Before moving on to the empirical chapters, it is important to understand more about the historical context of the government-citizen relationship in England. Some of these ambiguities in definitions and terminology of the citizen and the consumer arise from the ahistoricity of the analysis. Nineteen ninety-seven is not year zero for England's citizenship regime, and it is necessary to place the research in the broad context of the emergence of the modern state. The legacy of the Conservative governments in power between 1979 and 1997 is particularly relevant for understanding Labour's treatment of citizens after coming to power in the May 1997 general election. This historical inheritance is the focus of the next two chapters, with particular focus on the period since Thatcher took office as Prime Minister in 1979. These chapters explore two key strands within consumerist public service reforms: individualisation and marketisation. Chapter 4 considers the shifting relationship between government and citizen in the UK, including trends towards individualisation over the last 30 years. Chapter 5 focuses on the pro-market tendencies within public service reforms since 1979, outlining marketisation as a broader trend within which consumerisation needs to be positioned.

4
Public Services before New Labour: The Path to Consumerism

Underlying the regime approach is an assumption that different traditions of citizenship shape distinctive narratives of service provision. This chapter explores the relationship between state and citizen during the period up to 1997. It discusses the basis of the citizenship regimes that existed prior to New Labour coming to power, considering the social production role of government, the coalitions of state and non-state actors and the solution sets embraced.

The first section of the chapter sites the discussion of the relationship between government and the citizen in the longer trajectory of the state's welfare role from the nineteenth century. It considers the way that ideas about citizenship shaped the scope and content of public services in three periods: from the New Poor Law of 1834 to the end of the nineteenth century; from the election of the New Liberal government in 1905 to the Second World War; and from 1939 to the 1970s. In each case it seeks to extract the key assumptions about citizenship and the government's service delivery function in order to trace the citizenship regime of that era. The chapter then goes on to consider the reshaping of the citizenship regime by Conservative governments from 1979 to 1997, identifying moves towards individualised models of public service provision. The third section looks at how in the same period new accounts of the government-citizen relationship were being developed on the left, particularly at local level, to illustrate that a diversity of citizenship traditions were evident by 1997, although with common strands of individualism. The time periods are indicative rather than exact.

Government and the citizen, 1834–1979

In the transition from feudalism to capitalism and the social upheavals of the industrial revolution lie the roots of an administrative state.

From the Victorian period onwards citizens came to have direct experience of the social production role of government, rather than only its law enforcement function. Government interacted with citizens on an increasingly regularised basis such that it could be characterised as a citizenship regime. Through understanding the emergence of an activist state in the nineteenth century, and the development and retrenchment of the welfare state in the twentieth century, successive regimes can be identified.

The emergence of the administrative state

Before the nineteenth century the social production role of government was limited. 'Arsenals, dockyards, and the Post Office accounted for what the State did as a direct producer' (Fry, 1979, p. 104). The locally administered Poor Law, dating from 1601, provided relief in the case of extreme want (Birch, 1974, p. 3). Beyond that government ceded welfare responsibilities to families, private philanthropy and voluntary action (Fry, 1979, p. 104). By the early nineteenth century these arrangements had come to be seen as increasingly inadequate. The erosion of traditional clientelist linkages of an agrarian society undermined an organic sense of community, whilst industrialisation and urbanisation threw up new social needs that could not be met within families (Fry, 1979, pp. 104, 141; Marquand, 2004, p. 57). Increased dependence on the Poor Law created concerns that welfare allowances encouraged indolence (Birch, 1974, p. 10).

The New Poor Law of 1834 was a response to both the rise in welfare costs and to concerns about what state dependence might do to incentives to work. It offered relief based around the workhouse and the principle of 'less eligibility' (Birch, 1974, p. 10). The law marked the beginning of the state's modern role in welfare (Birch, 1974, p. 8; King, 1999, p. 227), and had three significant implications for future structures of service delivery. First, its method – 'that of inquiry, followed by report, followed by legislation, followed by inspection' (Birch, 1974, p. 12) – marked the triumph of a systematic approach to public administration that would become extensively used in the nineteenth and twentieth centuries to legitimise service reforms (Greenleaf, 2003, p. 164). Second, the practice of building coalitions between national policy-makers, local boards of guardians, philanthropic and charitable organisations to implement policies was to become common practice as the welfare state took shape (Fry, 1979, p. 143; Clarke *et al*, 1987, p. 21). Third, the New Poor Law, by imposing restrictions on the liberty of recipients and preventing access to political rights such as voting, signalled that those on welfare were not full citizens (Marshall, 1992, p. 15). The imprint of the ancient Roman principle – that a citizen, unlike a slave or a woman, was not in a position of dependence (Pocock, 1995) – was evident here. This disjuncture between welfare and full citizenship was sustained up until the Second World War. Paupers were not given the vote until 1918; recipients of public assistance were prevented from standing in local elections until 1946 (Harris, 1996, p. 134).

The expansion of the state's social production role during the nineteenth century is best characterised as incremental growth under the cloak of a dominant *laissez-faire* ideology (Fry, 1979, pp. 109–10). Dicey, Polanyi and Greenleaf are all agreed on a lack of deliberate planning behind the expanded state role in this period (Polanyi, 1957; Dicey, 1962; Greenleaf, 2003). Greenleaf describes how 'the edge of the collectivist wedge was more and more firmly inserted into the libertarian position,' as the state took on responsibilities in piecemeal fashion (Greenleaf, 2003, p. 26). As governments began to inquire into the condition of health, education, sanitation and housing of the populace, boards and commissions were established which created institutional support for a greater state role (Fry, 1979, pp. 141–51). *The Economist* in 1895 described the year-on-year growth of state responsibilities and expenditure as building up gradually, 'like a coral island, cell on cell' (Greenleaf, 2003, p. 32). From the middle of the century a system of multi-purpose local authorities was created, based on a rate-paying electorate, which administered national initiatives but also pressed for new powers to meet local needs (Fry, 1979, p. 157; Morton, 1991, p. 15; Hunt, 2004, p. 51). The expanded state role was presided over by a new generation of bureaucrats brought in after the 1854 Northcote Trevelyan report which called for a civil service recruited on merit, free of the taint of private business interests, and employing gifted amateurs to run the business of state.

Through the nascent administrative structures, a citizenship regime was developing that emphasised a significant, though *ad hoc*, role for the state in social production, and the incompatibility of citizenship with state dependence. The citizenship regime in this period derived much of its rationale from the assumptions of classical liberalism and its utilitarian variant. The scientific method and rational principles that animated utilitarian radicals were reflected in the reforming zeal of administrators such as Edwin Chadwick and more broadly in the Northcote-Trevelyan model of the civil service (Fry, 1979, pp. 15–22, 147). Deviations from *laissez-faire* were justified where it could be shown to contribute to individual self-development (Freeden, 1996, p. 153). The coalitions constructed in this period to respond to social need involved national government, local boards and municipal authorities, along with private philanthropy and the more 'solidaristic' ventures such as cooperatives and mutual societies (Dean, 1999, p. 214). A strong assumption endured, consistent with the communitarian tradition, that social need could be met through family and friends, providing mutual assistance in times of hardship (Clarke *et al*, 1987, p. 26). However the solution set of the second half of the nineteenth century, which admitted of the need for intervention to alleviate social need and for legislative protection for vulnerable members of society, came to require intervention that lay beyond that of private or local effort: 'government itself had to do so much more than supervise or coordinate these piecemeal responses' (Greenleaf, 2003, p. 116). Once the presumption of state action had been established, albeit incrementally, the space for charitable and cooperative ventures to operate began to shrink away.

New liberalism

Towards the end of the nineteenth century, in recognition of years of incremental change, the balance between non-intervention and individual development shifted into a new equilibrium. The state was urged to promote positive freedom through fostering the well-being of its citizens (Fry, 1979, p. 44). Under the tutelage of T.H. Green and the 'Oxford Idealists', a 'new liberalism' came to the attention of policymakers, recasting the relationship between government and the individual (Freeden, 1996, p. 194). Ideas of citizenship as bestowing equal membership of the political community were emerging and challenging the punitive and exclusionary aspects of the New Poor Law (Freeden, 1996, pp. 190, 200). Liberals such as Asquith, who were familiar with the teachings of Green and facing pressures from the swelling electorate, took steps to establish a more inclusionary and expansive citizenship regime (Fry, 1979, p. 41). The government of the 'New Liberals' from 1906 to 1914 expanded its social production role, assembling the apparatus of a welfare state by establishing old age pensions, Labour exchanges and national insurance for health and unemployment (Hennessy, 1990, p. 57).

These reforms created 'a great surge of state power in personal life and the national economy' (Hennessy, 1990, p. 58), establishing 'a vital new link between citizen and state' (Birch, 1974, p. 31). From the first decade of the twentieth century, government acquired a new relevance for the public, impacting on the lives of the populace to a greater extent than before – a transformation that Dicey deplored as a shift from individualism to collectivism in his 1905 *Lectures on Law and Public Opinion in England* (Dicey, 1962). Four years of war from 1914 and 1918 intensified such trends. The war extended the apparatus and capability of government, leaving a 'permanent residuum of policy' (Ministry of Reconstruction, quoted in Greenleaf, 2003, p. 66). The expansion of education and social housing provision after 1918 showed that government was willing to use its new fiscal and administrative capacity for social productive as well as military ends (Greenleaf, 1983, p. 70). A new solution set was emerging, based on the capacity of the state to work with coalition partners including Poor Law Guardians, Public Assistance Committees and the Unemployment Assistance Board, to provide for the welfare of poorer citizens (Clarke *et al*, 1987, pp. 85–6).

The economic deprivations of the interwar years further deepened the linkage between the citizenry and the state, as government took greater responsibility for providing health, housing and non-contributory unemployment relief (Birch, 1974, pp. 44–5). Greenleaf notes the significance of the depression in legitimising overall economic planning by the state, even if 'its implications were not always fully worked out in any detail' (2003, p. 144). By 1934, a century after the New Poor Law, a 'Social Service State' had been established, based on 'a national system of governmental social provision' (Fry, 1979, p. 198). The *Times* in 1935 described the growth of the role of the state as a 'Silent Revolution', highlighting again the incremental yet immense increase in the state's productive role (Greenleaf, 2003, p. 31).

This 'new liberal' solution set, which remained influential up to 1939, accepted the positive contribution that the state could make in securing for people the freedom from deprivation that would enhance their overall liberty. As Clarke *et al* say of the new liberals, 'What they did provide was a new political ideology which challenged *laissez-faire* individualism, and provided a political language about the state and its citizens which justified an expanded role for the state in collective welfare provision' (1987, p. 40). The use of contributory welfare schemes implied a solution set based on a contractual approach to welfare. Citizens were entitled to draw on the state if they had paid in their dues. The retention of the means test to assess eligibility, however, maintained the stigma of dependence. Reliance on welfare was a mark of exclusion rather than common identity. The years of widespread economic hardship during the depression exposed the limitations of the contributory model of insurance (Birch, 1974, p. 42), although it was not until the Second World War that support for a new solution set emerged.

The welfare state

The years after 1939 saw an enlargement of the social production role of government and of the scope of citizenship. As with the First World War, the wartime sacrifices of the people and the expansion of government capacity provided both motive and opportunity for state-based welfare provision. The capacity of the state to manage the war effort efficiently created national optimism about what the state could do in peacetime to secure prosperity (Greenleaf, 2003, p. 149). Depression-era strains in the new liberal conception of the welfare state combined with increased wartime faith in state capacity, brought to the fore social democratic traditions of citizenship and inclusive models of welfare (Clarke *et al*, 1987).

A universal contributory insurance was advocated by the 1942 Beveridge Report, and underpinned a welfare system of 'benefits paid not on the basis of the means-test and proof of need but as an automatic right of citizenship' (Harris, 1996, p. 122). In place of 'charity' and 'dependency' was 'a new ethic of social "citizenship"' (Harris, 1996, p. 122). Workers would be 'decommodified', no more would their welfare depend on the 'cash nexus' (Esping-Andersen, 1990, p. 21). The language of citizenship was invoked both by the reformers and by the academics that gave the reforms their *post hoc* rationale. The 1950 Labour Party Manifesto declared that 'Labour has honoured the pledge made in 1945 to make social security the birthright of every citizen' (quoted in Lister, 1990, p. 62). T.H. Marshall formalised the linkage between welfare and citizenship rights in his *Citizenship and Social Class*, first published in 1950, which positioned social rights as the third of a triumvirate, following civil and political rights (Marshall, 1992).

The reforms of the immediate postwar era established a citizenship regime in which welfare entitlements were a badge of equal citizenship rather than a disqualification. Most benefits were universal rather than means-tested, highlighting their inclusionary nature (Marshall, 1992, p. 28). The ills that the Beveridge-inspired reforms sought to address were conceived in collective rather than individual terms (Bevan, 1952, p. 1). The scope of government's social productive role in this era extended to managing national insurance and assistance schemes, running a centrally controlled National Health Service and undertaking mass building programmes for social housing. The administrative implications of expanded welfare provision were enormous. During the 1950s and 1960s Britain became, as Greenleaf puts it, 'a "much governed nation", with coalitions of councils, boards, departments, and authorities of many kinds exercising the numerous and extensive powers bestowed on them by modern legislation' (Greenleaf, 1983, p. 1). Nationalisation brought more of the UK's productive capacity under the direct control of the state. Welfare provision was assumed by central or local government, with reduced dependence on private or voluntary sector providers. Whilst the administrative state was transformed in scope, its operating principles remained those of Northcote-Trevelyan a century earlier (Fry, 1979, p. 205). Attempts to make internal civil service structures conform to more scientific theories of organisation and management – notably the Fulton Report of 1968 – were implemented only partially (Crowther Hunt and Kellner, 1980, p. 79).

In the solution set promoted during this era, group voice was favoured over the individual. Administrative structures developed routinised links with relevant groups – trade unions, professional associations and business interests – whose expertise and blocking power put them in an influential negotiating position (Jordan and Richardson, 1987, p. 11). In the delivery of welfare, the relevant unit was the family rather than the individual; there was no individualised right to social security benefits, a shortcoming highlighted by postwar feminists (Clarke *et al*, 1987, p. 105). Here communitarian traditions of citizenship retained a hold, even while the infrastructure of communitarian welfare was squeezed out by the state.

Professional power, based on the presumption that needs could be externally identified and evaluated by experts (Barry, 1990, p. 49), was particularly prized. Here the influence of the Fabian tradition, with its faith in the efficiency of professionalism, was evident (Clarke *et al*, 1987, p. 49). As Clarke *et al* say of the Beveridge Report, 'It supported the creation of an extensive professional bureaucracy whose main purpose of welfare provision included within it an explicit concern to police the poor' (1987, p. 90). The power of the professional producer was most overt in the NHS, but also evident in teaching and the personal social services (Clarke and Newman, 1997, p. 6). The designation of service users as clients captured the 'professional dependency' of their relationship (Gyford, 1991, p. 168). As Clarke and Newman put it:

In bureau-professional interactions, the power of service users was based on limited entitlements to certain universal services, with the fall-back possibility of expressing their interests or concerns to their MP or local councillor.

Clarke and Newman, 1997, p. 64

Integral to the importance of professional power was the assumption that professionals could identify the 'right solution', rising above 'mere opinion' (Robson, 1943, pp. 4–5, quoted in Clarke *et al*, 1987, p. 95). Asymmetries of power between professional and client were particularly evident in means-tested benefits. Whilst the welfare state was based on principles of equality and decommodification, the poor were reliant on lower status benefits, such as income support, and particularly vulnerable to being cast into a passive client role, reproducing some of the stigma of the undeserving poor (Esping-Andersen, 1990, p. 23). Interest in citizenship as a rationale for the state's welfare role declined, as the ideas of T.H. Marshall fell from fashion (Rees, 1996, p. 3; Kymlicka, 2002, p. 284). The role of citizen was often seen as an abstraction, particularly given the formal designation of Britons as subjects rather than citizens (Low, 2000, p. 180).

There was broad if uneasy agreement between the political parties in the two decades after the Second World War about the traditions on which the welfare state rested (Fraser, 2000, pp. 353–4). Progressives saw the welfare state as a way of integrating all members of society into full citizenship (Marshall, 1992, p. 26); conservatives saw it as a way to maintain social harmony (Freeden, 1996, p. 386). Both the Labour and Conservative parties in power continued and extended the practice of state provision of services, from social housing to schools and hospitals, incorporating services run by other institutions such as the church into a common framework of state services.

Hostile voices were not altogether silent. The libertarian tradition of citizenship drew strength from the work of Hayek, who warned of the totalitarian dangers of collectivism (Hayek, 1944). The 1950s saw a protracted debate within and between the major political parties about the sustainability of a welfare state based on universalism (Birch, 1974, p. 67). Doubts were raised over the effectiveness of administrative mechanisms that treated health, social care and housing as separate needs (Fry, 1979, p. 229). Constant tinkering with entitlements and structures of payment deepened the complexity of the administrative system designed by Beveridge to simplify the welfare state under an over-arching logic. Yet overall a majority within the two main political parties supported the welfare state, albeit for different reasons (Freeden, 1996, p. 386).

The rise of neo-liberalism

By the mid-1970s the hostile soloists were forming a choir. Diverse strands, including public choice theory, neo-liberal philosophy and monetary economics, were being threaded together into a comprehensive attack on the citizenship regime of the postwar welfare state. Public choice theory warned that a corporatist model of public administration gave too much power to producer interests, neglected users and encouraged bureaucratic waste (Niskanen, 1971; Buchanan *et al*, 1978). Neo-liberal philosophers and monetary economists warned that individual freedom and private enterprise were suffocated by government growth and welfarism (Hayek, 1944; Friedman, 1962; Nozick, 1974). Neo-conservatives bemoaned the 'moral hazard' of a welfare state that encouraged indolence and family breakdown (Murray, 1984; Barry, 1990, p. 73).

The size and expense of the state appalled many: by 1979 the state was spending 52 per cent of GDP, up from 26 per cent before World War Two; more than one in five workers was employed by a public agency in 1976, up from one in ten in the 1930s (Greenleaf, 2003, pp. 27, 33). Conservative and Labour governments of the 1970s became preoccupied with how to reduce state expenditure, at a time when the presumptions of full employment that underpinned the welfare state were proving misplaced (Clarke *et al*, 1987, p. 11). When fiscal crisis caused the Labour government to ask the International Monetary Fund for a loan in 1977, critics saw this as confirmation: the postwar citizenship regime was financially as well as morally bankrupt.

These critiques emerged from the right of politics, but some elements of their anti-Keynesianism found broader sympathy. Leftist critiques questioned the fiscal viability and legitimacy of postwar state capitalism (O'Connor, 1973; Habermas, 1976). By the 1970s, as Clarke *et al* explain, 'the post-1945 welfare state increasingly appear[ed] less as the centre-piece of political consensus than as an unhappy compromise to which few owed any continuing allegiance' (1987, p. 11). Welfare services characterised by efforts to achieve uniformity and standardisation of service, was increasingly looking out of step with new modes of production in the private sector (Hoggett, 1987; Murray, 1989; Stoker, 1989). One feature of these new modes of production was the freedom they gave to the increasingly 'affluent worker' (Goldthorpe *et al*, 1969), expressing their individuality through differentiated consumption patterns. Stoker notes that local authorities, which had copied Fordist industries in their 'commitment of scale, centralised planning, hierarchical control and the production of a standardised product', were 'caught up in the Fordist crisis' by the late 1970s (Stoker, 1989, p. 152).

Challenges to the traditional welfare state were also emerging on the left of politics, focused around the insensitivity of public services to individual users, particularly women and ethnic minorities (London Edinburgh Weekend Return Group, 1979; Wainwright, 1994; Panitch and Leys, 2001). The tendency of the welfare state 'to police and discipline the working class through the careful direction of funds and the supervision of officials and professionals, such as social workers' was criticised (Clarke *et al*, 1987, p. 128). A more participatory style of democracy was gaining support from the 'new left' and new social movements, emphasising a need for the users of services to play a greater role in their design and operation (London Edinburgh Weekend Return Group, 1979; Wainwright, 1981). Following the 1969 Skeffington Report, which called for greater public participation in land-use planning, public pressure grew for greater involvement in other areas (Boaden *et al*, 1982, pp. 53–4).

The two main political parties committed themselves to this more participatory account of citizenship. Labour's manifesto in February 1974 promised, 'we want to give a much bigger say to citizens in all their various capacities – as tenants, shoppers, patients and voters'. The Conservative manifesto of the same year called for greater worker participation in industry and parent involvement in schools (Klein, 2001, p. 82). The inclusionary but insensitive postwar tradition of citizenship was under attack from all sides.

In the period from the passage of the New Poor Law in 1834 to Margaret Thatcher's triumphant entry into Downing Street in May 1979, therefore, the citizenship regime underwent radical transformation. The solution set of policy goals expanded from minimal intervention to prevent destitution to universal access to health, education and welfare. Government took on a major social production role for the first time, with local authorities and national commissions of inquiry pushing forward the role of the state. New coalitions were constructed with local board, municipal authorities and private and cooperative bodies, although as time passed the state loomed larger and coalition partners smaller. The citizen, initially defined as free from dependence on the state, came to be defined in terms of shared access to welfare on the basis of common citizenship, although financial dependence on the state retained the stigma of second-class citizenship.

Missing from this account of the period are any indicators of the consumerist approach outlined in Chapter 2. Rather than customers or consumers, citizens were primarily conceived as clients of the welfare state (Gyford, 1991, pp. 15–16). Services were designed around principles of professional gatekeeping rather than user accessibility or choice (Marquand, 2004, p. 67). Social production was conceived as conferring collective benefits to meet social needs – the alleviation of disease, the spreading of literacy – delivering individual benefits as a side product rather than main stimulus. The state was responsive to pressure from groups but had few mechanisms in place to listen to the individual.

The Conservatives and consumerism

During 18 years of Conservative government from 1979 to 1997 a new citizenship regime was forged. Successive Conservative governments wrought substantial change to the administrative and productive structures of government. By the time the Conservatives left office in 1997, there had been a shift from a 'welfare state', in which government funded and produced a wide range of services, to a 'regulatory state' in which government regulated the production of a narrower range of public services (Loughlin and Scott, 1997, p. 205). As Labour came into power in May 1997 scholars were noting the emergence of a new consensus, this time incorporating low-inflation, fiscal constraint, privatisation and anti-trade unionism (Fraser, 2000, pp. 358–60; Flynn, 1997, p. 41), linked to a new citizenship regime based on privatised and individualised forms of social production (Clarke and Newman, 1997). This new citizenship regime drew on many of the consumerist criteria outlined in Chapter 3: first, there was a rhetorical shift which championed the user over the provider, the individual over the collective and the private sector over the public. Second, new opportunities were provided for individuals to exit the state and state dependence through the exercise of choice. Third, particularly under John Major, emphasis was placed on consulting and responding to individual service users, extending consumer rights into the public sector. Key elements of this regime are explored below.

Thatcher and the consumer

For the Conservatives, in place of ongoing group linkages between administrators and interest groups came an emphasis on individuals, freed from state control to pursue their own economic well-being. Thatcher's approach embodied a wider critique of the role of government. The Conservative manifesto for the 1979 election stated: 'No one who has lived in this country during the last five years can fail to be aware of how the balance of our society has been increasingly tilted in favour of the State at the expense of individual freedom' (Pollitt, 1993, p. 44).

The desire to make public services more responsive to their users and less responsive to producer groups was a central strand of the Conservative reforms (Thatcher, 1995, p. 149; Pollitt, 1993, p. 45). Waldegrave describes the government's attempts to increase responsiveness to individual service users, which in the past 'was routinely subverted in practice by producer interests' (Waldegrave, 1994, p. 82). Sir Peter Kemp who steered through the Next Steps reforms wrote, 'We must be consumer not producer-driven... We must ask our customers what they want of us and take account of this in developing services within the resources made available to us whether by taxpayers or by the customers direct' (Kemp, 1994, p. 57). Klein describes service users as 'both an end and a means' for the Thatcher governments:

> They were an end in so far as one of the aims of policy was to give them more choice. They were a means in so far as consumers were cast as the rank and file in the assault on provider power in the public services: the infantry who would follow up the ministerial artillery barrage.
>
> Klein, 2001, p. 116

Alongside extensive privatisations, a series of high profile business leaders were brought in to improve the management of those government functions that remained within the public sector. These advisors drew on an emerging orthodoxy, influenced by the widely read text *In Search of Excellence,* which illustrated how successful companies developed internal cultures that were customer-centric (Peters and Waterman, 1985, p. 14). An influential text on public service reform, *Reinventing Government,* borrowed explicitly from Peters and Waterman, and emphasised that a public sector organisation that placed the consumer at its core would also thrive (Osborne and Gaebler, 1992, p. 20). Roy Griffiths, managing director of Sainsburys authored a report on management in the NHS, published in 1983 (Klein, 2001, p. 124). The Griffiths report argued that the NHS ought to learn from private companies since successful companies, 'placed quality and customer satisfaction first and profit for a long time simply emerged as the by-product of effective service' (Griffiths, 1983 – quoted in Klein, 2001, p. 128).

As well as seeking to blunt producer influence, the Conservative governments' interest in the consumer was part of an effort to sever group linkages between government and the public and forge new connections between citizen and state (Klein, 2001, p. 116). Characteristic of the neo-liberal approach, 'was the notion that ultimately it was the individual rather than the group who was the only legitimate political and economic actor' (Gyford, 1991, p. 47). As a minister for local government under Thatcher, David (now Lord) Hunt put it:

> Margaret Thatcher thought more about the individual than she did about any collective organization. She tended to feel that as soon as you organized individuals on a collective basis, you started to get other pressures which moved away from the individual having real power. Margaret Thatcher thought power should go to the individual.
>
> Hunt, Interview, 9 June 2003

The consumer movement, for example, was snubbed by Conservative ministers. The incoming Thatcher government in 1979 cut central government funding for Consumer Advice Centres (Gabriel and Lang, 1995, p. 181). Efforts to get consumer affairs restored to a cabinet position were rejected as unnecessary 'since consumer affairs were "a top priority for the government as a whole"' (Hilton, 2003, p. 264). Pollitt highlights Conservative reluctance to encourage formal mechanisms for user representation, and the sidelining of Community Health Councils in the formation of the 1989 *Working for Patients* reforms (Pollitt, 1993, p. 185): 'The Conservative vision of consumer-responsiveness is more a matter of the robust individual consumer exercising informed choice and less a question of collective user representation in formal councils or boards' (Pollitt, 1993, p. 185). Support for Pollitt's argument comes from former minister David Hunt: 'I don't think we were ever greatly enamoured of the consumer lobby because they tend not necessarily to be representative and usually have a particular hobby horse to run' (Hunt, Interview, 9 June 2003).

A consumer orientation was also a reassertion of the principle that the citizen should not be reliant on the state. Those who continued to use public services should not do so from a position of passive long-term dependence (Thatcher, 1995, p. 148). Consumption rather than political participation or state provision was represented as the route to individual autonomy, with home ownership and share-holding offering economic rather than political forms of empowerment (Faulks, 1998, p. 145). Lister noted that, 'Lurking behind the active citizen is the successful, self-reliant, enterprising citizen, alias the consuming, property-owning citizen' (Lister, 1990, p. 15). The Conservatives' 1987 manifesto heralded, 'A capital-owning democracy... a profound and progressive transformation – popular capitalism' (Conservative Party, 1987, pp. 15–16 – quoted in Heater, 1990, p. 269). The extension of property owning increased divisions between the taxpaying majority and the welfare dependent minority, a tension highlighted by the community charge (or 'poll tax') initiative. As Jordan puts it, the welfare state became 'an instrument of division rather than solidarity'. Better paid workers were integrated into the market sector as home-owners, 'with their interests as ratepayers and taxpayers opposed to the excluded, casualised sector of welfare beneficiaries (Jordan, 1989, p. 7).

This empowerment of the individual was developed in part through a new emphasis on choice. Thatcher spoke out strongly in favour of the right of the individual to choose:

> Choice is the essence of morality. It is the essence of all religion. If you are to take away so much in tax that people don't have choice, to take away from them responsibility for their families and their children, I would say that was the immoral route.
>
> Thatcher, 1987 – quoted in Jordan, 1989, 19

The Education Act 1980 gave statutory backing to the rights of parents to choose schools (Pollitt, 1993, pp. 63, 76). The importance of user choice in public services was embodied in a series of further statutes, including the Education Acts of 1988, 1993 and 1996, the Housing and Local Government Act of 1989, and the NHS and Community Care Act of 1990 (Faulks, 1998, p. 133). These were in part measures to allow greater choice within the public sector, on the assumption that this would drive up service quality. The Conservatives were also keen to encourage the use of private sector provision, through the right to buy scheme in social housing, tax concessions for private health care and initiatives such as nursery vouchers (Durden, 2001, p. 140; Klein, 2001, p. 132; Crouch *et al*, 2001, p. 127). More diversity of school provision was attempted through the creation of City Technology Colleges and grant maintained schools (Whitty *et al*, 1993).

Choice was primarily seen as an exit right, part of a broader neo-liberal strategy to push social responsibilities from the public to the private sphere (Clarke, 2004, p. 32). As Clarke puts it, 'if there is a public interest, it takes the form of a consumerist desire for efficient and high-quality services, which will be best served by private pro-vision and private choices' (2004, p. 34).

Major and the Citizen's Charter

Whilst choice as exit from the public sector was a theme of the Thatcher governments. John Major, who replaced Thatcher as Prime Minister in November 1990, took a different approach. According to Sarah (now Baroness) Hogg, former head of Major's Policy Unit, the emphasis moved from the empowerment of citizens outside the state to the empowerment of those who continued to use public services (Hogg, Interview, 8 March 2000). Within eight months of taking office, Major launched the Citizen's Charter initiative, which placed the user of the service firmly at the centre of its universe, and attributed the language of citizenship to the service user, not those liberated from public dependence. An idea borrowed from local authorities such as York, the Charter was described by Major as 'the centrepiece of our policies for the 1990s' (Hogg and Hill, 1995, p. 135). In the preface to the Citizen's Charter white paper Major wrote: 'To make public services better answer the wishes of their users, and to raise their quality overall, have been ambitions of mine ever since I was a local councillor in Lambeth over 20 years ago' (Cabinet Office, 1991, p. 2). The implication from this was that user empowerment was not a means to achieve other ends; rather, improved services for users was to be a core aim of government. Plant notes that free marketeers at the time disliked the charters since, 'they were seen as administrative devices, not even second best compared to a genuine market because they assume a degree of commitment on the part of the average citizen to be aware of, interested in and prepared to act on a set of administrative standards' (Plant, 2003, pp. 575–6).

The Charter offered not enhanced exit rights but new mechanisms within the public sector to ensure that services were accountable to their users. It required, 'consultation with the customer to find out what his or her real wants and needs are' (Waldegrave, 1994, p. 83). Older models of political accountability were criticised for failing to be responsive to the needs of users. William Waldegrave, the minister with departmental responsibility for implementing the Citizen's Charter, argued, 'Services are not necessarily made to respond to the public simply by giving citizens a democratic voice, and a distant and diffuse one at that, in their make-up' (Waldegrave, 1993, p. 13). The Citizen's Charter concept evoked an explicitly contractual relationship between the individual and the state, in which service users were told what to expect from public services and how to seek redress if it was not delivered (Cabinet Office, 1991). As Tyson puts it, 'The Citizen's Charter is intended to set performance standards and to give the public dealing with various government departments "customer" rather than claimant status' (Tyson, 1994, p. 67). Stewart wrote critically of the diminishment of accountability implied by the Charter and associated reforms: 'The citizen as customer can then replace the citizen as voter, and this is the position taken implicitly, if not always explicitly, by the white paper on the Citizen's Charter' (Stewart, 1994, p. 77).

The model for the charter rights were the guarantees designed to protect consumers in the private sector, and as such came from a legal tradition rather than being rights in the political or social sense. Its main objective as Taylor put it, 'was to extend the principles of market consumption to the user of public services...rather than enhancing his or her rights as a citizen through new legal and political rights or social entitlements' (Taylor, 1999, pp. 197–8). The link between public and private consumption was made explicitly by David Willetts. Reflecting on the introduction of the Citizen's Charter, the former public services minister observed, 'The public sector was catching up with consumerist attitudes. People's expectations changed – shopping changed. And they had more consumerist attitudes when they came to use public services' (Willetts, Interview, 28 June 2000). Waldegrave rejected arguments from Charter critics for constitutional protection for social rights: 'Would a Bill of Rights provide compensation for commuters stranded on a wet railway platform? Of course not' (Waldegrave, 1994, p. 85).

In practice few charter rights were legally enforceable, however. According to Taylor, 'One of the main weaknesses of the Charter is its inability to offer the same level of protection to the consumer of public services as is enjoyed or expected in the private/commercial sector...' (Taylor, 1999, p. 200). David Willetts acknowledges this shortcoming:

> One question that was asked at the time was to what extent the charters were legally enforceable and offered guarantees that were equivalent to those on offer in the private sector. And clearly if you give someone a new hip, you can't give them a guarantee certificate in the same way as you can if you buy something in a shop.
>
> Willetts, Interview, 28 June 2000

In the place of legally enforceable guarantees, the charters offered entitlements such as access to performance information and in some cases compensation (Lewis and Birkinshaw, 1993, p. 35). Hogg explains that through the Citizen's Charter initiative, 'information was used as a surrogate for the market' (Hogg, Interview, 8 March 2000). Performance Indicators (PIs) had been introduced into most of the public sector during the 1980s, to improve the accountability of devolved bodies to their host department (Carter, 1991, p. 87). The Citizen's Charter proposed that PIs would become a tool of public accountability (Cabinet Office, 1991), with greater emphasis placed on customer service aspects (Christie, 1994, p. 46). Citizens were to be more extensively consulted about services, through new techniques such as customer satisfaction surveys and feedback forms (Lewis, 1993, p. 320). Service-facing parts of the administration were forced to inform and engage their users. Through name badges and 'service with a smile' administrators gained a human face (Cabinet Office, 1993, ch. 2). An Office of Public Services in the Cabinet Office oversaw the development of charters across the public services and local government. By late 1997, there were 40 national charters (Kilfoyle, 1997, Col. 471). They included a Redundancy Payments Service Charter, a Traveller's Charter (from Customs and Excise) and a London Bus Passenger's Charter. Most offered information about current and future performance and in some cases offered financial compensation if standards were not met (Lewis and Birkinshaw, 1993, pp. 34–8).

The charters blended the rhetoric of citizenship with consumerist language, aiming to 'give the citizen a better deal through extending consumer choice and competition' (Cabinet Office, 1991, p. 4). The terms citizen and consumer were used interchangeably, and with a presumption of shared interests (Elcock, 1996, p. 24). Emphasis was firmly placed on the individual citizen-consumer, as the apostrophe in Citizen's Charter indicated. Asked about the apostrophe, Hogg explained, 'The philosophy of the individual was central. Markets work as an aggregate of individuals' (Hogg, Interview, 8 March 2000). According to Hunt:

[The Citizen's Charter] was a sea change in that people's individual views started to matter once more... Before it was much more important to find out what the trade unions, the consumer organisations and the political parties thought. Now it's the individual that matters.

Hunt, Interview, 9 June 2003

The Charter was seen by many as heralding a cultural shift within the public sector. Rhodes describes it as confirming the predominance of consumers over producers (1994, p. 4). Willetts argues, 'The Citizen's Charter's success was that it created the expectation that every public sector body should have a useable information point. That barely existed ten to fifteen years earlier' (Willetts, Interview, 28 June 2000). The initiative gained endorsement, with minor reservations, from the National Consumer Council (Gabriel and Lang, 1995, p. 178). A number of interviewees for this book cited the Charter as the watershed in the emergence of a formal endorsement of the principle that responsiveness to the service user should be a key aim (Bunting, Interview, 19 May 1999; Steel, Interview, 19 May 1999; Hunt, Interview, 9 June 2003).

However, critics pointed to the Charter's continued reliance on individualised and passive forms of consumer empowerment. Doubts were expressed about the extent to which the Charter marked a significant shift in the relationship between government and citizen. Critics attacked the Charter for its anaemic version of citizenship, in which the citizen was equated with a private sector consumer (Butcher, 1997, p. 56; Deakin, 1994, p. 54). Taylor argued, 'The Citizen's Charter is essentially a charter for consumers of public services rather than a blueprint for enhancing the constitutional and political rights of the citizen' (1999, p. 197). Further he argued, '[B]y empowering the consumer, the Charter was personalizing consumption at the expense of the ethos of collective provision and consumption of universal services' (Taylor, 1999, p. 199).

Although the individual public service consumer received more attention under the Conservatives than before 1979, there are a number of reasons to doubt the Conservatives' commitment to the consumer. Tensions between consumer and taxpayer interests tended to be resolved in favour of the taxpayer. There were renewed concerns about allowing welfare dependents too much political power, harking back to early limits on the political rights of paupers. Those who paid low or no tax were suspected of voting in favour of expansive welfare services (Department of the Environment, 1986). David Hunt, local government minister under Thatcher, emphasised the rationale behind the community charge:

> If you had 36 million people paying for services that 36 million people used, that would be a far better way to make local authorities answerable, than just asking 18 million people to pay for the services used by 36 million people.
>
> Hunt, Interview, 9 June 2003

Responsiveness to service users was secondary, therefore, to responsiveness to taxpayers, a reflection of the government's efficiency agenda. In the many aspects of public service delivery where markets were infeasible or inappropriate, the service user remained relatively impotent.

Indeed, Conservative suspicion of consumerism was also evident in this period. Ignatieff highlights the conservative distaste for the culture of the marketplace: 'its pandering to the taste of the lowest common denominator, the vulgarity, and sexuality that seem to be what sells in a market culture' (1995, p. 73). According to Aldridge:

> Whenever it was forced to choose between them, Thatcherite neoliberalism upheld the conservative self. The sovereign consumer was not free to choose 'permissiveness', and educators were forbidden from 'promoting' homosexuality. Consumer sovereignty was thus constrained by the need to have conservative values.
>
> Aldridge, 2003, pp. 92–3

Under the Conservatives, therefore, the citizen-consumer was an occasional ally, whose choices and rights would discipline errant producer interests, drive down costs and improve service quality, so long as permissiveness was kept in check. In the 18 years of Conservative government a new vision of the government-citizen relationship was on offer, which discouraged dependency on the state and encouraged citizens to utilise choice, information and consultation to become empowered service users. However the inconsistencies in the Conservative approach to the consumer, and continued resistance to strands of consumerism, suggests that the citizenship regime promoted by the Conservatives was not fully consumerised.

The Labour Party in opposition

The Labour Party was more firmly wedded to the postwar welfare state than the Conservatives, and during years of opposition the achievements of the Attlee government in securing the welfare state became ever more mythologised (Klein, 2001, p. 48). However, strands of the left remained highly critical of the welfare state for its failure to respond to the diverse needs of women, ethnic minorities and the disabled, and supportive of participatory, localised, self-help ventures in opposition to the bureaucratic state (Benn, 1970; London Edinburgh Weekend Return Group, 1979; Wainwright, 1981; Hall, 1979). Also critical of the welfare state were the writers associated with *Marxism Today* and the 'New Times' manifesto (Corrigan *et al*, 1988; Hall and Jacques, 1989; Mulgan, 1991). Authors such as Stuart Hall called for the left to recognise the social significance of consumption, noting the potency of Thatcherite rhetoric on state dependence and social hierarchy (Hall, 1988). In an account of the transition from Fordism to post-Fordism, Robin Murray wrote: 'The perspective of consumption – so central to the early socialist movement – is emerging from under the tarpaulin of production...[T]he relations of consumption have been given only walk-on parts in party programmes. They should now come to the centre of the stage' (1989, pp. 48–9).

The Labour Party's electoral weakness during the 1980s, its traditional producer-oriented stance and its defensiveness towards a welfare state under attack from the Thatcher governments, meant that it came only slowly to call for new forms of accountability and responsiveness in the welfare state (Rouse and Smith, 1999, p. 244). Party modernisers under Neil Kinnock from the mid-1980s came to develop new policy initiatives to improve the responsiveness of public services to users, although without the radicalism of the new left project to transform and democratise the state (Panitch and Leys, 2001, p. 13). The party's conversion to a service user orientation stemmed from a combination of local success and national failure. At local level pioneering Labour councils, influenced by the participative ethos of the new left and the decline of traditional forms of political mobilisation, introduced more participatory and decentralised forms of service delivery (Rouse and Smith, 1999, p. 244; Gyford, 1991, p. 48). Citizen's Charters were pioneered in York and Lewisham during the late 1980s, specifying standards of service and availability of information (Rouse and Smith, 1999, p. 245). Whilst the organised consumer movement attracted little government sympathy in this period, it fed into more receptive strands within local government and the Labour Party which themselves contributed to the national debate (Gyford, 1991, p. 167).

Local authority discretion over service delivery was limited during the 1980s as council responsibilities were parcelled out between quangos, agencies and the voluntary sector, and the 'enabling authority' was born (Ridley, 1988). Local innovation flourished despite, or perhaps because of, this reduction in autonomy (Stoker, 1989, p. 153). The Public Service Orientation (PSO), developed at local level as a centre-left alternative to new public management, called on local authorities 'to look at their services from the viewpoint of the public rather than simply from the standpoint of the organisation' (Stoker, 1988, p. 117). PSO claimed a 'values' dimension, emphasising the importance and distinctiveness of public service, which was absent from the private sector-infused Conservative agenda (Rhodes, 1987,

p. 63; Stewart and Clarke, 1987, p. 161). This approach highlighted the importance of responsiveness to users without assuming that private sector models were the only inspiration for public service improvement. The endorsement of PSO approaches by prominent Labour-led councils gave it a reputation as a movement of the 'urban left' (Stoker, 1988, p. 203) – although enthusiasm for this approach also came from the centre parties (Pollitt, 1993, p. 154).

At national level a succession of election defeats led Labour to overhaul its policy agenda, which in part meant signalling a shift away from union domination (Rouse and Smith, 1999, p. 244). The party's 1989 Policy Review document stated:

> In the past, Labour has had the reputation of being more concerned with protecting the interests of the *producers* of goods and services rather than the interests of consumers. That was never accurate... Labour is naturally the party of the consumer.
>
> Labour Party, 1989, pp. 7, 41 – emphasis in the original

For Labour this approach meant, 'a new framework for public *and* private services which put people first (Labour Party, 1989, p. 7 – emphasis in the original). Labour published its own Citizen's Charter in 1992, subtitled 'Labour's better deal for consumers and citizens' (Labour Party, 1992).

After the election of Tony Blair as leader of the party in 1994 efforts to shift the party towards the centre of politics were intensified, and a 'New Labour' Party born. A focus on the user of services became a useful signal of the party's freedom from trade union influence. Blair made clear that he believed the Labour Party in the past had been too closely associated with 'producer interests' (Blair, 1995, quoted in Driver and Martell, 1999, p. 61). Many of those on the left that had contributed to earlier calls for public services to be more sensitive to their users became advisers to the new Labour leader (Leadbeater, 1988; Corrigan *et al*, 1988; Mulgan, 1991). By 1997, in response to four successive defeats and a radical reform agenda from the Conservatives, Labour had changed its name, its constitution, its internal decision-making processes and many of its policies (Driver and Martell, 1999, ch. 1). Its approach to public services emphasised fiscal discipline and services that were effective in meeting the needs of users (Labour Party, 1997).

Thus the service user had come to the attention of the major parties by 1997. Writing in 1994, Thomson argued 'Service quality and customer care are likely to be of continuing significance for management in the public sector for the foreseeable future since the focus (though articulated in different ways) is shared by all three political parties' (1994, p. 36). Indeed scholars began to speculate whether there was any alternative to the consumer orientation. As Clarke and Newman put it, in discussing public services, 'Opposing the opening out of services through consumerist initiatives is untenable, because it implies simply seeking to conserve professional power' (Clarke and Newman, 1997, p. 53). Bauman went further identifying a consumer-based social system that was so all encompassing that it closed down other options, noting 'its success in denigrating, marginalizing or rendering invisible all alternatives to itself except blatant bureaucratic domination' (Bauman, 1988, p. 93).

Conclusion

The transition from the Poor Law of the 1830s to the regulatory state of the 1990s marked a transformation not only in the role of government but also in the traditions of citizenship that underpinned it. The triumph of the postwar welfare state was to develop public services on the basis of an empowering universal citizenship, rather than as a condition of dependence and stigma. However, the emphasis on professional expertise within welfare left little scope for responsiveness to the individual users of services. During the 1980s and 1990s a shift in citizenship regime took place, with a move away from welfarist linkages towards those that cast the citizen as an individualised public sector consumer. This shift was associated with Conservative governments in central government, but aspects of it also found favour with a broader coalition of interests, particularly within local government.

Under the Conservatives, some aspects of consumerism – the adoption of private providers, expanded user choice and charter rights – were given a high profile, although users were given few new opportunities for choice beyond an enhanced exit right. Neither Thatcher nor Major oversaw the coherent adoption of a fully consumerist set of public service reforms. Often responsiveness to consumers appeared to be a pragmatic response to another political agenda, particularly disciplining producer interests. Support for the frugality of the taxpayer trumped endorsement of potentially inflationary consumer demands.

In opposition, Labour was undergoing its own conversion to the principled and pragmatic advantages of an individualised consumer orientation, particularly after Blair became leader in 1994. To under-stand the way that New Labour has framed public services and those that use them, it is necessary to do two things. The first is to outline the key themes of New Labour's public service reforms, and the second is to look in detail at the speeches and documents from the New Labour period – testing how far these are oriented to the individual or the community, to service users or to people in non-service conditional roles, and what balance is established between the three public service narratives identified in Chapter 3. The next chapter provides a broad account of public service reform under New Labour, shifting from this chapter's assessment of the rise of individualism in public services towards the theme of marketisation in public service reforms. Sub-sequent chapters go on to undertake detailed analysis of New Labour texts to understand how consumerism is manifested in the con-struction of narratives of public service reform.

5
The Context of Public Service Reform under New Labour: Marketising the Welfare State

To compare and evaluate the narratives of public service constructed by New Labour policy actors it is necessary to undertake a process of fragmentation, using content analytic methods to examine speeches and policy documents, bringing out differences across institutions, between service areas and over time. The quantitative methods used in subsequent chapters allow this textual deconstruction. However, to make sense of the component parts, it is first necessary to understand the broad outlines of public service provision under New Labour. It is also vital to place consumerism within the broader trends reshaping public service reform during New Labour's time in office.

As Chapter 4 made clear, a series of governments across several centuries have played a cumulative role in shaping public service provision in UK, and New Labour's public service reforms need to be understood as a continuation of this evolutionary practice. Most recently, the period of Conservative dominance of government under Thatcher and Major from 1979–1997 saw substantial restructuring of the state and redefinition of public service scope and entitlement. The Thatcher/Major era is relevant not only in providing a policy inheritance for New Labour but also in embedding a set of new public management-type assumptions into public service provision which New Labour has largely continued. Thus the broad story of public service reform under New Labour can best be told by identifying a series of changes introduced by the Thatcher, Major and Blair governments, all of which fit within a 'new public management' paradigm. Although the periodisation is rough, and the integrity of the paradigm disputed, discussion of public service reforms since 1979 provides the context within which to explore New Labour's narratives in future chapters.

New public management

The term new public management (NPM) has been invoked to cover the broad package of administrative reforms introduced by central governments since 1979, although the extent to which it is possible to speak of *the* new public management is disputed (Gray *et al*, 1991, p. 53; Hood, 1991, p. 3; Pollitt, 1993, p. 45; Ferlie *et al*, 1996, p. 14). Pollitt draws a line between efficiency-oriented reforms of the early 1980s, such as the improvement of financial management within the civil service, and later quality-oriented reforms such as Next Steps, quasi-markets and the Citizen's Charter (Pollitt, 1993, p. 183). He defines the early period as neo-Taylorism, given its emphasis on tightening line management within the civil service, and reserves the NPM label for the later period (Pollitt, 1993, p. 183). In a different approach, Ferlie *et al*, identify four new public managements, based respectively on efficiency, decentralisation, effectiveness and a 'public service orientation' (Ferlie *et al*, 1996, p. 14). Hood contrasts the new institutional economics strand of NPM with its business-type managerialism strand, noting 'Free to manage is a rather different slogan from free to choose' (1991, p. 6).

Despite its limitations as a coherent paradigm, the NPM model captures an approach to government that was gaining support from the mid-1970s, but is particularly associated with the Conservative governments, from 1979 to 1997, and then with New Labour after 1997. Since some of New Labour's reforms were introduced explicitly to tackle shortcomings of Conservative policies – calls for 'joined up government' and a 'new deal' on welfare, for example – it is important not to overstate the continuities. Yet the common rationale underpinning administrative and service reform in the Thatcher, Major and Blair governments commands attention. Running through these governments are a set of shared assumptions that fit the broad trajectory of NPM, and maintain its internal incoherence. Concerns over productive efficiency (the ratio of inputs to outputs) and a results orientation have been ongoing since the Thatcher era. Similarly, there has been a common approach to state restructuring as a series of principal-agent problems, best solved through separating the purchaser of services from the provider (Erridge, 2003). The twin (and sometimes conflicting) goals of strengthening management and empowering consumers have driven reforms since 1979, squeezing professional discretion from both sides (Pollitt, 1993, p. 43; Gray and Jenkins, 1995, p. 81). An assumption of the Thatcher, Major and Blair governments has been that public services will flourish through adopting the entrepreneurialism, efficiency and customer focus of the market (Blackmore, 1997, p. 30; Cairney, 2002, p. 380). Finlayson draws attention to the common strands of public choice theory underpinning reforms across this period (Finlayson, 2003b). Other authors have used the term marketisation to capture commonalities, given that the reforms have sought to shrink or ignore the difference between public services and those provided in a market (Crouch, 2003, 2007; Clarke, 2004; Whitfield, 2006; Finlayson, 2007).

The impact of NPM-type assumptions on public services can best be seen by tracing the development of three trends in service reform since 1979: cost-containment, decentralisation and risk-transfer. These three aspects of reform are considered below before going on to look in more detail at the over-arching theme of marketisation.

Cost-containment

The challenge to create 'a government that works better and costs less' was laid down by United States Vice-President and government reformer Al Gore (1993), but it can also be seen as the underlying rationale of the Conservative and Labour governments since 1979. The cost-cutting motives of the Thatcherite reforms were apparent from the efficiency reviews and Financial Management Initiative (FMI) of the early 1980s (Hennessy, 1990, p. 595). Pollitt describes cost-cutting as a key theme of administrative reforms in this era, identifying:

> [a] strong emphasis on the tighter control of civil service spending, both at the macro and middle levels (cash limits, cash planning and tighter ministerial control over civil service pay) and at the level of detail (FMI, cuts in civil service numbers, competitive tendering).
>
> Pollitt, 1993, p. 55

King quotes the government's expenditure plans for 1980–1983: 'The Government is determined not merely to halt the growth of public expenditure but progressively to reduce it' (HM Treasury, 1980, p. 5 – quoted in King, 1987, p. 120). Although the overall share of GDP taken up by state spending changed little under the Conservatives, there was a marked lack of investment in public service infrastructure (Hills, 1990). The final years of the Major governments sought to introduce tight spending controls, pushing the share of GDP spent by the state down to 37 per cent (Emmerson *et al*, 2004).

When Labour came to power in May 1997, it promised to reverse years of under-investment in public services, whilst also sticking to Conservative spending targets for two years and leaving income tax levels unchanged (Labour Party, 1997). The broad trajectory of public spending since 1999 has been upward – increasing public expenditure as a percentage of GDP to 42 per cent (Emmerson *et al*, 2004). However ministers have emphasised the need for increased investment to be accompanied by an improved ratio between inputs and outputs, to ensure that the result of greater spending was 'much more for a little more' (Pottier, 2005). To drive forward the efficiency agenda, an independent review was set up in 2003 led by Sir Peter Gershon, dubbed the 'waste-finder general' (Walker, 2004). The first stage of the Gershon review, published in July 2004, called on government to find £21.5 billion in 'efficiency savings' (Gershon, 2004). Spending money on procurement rather than in-house staffing was seen by Gershon as a way to tackle the principal-agent problems that inhibited efficient resource use, through a clearer definition of roles (ODPM, 2003; Gershon, 2004, p. 9). Alongside Gershon the government also commissioned reports into improving government productivity measures (Atkinson, 2005), and relocating public servants out of London (Lyons, 2004).

Across public services, increased pay has been conditional on service restructuring and increases in productivity (HM Treasury, 2003). The users of some public services have also had to accept new forms of conditionality. The cost-containment agenda in social housing has driven the process of large-scale voluntary transfers of council housing stock to so-called 'arms-length' management organisations (ALMOs). Tenants balloted on transfer are told that repair backlogs will only be dealt with if they support the transfer, leading some to reject a deal that they see as offering no real choice at all (Daly *et al*, 2004). Plans have been floated to make public service provision in general more conditional on lifestyle choices, as part of a new state-citizen contract (Strategy Unit, 2006). In welfare, Labour has expanded the use of means-testing of benefit payments, primarily through the use of tax credits, emphasising the importance of targeting resources rather than providing universal cover (Lister, 2003, p. 431; Smith, 2004, p. 223). Whilst such concerns for allocative efficiency (focusing resources where they are most useful) were assumed to be compatible with broader concerns to secure productive efficiency (i.e. to improve the ratio of inputs to outputs), they were not necessarily pulling in the same direction. A Parliamentary report on the U.K. tax credits system in June 2005, for example, highlighted the wastefulness and ineffectiveness of the complex payment system (Parliamentary Ombudsman, 2005).

The cost-containment agenda has also been pushed forward through the expansion of co-payments, asking users to contribute directly to the costs of services that were previously funded through general taxation. Road tolls have been introduced in London and on some major trunk roads, with plans for further expansion (Eddington, 2006). University students have been required to pay tuition fees of up to £3000 a year from 2006, a cap which looks set to be lifted when it is reviewed in 2008–2009 (Smith, 2006). Blair has indicated his willingness to explore other ways in which co-payments can be introduced into service provision (2003), although concerns have been expressed about high administration costs and detrimental impact on access to services for poorer citizens (Wanless, 2002, §4.40–§4.44).

Decentralisation

Running through these cost containment initiatives has been an impetus to decentralise and diversify service provision as part of moves to increase efficiency (Gray and Jenkins, 1995, p. 86). This idea, that central government should concentrate on 'steering not rowing' (Osborne and Gaebler, 1992), was endorsed by the Thatcher government and Major governments (Butler, 1994; Gray and Jenkins, 1995, p. 81), as well as by New Labour (Blair and Schröder, 1999). The process of decentralising service provision has involved ceding operational control of policy implementation whilst maintaining strategic and financial oversight (Rhodes, 1997). Under the Conservatives, this agenda can be seen in a range of initiatives from the creation of 'next steps' agencies to the contracting out of services to the private and voluntary sectors. From waste collection to the provision of care homes for the elderly, the state increasingly became the commissioner of services provided by non-state bodies. Strategic oversight was maintained through performance measures, in what Michael Power calls an 'audit explosion' (1994, p. 1). Financial control was intensified rather than loosened, as evidenced by measures to strip away local government financial autonomy (Travers and Esposito, 2003).

Rather than rejecting the performance targets and efficiency measures of their predecessors, New Labour in power after 1997 sought to extend and improve them. Alongside tough audit regimes for local government, central government departments were required to sign Public Service Agreements with the Treasury, making future funding conditional on meeting a series of targets (Painter, 1999). The creation of new units within central government departments to monitor and enforce delivery marked the intensification of a focus on results (Prabhakar, 2004, pp. 167–9). However, the government has argued that targets are not a tool for centralisation but quite the opposite: they are characteristics of 'lean headquarters that set clear targets, set the incentives and rewards, provide the freedom for local managers to deliver...' (Brown, 2003). Thus they are presented as a mechanism to foster the autonomy of service providers, rather than a centralising force – although as Clarke points out this only holds, 'so long as local autonomy is exercised in the right directions' (2004, p. 38).

The Labour governments' approach to service decentralisation has been more focused on partnerships and networks than that of their predecessors. Area-based partnerships in public services, such as the Sure Start programme and Local Strategic Partnerships, have sought to address service fragmentation, for example between education, health and social service providers (Painter, 1999, p. 110). To encourage local partnerships, ministers have indicated a willingness to explore light-touch audit regimes, particularly for high performing authorities (Brown, 2003). Ministers have come to talk of a 'new localism' and 'double devolution' reducing the numbers of national targets and encouraging local authorities to explore innovative approaches to service delivery involving the profit and not-for-profit sectors (Miliband, 2006; Communities and Local Government, 2006).

Harnessing the creativity and flexibility of voluntary sector organisations (also known as social enterprises or the third sector) in the delivery of services has been a key priority for New Labour (Blair, 1999), leading to the signing of a national Compact between the government and the voluntary and community sector and the creation of a Minister for Social Enterprise. The 2005 Labour Party manifesto stated that new opportunities would be created for such enterprises to run core aspects of state provision, from job centres to probation services and primary care facilities in health (Labour Party, 2005). The government has indicated that it sees 'communities' as important stakeholders in the improvement of public services, and seeks to give new powers to communities to deliver services as well as to tackle those who threaten the community through anti-social behaviour (Lister, 2003, p. 428).

To extend decentralisation, both the Conservatives and New Labour have experimented with new forms of para-state institutions, combining private and public management and finance. City Technology

Colleges (CTCs), for example, were introduced by the Education Reform Act 1988, as high-tech 'state-independent' schools based in inner cities, with capital funding and management expertise provided by the private sector, and ongoing resource funding provided by the state. They were to be a 'unique partnership between government and business', although only 15 were ever created (DES, 1986 – quoted in Whitty *et al*, 1993, p. 2). The Labour government resuscitated the initiative with its school academies programme (Catalyst/Public World, 2006). The academy initiative closes 'failing' schools and brings in a small amount of private finance to contribute to the costs of new premises. For sponsorship of to £2 million, private investors get to name the school and to nominate a majority of the members of the governing board. The financial risks of academies remain with the public sector as all future costs (including capital overspend, salaries, overheads) are borne by the state in perpetuity. The Education and Inspections Act 2006 opened the way for more schools to develop partnerships with the private and voluntary sectors.

In the NHS since 2004 high-performing hospital trusts have been able to become public interest companies with foundation trust status. Foundation hospitals have greater freedoms than other hospitals to manage their finances and sell off capital assets. Representatives of local communities are elected to the management board of the trusts, in an effort to strengthen accountability to local populations (Walshe, 2003). In health, as in education, new institutional forms are premised on greater involvement of service users and the private sector, whilst the role of elected local government is downgraded.

There are ongoing debates about whether two decades of decentralisation have 'hollowed out' the centre of government or enhanced its core strategic capacity (Rhodes, 1997; Newman, 2001, p. 125). Certainly, there is an ongoing tendency of central government, be it run by the Conservatives or Labour, to insist on audit mechanisms to check local performance and to retain Treasury control over public sector borrowing (Peston, 2006, p. 296).

Risk-transfer

Running through all these initiatives have been efforts to transfer risk away from central political institutions. A theory of 'risk society' underpinned the third way ideology endorsed by New Labour (Giddens, 1998), although it is possible to see risk transfer as an underlying rationale for earlier Conservative Party reforms (Corry, 1998, p. 91), inspired themselves by 1970s fears of government 'overload' and 'crisis' (O'Connor, 1973; Crozier *et al*, 1975; King, 1975; Habermas, 1976). A key priority for Thatcher and Major was the transfer of assets to the private sector through the privatisation of nationalised industries and utilities, including gas, water, electricity, telecommunications and the railways. Those assets that remained in state hands were moved from the core state into agencies and quangos, or were managed (if not owned) by private providers.

Under New Labour, privatisation has taken a different route, primarily through the use of private finance in public sector projects. The Private Finance Initiative and Public Private Partnerships are designed to reduce state risks and costs through harnessing the efficiency incentives of private sector operatives. Infrastructure investment projects, such as the Building Schools for the Future programme which aims to update all secondary school building stock within the next ten years, are conditional on the use of private finance schemes to design, build, finance and operate the properties (Painter, 1999, p. 105). Core aspects of state provision such as social housing are now built and run by private companies and social enterprises with minimal state oversight. One of the most radical and controversial uses of outsourcing has been the use of Independent Sector Treatment Centres by the NHS to cut waiting lists for elective surgery.

A paradox of privatisation, private finance initiatives (PFI) and public private partnerships (PPP) has been that a rationale of risk transfer has been accompanied by a tendency to shield private contractors from major risks to induce participation (Corry, 1998, p. 91; Grieve Smith, 2002, p. 9). The large-scale privatisations of the 1980s often created monopolies with protected status for at least the first few years of flotation, along with cosy relationships with regulators (Corry, 1998, p. 95; Pollitt, 2003, p. 13). Under PFI, the political costs of failure in big capital projects remain so high that central and local governments have to bail out poor performers, diminishing any sense of risk-transfer. A Public Accounts Committee's report of the enormous windfall profits made by PFI schemes, revealed how refinancing deals were negotiated on the basis of insulation from risk (Hencke, 2005). PPP schemes often involve 20–25 year contracts for services such as upgrading GP surgeries and providing school meals, making it very difficult for the government to extract itself when the services provided under contract do not meet changing user needs (Pollock, 2004).

A second form of risk-transfer, undertaken within those parts of the state that are not suitable for privatisation, has been from the centre to individual service providers, through the use of internal markets. From 1991 the key change in the NHS was the shift to GP fundholding and an internal market between the purchasers of healthcare (doctors) and the providers (hospitals and community services) (Klein, 2001). Hospitals became financially independent corporations, required to generate enough income to break even (Pollock, 2004). Although nominally abolishing the internal market after 1997, the Labour governments have maintained the purchaser/provider split and moved further in the direction of an internal market by introducing a payment-by-results system. In 2005 the government announced plans to further restructure primary care such that the NHS was the commissioner rather than provider of services, with contracts being awarded to the private and voluntary sectors to provide care (DoH, 2005a).

A third form of risk-transfer that has been pursued is from government to the individual. There are signs of this emergent agenda under the Conservatives in its policies on right-to-buy in housing, private pensions and subsidies for health insurance. As Smith puts it, 'The goal of Conservative policy was to free individuals from the state, the dependency culture and from taxation, to enable them to make their own choices and create their own opportunities' (2004, p. 215). Under Labour, risk transfer has been part of a response to the perceived exigencies of globalisation, equipping workers with the skills to respond to a global knowledge economy whilst creating a more 'flexible' labour market (Moss and O'Loughlin, 2005; Finlayson, 2007, p. 42; Coats, 2007, p. 133). Asset-based forms of welfare – such as the Child Trust Fund and Savings Gateway – promote individual rather than collective provision for future needs in the 'social investment state' (Lister, 2003, p. 427; Whitfield, 2006, p. 60).

The growth of compulsory work schemes in the UK shifts responsibility for unemployment to the individual, focusing on individual sanctions rather than tackling high levels of structural unemployment in declining areas (Bennett, 2002, p. 31). From the Conservatives Jobseekers Allowance to New Labour's New Deal, benefits are conditional on recipients actively seeking work or training. As Finlayson puts it, 'The welfare claimant must understand him or herself as in need of retraining, reskilling and rebranding so that they can get back on the market' (2007, p. 43).

The rhetoric of user choice, which has been central to public service reform under Thatcher, Major and Blair, can also be seen as a form of individual risk-transfer. Choice has been put forward in a wide range of different services and processes – schools, hospitals, housing, social care – many of which are potentially liberating for service users, but some of which raise concerns about risk, capacity and equity. New forms of information are made available, and new technologies harnessed – hospital mortality rates, school league tables, National Student Survey – to make users more aware of their choices and the risks associated with them.

Extending choice to social housing applicants, for example, was a core element of New Labour's approach to social housing. The Homelessness Act 2002 required local authorities to offer people, 'a choice of housing accommodation' or 'the opportunity to express preferences about the housing accommodation to be allocated to them' (HMSO, 2002, §167 (1A)). Local authorities were encouraged to move to a 'choice-based letting service' in which waiting time becomes the 'currency' of the social housing market (DETR, 2000a, §9.21). The choice-based approach was said to 'enable people to balance their own "felt" need, as measured by the time they felt able to wait, against the availability of the properties they might be able to secure' (DETR, 2000a, §9.20). Thus people take their own decisions about how desperate they are for accommodation and what types of housing they are prepared to accept.

In the NHS a range of initiatives have sought to involve users more directly in bearing the risks of health-management. The expert patient scheme has engaged those with chronic ill health in managing their own conditions (Greener, 2005). The DoH's *Expert Patient* document noted that patients can 'become key decision-makers in the treatment process' and encouraged NHS trusts to pilot expert patient schemes (Appleby *et al*, 2003, p. 10). The public health white paper, *Choosing Health*, published in 2004, made clear that people were expected to take responsibility for producing their own healthy lives, through the avoidance of damaging foods and substances (DoH, 2004).

The introduction of co-payments is also part of the risk-transfer agenda. Tuition fees for higher education, for example, are justified on the basis of the higher future earnings of graduates compared to non-graduates, although concerns have been raised about the extent to which such income differentials will be maintained as the market becomes saturated with graduates (Hoare, 2002). Another form of risk-transfer pursued by the government has been the direct payment of care budgets to those eligible for state support. An initiative piloted by the Conservatives at the end of their last term has been extended to cover a wide range of recipients of social care (Ungerson, 2004). Budget-holders are given greater freedom to manage their own package of care, including the payment and management of care providers, giving people the freedom to buy in the services they need on an individual basis. Users of services become the employers and commissioners of their own care provision (Frew, 2006). Underpinning the reforms is an assumption that service users are best equipped to make their own choices, and that freedom of choice improves services whilst promoting independence. Whilst such an initiative is empowering for many users, it passes the responsibility for the selection of appropriate service and personnel from the state to the individual.

Marketisation and consumerism

Cost-containment, decentralisation and risk-transfer can all be interpreted as trends that seek to bring the public sector in line with the market. The distinctiveness of public services, highlighted in Chapter 2, becomes eroded by the introduction of markets into service provision – either in direct form (privatisation) or as hybrid forms such as quasi-markets (purchaser-provider splits), pseudo-markets (a customer service ethos) or other forms of 'market replication' (such as reliance on business advisers) (Le Grand and Bartlett, 1993; Brereton and Temple, 1999; Crouch, 2003, p. 4, 2007, p. 53).

Clarke characterises the neo-liberal restructuring of the state under Thatcher, Major and Blair as a form of marketisation, in which 'the universality and superiority of the market as a decision-making mechanism' is asserted (2004, p. 35). Whitfield particularly associates marketisation with New Labour's reforms of public services, arguing 'New Labour has gone much further in the marketisation of public services and the welfare state than the Tories did between 1979–97' (2006, p. 12). Titles of recent books on New Labour's public service reforms, including *Market-Driven Politics* (Leys, 2003) and *NHS Plc* (Pollock, 2004), highlight the recurrence of market-oriented interpretations.

For other authors, New Labour has pulled back from the high water mark of marketisation under the Conservatives, and reasserted the importance of community, equality, responsibility and the social sphere. Certainly, the third way approach embraced by New Labour was presented as 'an alternative to both the untrammelled free market (of neo-liberalism) and the strong state (of social democracy)' (Levitas, 2000, p. 191). Smith has pointed to discontinuities between the Conservative and New Labour approaches to welfare arguing: '[A] key difference exists in that the role of the private sector [under New Labour] is to supplement and in a way improve, the provision of public goods rather than to replace them' (2004, p. 224). Finlayson also sees some difference with the neo-liberal Conservative project: 'New Labour has not simply capitulated to neo-liberal marketisation. But in seeking to reinvent the state for the neo-liberal era it has failed to think beyond it, and has come to understand freedom and equality in market terms' (2007, p. 44).

A number of authors have noted the international pressures that are pushing UK governments more resolutely to embrace the market (Leys, 2003; Whitfield, 2006). A series of European Court of Justice rulings seem to call into question the subsidies that member-states pay to maintain public services (known at the European Union level as 'services of general interest'), such as energy, postal and transport services. In 2005 the European Commission considered a new services directive (the so-called 'Bolkenstein Directive'), which sought to create a single market in all services, including some provided by governments. Although the directive was successfully resisted it is likely to be an area to which the Commission will return (Rowland *et al*, 2004). Pressures are also intensifying from the World Trade Organisation, which seeks to expand the General Agreement on Trade in Services to cover a wider range of sectors, including some traditionally in the public domain (Martin, 2001).

These international market pressures, coming after almost 20 years of domestic market-type reforms to the public service in the UK, have profound consequences for the UK's citizenship regime. The implications of marketisation stretch beyond public services, as Finlayson concludes:

> The problem to which Blairism is the answer is that of how most effectively to subordinate first social policy and then more and more areas of social life to market commodification, in the belief that this enhances freedom, fairness and equality... The space between the private activity of market exchange (self-oriented and instrumental in its approach to the world) and the public activity of society-making (other-oriented and ethical in approach) is becoming lost.
>
> Finlayson, 2007, pp. 43, 45

It is clear that in such a context, those forms of citizenship most closely aligned with private economic interests are likely to flourish, whilst civic republican and communitarian approaches will suffocate. In particular, when the marketised public services discussed here combine with the individualised accounts of the public service user outlined in the previous chapter, conditions are created for the dominance of the citizen as consumer.

Conclusion

The broad accounts of public service development and reform presented here and in Chapter 4 outline the context within which New Labour has developed its public service agenda. In particular the twin themes of individualisation and marketisation of public services demonstrate an environment of public service provision highly conducive to a consumerist citizenship regime. Yet, as discussed in the first part of the book, there are various dimensions to the public service consumer, likely to be expressed differently across levels of government, between services, and over time. Marketised public services can easily accommodate the user as consumer, but are also oriented to the efficiency concerns of the individual as taxpayer (Clarke, 2004, p. 40). As discussed in Chapter 4, individualised services have been oriented to the citizen, as well as the consumer and customer. Differences between services also command attention. Traditional notions of the service user as client have been more important historically in welfare than in health or education, whereas the notion of user as customer is easier to reconcile with transport services than with policing. New Labour's well-developed tendency to orient services to the community as well as the individual service user demands that attention be paid to collective aspects of delivery as well. The three narratives of public service – standardisation, differentiation and coproduction – all interact differently with the themes of individualisation and marketisation, and their balance and significance in the New Labour project need to be understood better. It is necessary therefore to move from the broad contours of public service reform into a more detailed and comparative textual account of New Labour's public service policies.

6
Tony Blair: Consumerism and Community

The theoretical and historical discussion undertaken so far indicates that political, economic and social shifts by 1997 had combined to give greater power and significance to the individual as the consumer of public services. However, the Conservatives had not consolidated a consumerist citizenship regime by 1997, and were resistant to some of the inflationary pressures of consumerism in public services. When New Labour came to power therefore it found a transitional citizenship regime, with new charter rights for users and some extension of choice, but little sign that services themselves were being reworked around their users. Policy actors therefore had the option of moving more resolutely in the direction of consumerism, or of pursuing an alternative citizenship regime.

The three chapters that follow use content analysis of speeches and documents, along with interview data, to explore different aspects of New Labour's approach to public services and assess how far it opted for the consumerist approach. The definition of a consumerist citizenship regime is as identified in Chapter 3: focusing on the individual service user; driven by the user's subjective preferences; and utilising the standardisation or differentiation narratives of public service. A set of keywords are identified here to explore the language used to refer to the users of public services and the narratives constructed around them.

This chapter analyses the speeches of Tony Blair, who became Prime Minister after Labour's election victory in May 1997. The next chapter explores the detailed policy aspects of the citizenship regime by considering government white and green papers. The citizenship regime at local level is the focus of Chapter 8. Together these chapters help to provide an insight into the extent to which a consistent consumerist solution set is being developed between levels of government, between services and over time. The chapter begins by discussing the measures of consumerism, building on the discussion of consumerism and public service narratives in Chapter 3. It then goes on to analyse the use of language in the 193 speeches made by Blair from May 1997 to December 2005.

Developing measures of consumerism

As discussed in Chapter 2, a key indicator of the citizenship regime is the discourse used by policy actors (politicians and bureaucrats) within central and local government. To understand how they frame the solution set it is necessary to understand the narratives they construct around public services. In particular sources need to be identified that test the following:

1. In the texts, how do policy actors refer to people: do they use service conditional or non-service conditional terms?
2. In the texts, do policy actors accord particular weight to the subjective preferences and expectations of users, over other sources of knowledge?
3. In the texts, do policy actors take a consequentialist position, prioritising individual utility maximisation over structural or ideological aspects of service delivery?
4. How significant are the three narratives in the texts (standardisation, differentiation or coproduction) and what is the balance between them?

There are various potential sources for policy actors' discourse on public services, including speeches, documents and interviews. To develop valid and reliable insights into the perspectives of policy actors it is helpful to make use of a diverse range of material. Validity in this context is best explained as 'the extent to which a measuring procedure represents the intended, and only the intended, concept' (Neuendorf, 2002, p. 112). Through triangulating different methods, each utilising different sources, it is possible to maximise the validity of the analysis, using the results of documentary content analysis and interviewing to corroborate each other, for example (Webb *et al*, 1996, pp. 12–7; Davies, 2001, p. 75).

Here, content analysis of documents was combined with qualitative analysis of interviews and focus group data, to test for an orientation towards the service user and the privileging of the user's perspective, and to probe the balance between narratives. Speeches of the Prime

Minister, white and green papers from national government, and corporate plans from local government were gathered together and analysed using content analytic methods. Content analysis, as Weber explains, 'is a research method that uses a set of procedures to make valid inferences from text' (1990, p. 9. See also Berelson, 1952). Two sets of keyword searches were undertaken on the speeches and documents. Keywords are the 'manifest variables', which reveal 'latent variables', in this case a consumerist solution set (Neuendorf, 2002, p. 23). The first set of keywords were designed to assess the terminology used to refer to people in the speeches and documents, and in particular the balance between community and individual terms, and between terms that are conditional and non-conditional on service use. The same number of keywords was chosen for each category to assist comparative quantitative analysis between categories.

A first group of keywords was selected that contained terms not conditional on service use. Three keywords were chosen which have been central to debates about New Labour and public service reform:

– Community
– Citizen
– Taxpayer

A second group of keywords contained terms that are conditional on service use, but not specific to any particular service. Three terms were selected here that have been applied to the users of public services:

– Client
– Consumer
– Customer

A third category contained keywords that refer to individuals (or aggregates of individuals) as users of specific public services. Three terms were chosen which are relevant to key public services:

– Pupil
– Parent
– Patient

Clearly these nine terms are overlapping, and in practice people perform all of these roles, often on a daily basis. However, the roles are indicative of different relationships between the state and the public. The citizen stands in a different relationship to the state than the community, the taxpayer, the consumer or the patient. An assumption is made here that the usage of one of these terms rather than another in a speech or policy document is suggestive of the solution set that policy actors construct about the roles and status of that group or individual. In the way in which the terms are used, and the assumptions that are made about their preferences and expectations, otherwise latent aspects of the citizenship regime can be explored.

The keywords were chosen as nine of the most significant words relating to public service users rather than a comprehensive list designed to cover every word that policy actors might use to refer to people. By looking at their relative weighting and the context in which they are used it should be possible to draw out some of the themes that are significant to an understanding of the citizenship regime. Of particular interest is the balance between the service conditional and non-service conditional terms. In a consumerist solution set, it would be expected that services would be talked about most in relation to the individuals that benefit from them (consumers, customers, clients, pupils, parents, patients), rather than non-service conditional terms (community, citizen, taxpayer).

A second set of keywords was developed to explore the balance between the three public service narratives in the speeches and documents. Since the first narrative highlights the importance of delivering standardised and accessible services, keywords here were selected as common terms likely to be indicative of standard public services. It is impossible to identify or include all such words but the list below offers six that have a claim to be associated with consistent and high quality services:

- Access
- Inform
- Standard
- Target
- Convenient
- Right

The second narrative focuses on delivering a differentiated service for each user, so again six keywords were identified which were likely to tap into efforts to provide differentiated public services. These terms are all associated with moves to design services to more closely reflect the needs of individual users:

- Choice
- Individual
- Personal
- Responsive
- Diverse
- Tailor

In the third narrative, users participate in shaping service outcomes, and so key words selected here were those that indicated an active role for the service user. All of the words below have been associated with efforts to give users a more productive role in shaping service delivery:

- Opportunity
- Engage
- Involve
- Empower
- Participate
- Responsible

Together, these keywords allow for an exploration of New Labour's public service solution set, across levels of government and between services. The words have face validity: 'the extent to which a measure "on the face of things," seems to tap the desired concept' (Neuendorf, 2002, p. 115). They were also selected to be semantically valid: '[w]ords or other coding units classified together need to possess similar connotations' (Weber, 1990, p. 21. See also Bara and Budge, 2001, p. 14). The measures have construct validity, in the sense of meshing with other accounts of New Labour. As discussed in Chapter 3 a number of authors have highlighted aspects of New Labour that are consistent with the criteria of consumerism identified here.

The frequency with which the keywords were used in the speeches and documents was explored through generating word counts in the software package N6. Weber explains that although counting the number of keywords can be a blunt tool to assess the nuance of documents, it can also serve useful purposes:

First, counting generates results that allow for more precise comparisons among texts. Second, we want to know how much more (or less) attention is devoted to some issues than others. Third, quantitative analytical procedures often reveal similarities and differences among texts that would be difficult, if not impossible, to detect otherwise.

Weber, 1990, p. 74

All texts were coded using the sentence as the unit of analysis. Findings could thus be given as a proportion of the text units in that document, facilitating comparison between longer and shorter documents. In undertaking the keyword counts, word roots were used, allowing a range of suffixes. A search for 'communit*' for example generated hits for community, community's, communities, communities', and so on. More details on the content analytic methodology, including measures of reliability, are provided in Appendix 1.

Whilst word counting can be a useful guide to patterns across a large number of texts, it is also important to remain alert to the context within which the terms are used. Thus alongside the quantitative study, qualitative analysis of key-word-in-context lists was conducted. This analysis allowed an exploration of how the terms were used, and whether the indicators of consumerism – a subject orientation towards user preferences, an emphasis on outcomes rather than structures of delivery – were evident in the speeches, command papers and corporate plans. Alongside the analysis of keywords, interview data from central and local government was used to probe some of the distinctive aspects of the New Labour solution set. A full list of interviewees is given in Appendix 2, along with details of the interview design. Focus groups were also used to understand how people talk about public services and to explore the congruence between New Labour's arguments and public attitudes.

Consumerism in public services

Chapter 4 revealed the contingent and shifting nature of the package of social production activities clustered within the term welfare state or public services. It also showed how the particular bundle of services on offer at any point was linked to conceptions of citizenship, accounts of human nature and productive practices within the private sector. Studying public services therefore reveals something about the way that policy actors frame the government-citizen relationship, as well as exposing the service specific discourses. As a 2005 government green paper states: 'Our public services define what we want our society to be, and reflect its values and commitment to social justice and equity' (DoH, 2005b). Thus studying public services provides a way of analysing how policy actors construct problems, offer solutions and express the values that lie behind their vision of society.

The focus here is on a range of public services, including education, health, welfare (incorporating benefits, housing and social care), law and order and transport, to draw out the extent to which a consumer orientation is evident. These five policy areas provide useful case studies for exploring consumerism because they construct the government-citizen relationship in different ways. As discussed in Chapter 2, education, health and welfare are private goods provided by government because of their perceived 'merit' and positive externalities (Savas, 1987, p. 55). Law and order, in contrast, is a classic public good in the sense that it is non-rival and non-excludable (Samuelson, 1954). Public transport is excludable and rationed through a user charge, as a 'toll good' (Savas, 1987, p. 47; Ostrom, 1989, p. 47).

Although users 'consume' all of these services, they do so in different ways, dependent in part on the nature of the good and in part on the historical development of that good in a particular state. All those within the borders of the state fall under the jurisdiction of policing and criminal justice services, and there is little scope to opt out, aside from diplomatic immunity and the use of private security guards. Thus security has been a characteristic function of the state both theoretically and historically, whereas other services are more historically contingent. State education from 5 to 16, for example, is a legal requirement in the UK, and as a universal service shares some of the features of security, but is firmly rooted in postwar notions of the importance of education and the responsibilities of government. Public health and social care services are similarly universal, in terms of entitlement, but are provided only on the basis of professional assessment of need. Welfare benefits and social housing are means-tested, and allocated only to those who lack financial resources. In the UK, all these services are tax-funded, although there may also be means-tested forms of copayment, such as prescription charges and rent payments. Public transport is available to all who choose to use it and, although services may be tax-subsidised, they are also paid for at the point of use.

Thus whereas the postwar welfare state tended to characterise its users as clients, as discussed in Chapter 4, a client (a user dependent on professional expertise) seems most the appropriate term for rationed services such as health and welfare. Public transport users are more closely analogous to the payment-oriented definition of customer given in Chapter 3. Since education from 5 to 16 and criminal justice services are provided as a condition of being resident in a state – and involve little or no volition from the user – they could be characterised as applying to users as citizens or residents, rather than customers or clients.

The three public service narratives are likely to be unequally balanced between the different services. In public transport, a standardised, accessible service, would seem to be more important than a differentiated service or one that seeks to involve its users. Within education, health and welfare, the narratives may be more balanced: users are likely to want standardised and accessible services, which respond to their individual needs but may also want opportunities to be engaged in the service process. Within all three services, however, choice is constrained by legal requirements, medical exigencies and professional gatekeeping. Law and order is a different type of service. It requires people to have a shared responsibility for law enforcement, but is often used by people – victims and perpetrators of crime – that are unwilling consumers, and may wish to play little role in coproducing outcomes. It is difficult to see choice or personalisation playing much of a role in policing, whereas rights and access to legal services are important. Most obvious in the law and order context, but also having resonance for other services, is the question of who is the user. All of these services are provided by the state, in part at least, because they have externalities: communities benefit from integrated transport systems, a skilled workforce, low rates of contagious disease, low risk of destitution, and protection by the police. The consumer approach encourages attention to be focused on the direct beneficiary, but this may distort patterns of service delivery. In some services the main beneficiary may be unclear; consider, for example, the debate about whether parents or pupils are the consumers of education.

Through analysing the speeches of the Prime Minister – and in later chapters other government texts – it is possible to assess how far the narratives constructed around public services are consistent with the different features of these services, reflect the ambiguities in their delivery and link into the traditional postwar conceptions of service delivery. Although content analysis can be a blunt tool for understanding the nuanced accounts that policy-makers give, it has the advantage of helping to identify patterns across documents and over time, revealing consistencies and shifts that might otherwise remain hidden.

As leader of the government through two full terms and part of a third, Tony Blair's speeches are a useful starting point for considering New Labour's solution set. The speeches can be searched to analyse their theme and keywords and to assess the relative importance that

Blair accords to particular topics and vocabulary. Since the speeches are scripted, unlike the *ad hoc* responses that the Prime Minister might give in interviews or press conferences, they can be used to understand the deliberate construction of public service narratives.

A corpus of Blair speeches as Prime Minister between May 1997 and December 2005 was constructed from the archive of speeches on the 10 Downing Street website. These are the formal speeches that Blair gave in his capacity as Prime Minister during this period. They exclude the political speeches he gave as party leader – for example his speeches to the Labour Party annual conference or to affiliate organisations – which are not systematically archived. However since the analysis focuses on Blair's role as leader of government, the exclusion of party leader speeches does not undermine the validity of the findings. A total of 193 speeches were downloaded from the Downing Street website and saved into N6 software to allow coding and searches.

Speeches were coded by policy theme (such as public services, foreign policy and the economy) to allow later disaggregation of keyword findings by policy. A dictionary of policy categories for coding the speeches was developed inductively by reading through the speeches to extract key themes. The speeches were then coded using the dictionary as a codebook, as detailed in Appendix 1.

Table 6.1 shows the total number of speeches made by Blair between May 1997 and December 2005. It also shows the total number of text units (sentences), and breaks the data down into first, second and third terms and monthly averages. Total and average text units are also given. The first and second terms are included in their entirety. A small amount of data from the third term is utilised, drawn from the period May to December 2005 to illustrate the extent to which Blair is carrying forward themes from the second term into the third.

As the table shows, Blair made just under two speeches a month on average during the full period, and his speeches got slightly longer over time. However, there is generally little fluctuation over the period, helping to provide stable comparisons over time. Given that a much smaller set of speeches are available for the third term, all data from this period must be treated with some circumspection. More reliable patterns can be inferred from the larger data sets of the first and second terms.

In the discussion below where extracts from speeches are used, they are referenced with the date of the speech. The full text of all speeches is available from the 10 Downing Street website: www.number10.gov.uk. The discussion below does not disaggregate speeches according to their

Table 6.1 Blair speeches, 1997–2005

Term	Time period	Length (months)	Number of speeches	Average speeches/ month	Total text units	Average text units/ speech
First term	1 May 1997–7 June 2001	51	101	1.98	11,590	115
Second term	8 June 2001–5 May 2005	47	79	1.68	9,390	119
Third term	6 May 2005–31 December 2005	8	13	1.63	1,566	121
Total	1 May 1997–31 December 2005	106	193	1.82	22,546	117

audience; although context does matter – Blair is unlikely to give the same speech to a group of nurses as to the Confederation of British Industry – an assumption is made here that all Blair's speeches are made for the national and international audience that hear them through newspapers, television, radio and the Internet.

Policy themes in Blair's speeches

Blair has described public service reform as the government's 'crusade' (14 July 2001) and 'defining priority' (10 June 2002). How far public services have played such a central role in Blair's premiership can be explored in a variety of ways. The increased investment in public services, particularly health and education, for example, is one indicator that public services have been a priority for the New Labour administrations to greater extent than their predecessors (Prabhakar, 2004).

Here attention focuses on the priority that Blair accorded to public services in his speeches, and the way that priorities shifted between services over time. All the text units in the 193 speeches were coded by policy area using the categories set out in the codebook. Transport is included as a public service category even though government has little direct role in running transport services, because policy actors continue to play an important part in regulating and steering provision. The general service category includes sentences that mention more than one public service or public services in general, although where possible sentences were coded into a specific area rather than this general category. Table 6.2 below shows the total number of text units and speeches for each of the policy areas. Some speeches include more than one theme so the columns showing the number of speeches do not add up to the total number of speeches.

The table provides a guide to the way that Blair ranges across the different themes in his speeches. Overall, he talks most about public services and the combined category of Europe and foreign affairs, devoting about the same proportion of text units to both of these topics. The distribution over time is worth noting. Public services are the most talked about policy area in the first and third terms whereas foreign policy dominates the second term. The influence of events is evident here, with the attacks of 11 September 2001 coming only three months into Labour's second term, and followed by interventions in Afghanistan and Iraq. In Labour's first term, Kosovo was the only major overseas intervention. Moving into the third term, Blair raises foreign affairs in more speeches than public services, but devotes more

Table 6.2   Blair speeches by theme

	First term Units	First term Speeches	Second term Units	Second term Speeches	Third term Units	Third term Speeches	Total Units	Total Speeches
Public services, all	3,340 (28.8%)	63 (62.4%)	3,192 (34.0%)	40 (50.6%)	569 (37.6%)	8 (61.5%)	7,191 (32.0%)	111 (57.5%)
General	526 (4.5%)	32 (31.7%)	594 (6.3%)	20 (25.3%)	123 (8.1%)	8 (61.5%)	1,243 (5.5%)	60 (31.1%)
Education	1,092 (9.4%)	32 (31.7%)	1,027 (10.9%)	24 (30.4%)	336 (22.2%)	5 (38.5%)	2,455 (10.9%)	61 (31.6%)
Health	875 (7.6%)	14 (13.9%)	237 (2.5%)	14 (17.7%)	13 (0.9%)	2 (15.4%)	1,125 (5.0%)	30 (15.5%)
Welfare	375 (3.2%)	24 (23.8%)	504 (5.4%)	15 (19.0%)	35 (2.3%)	4 (30.8%)	914 (4.1%)	42 (21.8%)
Transport	199 1.7%	9 (8.9%)	50 (0.5%)	8 (10.1%)	12 (0.8%)	1 (7.7%)	261 (1.2%)	18 (9.3%)
Law and order	363 (3.1%)	11 (10.9%)	780 (8.3%)	18 (22.8%)	50 (3.3%)	1 (7.7%)	1,193 (5.3%)	30 (15.5%)
Europe and foreign affairs	2,929 (25.3%)	47 (46.5%)	3,960 (42.2%)	45 (57.0%)	474 (31.3%)	9 (69.2%)	7,363 (32.7%)	101 (52.3%)
Economy, industry and technology	1,931 (16.7%)	33 (32.7%)	1,008 (10.7%)	17 (21.5%)	160 (10.6%)	4 (30.8%)	3,099 (13.8%)	54 (28.0%)
Government-citizen relationship	1,529 (13.2%)	39 (38.6%)	228 (2.4%)	11 (13.9%)	235 (15.5%)	7 (53.9%)	1,992 (8.9%)	57 (29.5%)
Constitution/ civil service	925 (8.0%)	26 (25.7%)	544 (5.9%)	6 (7.6%)	10 (0.7%)	1 (7.7%)	1,489 (6.6%)	33 (17.1%)
Environment and agriculture	657 (5.7%)	10 (9.9%)	448 (4.8%)	7 (8.9%)	14 (0.9%)	2 (15.4%)	1,119 (5.0%)	19 (9.8%)
Culture, media and sport	189 (1.6%)	5 (5.0%)	0 (0.0%)	0 (0.0%)	52 (3.4%)	4 (30.8%)	241 (1.1%)	9 (4.7%)
Total	11,590 (100.0%)	101 (100.0%)	9,390 (100.0%)	79 (100.0%)	1,514 (100.0%)	13 (100.0%)	22,494 (100.0%)	193 (100.0%)

Percentages show keyword usage as a proportion of total public service text units, i.e. sentences, for each term.

sentences to talking about public services. There is an indicator here of Blair seeking to move the territory back onto public services after the 2005 election – in which Labour won on the support of less than a quarter of the electorate – whilst having to make reference to ongoing instability in Iraq and elsewhere.

Disaggregating the public service category reveals some interesting patterns in Blair's speeches. The most popular category (discussed almost twice as often as any other single public service or public services in general) is education. Blair raises this theme in almost a third of speeches. This fits with his much-cited claim before coming into office that New Labour's three key themes would be 'education, education, education' (Blair, 1996). However, it is in Labour's third term that education is particularly significant for Blair (raised in 22 per cent of sentences), a time when he is defending Labour's controversial education white paper, proposing to give the private and voluntary sectors more of a role in running schools. In earlier periods, although education is raised in around a third of speeches it accounts for only around 10 per cent of sentences.

Upgrading the National Health Service and being 'tough on crime' are often seen as key themes of New Labour's public service reforms, alongside education. Indeed, health and law and order are the services most commonly talked about by Blair, after education and the general public service category. Again, though, the picture is differentiated over time, and appears to show a substitution effect. Blair talks about health in 8 per cent of sentences in the first term, whereas law and order is raised in only 3 per cent. In the second term, the positions switch: Blair appears to lose interest in health in the second term, and to become more focused on the punitive aspects of public services. Health is down to 3 per cent, law and order up to 8 per cent. The term 'anti-social behaviour', for example, is not used by Blair until 2000, and occurs only eight times in Labour's first term compared to 42 times in its second. Both services drop again in the third term, to 1 per cent for health and 3 per cent for law and order, as Blair focuses on education in the autumn of 2005.

Welfare and transport are the public services where the gap between the proportion of sentences and the proportion of speeches in which they occur is biggest, indicating that they are name-checked in speeches without being given detailed attention. Transport is the most obvious loser here, being covered in less than one in 50 of Blair's sentences. Welfare gets more attention, and rises from 3 to 5 per cent of text units in Labour's second term, falling back to 2 per cent in the third term. It is interesting to note that the pattern here mirrors that of law and order, peaking in the second term of the Labour government. Links between welfare and law and order are historically strong, associated with discourses of deviancy and inadequacy, a need for social control and loss of autonomy (Foucault, 1986; Barry *et al*, 1996). Exploring these aspects in qualitative analysis below helps to bring out the relationship between the two services in the New Labour solution set.

Having isolated the public service text units, it is now possible to explore the ways that Blair talks about these public services, and the extent to which consumerist patterns are evident. The remainder of the chapter conducts searches only on those parts of the speeches that refer to public services. Other topics are set to one side.

The individual and the community

In talking about public services, Blair makes reference to the people that will receive and be affected by the service. Table 6.3 shows the frequency with which the service conditional and non-service conditional keywords occur in Blair's sentences and speeches. Percentages of the total text units and speeches are shown in brackets. Although the percentage of keyword hits is low, with most of the results falling between 0 and 5 per cent overall, low scores are to be expected in this kind of keyword searching, where the sample text units range over a variety of themes. Bara (2005: 17) for example, uses 0.08 per cent as a minimum measure of the importance of a keyword in a party manifesto. Here, since the emphasis is on the balance between the keywords, relative placings are more important than absolute and no minimum is established.

As Table 6.3 shows, overall Blair uses the term parent more than any other. Parent is used 246 times by Blair, and appears in 3.4 per cent of sentences and half of the speeches. The usage increases in frequency across the three terms, outpacing patient only after the first term. Overall Blair talks about parents more than community, often seen as a key motif in New Labour's governing agenda. Community is the second most popular term overall, used in 3.1 per cent of sentences, and cited in more speeches than any other term (55 per cent). Other terms used relatively frequently by Blair are patient (2.2 per cent) and pupil (1.9 per cent). These findings indicate that Blair talks about public services either in terms of specific users or the community. The more abstract roles, such as client and taxpayer, customer and consumer, are invoked relatively little.

Breaking the results down by service area reveals the way in which Blair's vocabulary shifts between services, as Table 6.4 shows. By far the most community-oriented service is law and order. Given the earlier discussion of the collective impact of policing services, and the difficulty of identifying specific beneficiaries, this is unsurprising. Education and welfare are also services that Blair frequently links to community. Qualitative analysis of the text units containing community shows that the term is used both as an adjective and a noun. It is a descriptor for a range of services, for example community schools, community hospitals, community nurses, community policing and community

Table 6.3   Service conditional and non-service conditional keywords, over time, in Blair's speeches

	First term		Second term		Third term		Total	
	Units	Speeches	Units	Speeches	Units	Speeches	Units	Speeches
Community	69	30	138	27	18	4	225	61
	(2.1%)	(47.6%)	(4.3%)	(67.5%)	(3.2%)	(50.0%)	(3.1%)	(55.0%)
Taxpayer	5	4	5	4	1	1	11	9
	(0.2%)	(6.3%)	(0.2%)	(10.0%)	(0.2%)	(12.5%)	(0.2%)	(8.1%)
Citizen	9	8	16	13	2	2	27	23
	(0.3%)	(12.7%)	(0.5%)	(32.5%)	(0.4%)	(25.0%)	(0.4%)	(20.7%)
Client	0	0	5	2	0	0	5	2
	(0.0%)	(0.0%)	(0.2%)	(5.0%)	(0.0%)	(0.0%)	(0.1%)	(1.8%)
Consumer	2	2	24	9	1	1	27	12
	(0.1%)	(3.2%)	(0.8%)	(22.5%)	(0.2%)	(12.5%)	(0.4%)	(10.8%)
Customer	5	2	7	4	0	0	12	6
	(0.2%)	(3.2%)	(0.2%)	(10.0%)	(0.0%)	(0.0%)	(0.2%)	(5.4%)
Patient	110	15	45	12	6	2	161	29
	(3.3%)	(23.8%)	(1.4%)	(30.0%)	(1.1%)	(25.0%)	(2.2%)	(26.1%)
Pupil	46	15	64	18	24	4	134	37
	(1.3%)	(23.8%)	(2.0%)	(45.0%)	(4.2%)	(50.0%)	(1.9%)	(33.3%)
Parent	58	28	136	22	52	4	246	54
	(1.7%)	(44.4%)	(4.3%)	(55.0%)	(9.1%)	(50.0%)	(3.4%)	(48.6%)
Total hits	304	46	440	37	104	6	848	89
	(9.1%)	(73.0%)	(13.8%)	(92.5%)	(18.3%)	(75.0%)	(11.8%)	(80.2%)
Total units/ speeches	3,340	63	3,192	40	569	8	7,191	111
	(100%)	(100%)	(100%)	(100%)	(100%)	(100%)	(100%)	(100%)

Percentages show keyword usage as a proportion of total public service text units, i.e. sentences, for each term.

sentences. These services seem to have little in common other than being delivered close to target populations.

As a noun, public services can improve communities (especially deprived ones), can foster responsible communities and can limit the damage done to communities by crime. Public service providers are encouraged to work in partnership with the community. Community is also a value for Blair, an alternative to 'selfish individualism', combining opportunity with responsibility (16 July 2001). As Blair says, 'It is a simple equation – we give opportunity, we demand responsibility, and that's how we build strong communities' (18 September 2002). This juxtaposition of opportunity, responsibility, community, borrowed from Clinton (Needham, 2005, p. 353), highlights the character

Table 6.4   Service conditional and non-service conditional keywords, by service area, in Blair's speeches

	General	Education	Health	Welfare	Transport	Law/order	Total
	Units (%)	Units (%)	Units (%)	Units (%)	Units (%)	Units (%)	Units (%)
Community	35	62	7	25	0	95	224
	(2.8%)	(2.5%)	(0.6%)	(2.7%)	(0.0%)	(8.0%)	(3.1%)
Taxpayer	5	2	1	3	0	0	11
	(0.4%)	(0.1%)	(0.1%)	(0.3%)	(0.0%)	(0.0%)	(0.2%)
Citizen	6	6	1	2	0	12	27
	(0.5%)	(0.2%)	(0.1%)	(0.2%)	(0.0%)	(1.0%)	(0.4%)
Client	0	0	0	4	0	0	4
	(0.0%)	(0.0%)	(0.0%)	(0.4%)	(0.0%)	(0.0%)	(0.1%)
Consumer	22	0	5	0	0	0	27
	(1.8%)	(0.0%)	(0.4%)	(0.0%)	(0.0%)	(0.0%)	(0.4%)
Customer	2	0	1	4	4	0	11
	(0.2%)	(0.0%)	(0.1%)	(0.4%)	(1.5%)	(0.0%)	(0.2%)
Patient	19	0	142	0	0	0	161
	(1.5%)	(0.0%)	(12.6%)	(0.0%)	(0.0%)	(0.0%)	(2.2%)
Pupil	7	123	1	1	0	2	134
	(0.6%)	(5.0%)	(0.1%)	(0.1%)	(0.0%)	(0.2%)	(1.9%)
Parent	19	133	2	78	3	11	246
	(1.5%)	(5.4%)	(0.2%)	(8.5%)	(1.2%)	(0.9%)	(3.4%)
Total hits	115	326	160	117	7	120	845
	(9.3%)	(13.3%)	(14.2%)	(12.8%)	(2.7%)	(10.1%)	(11.8%)
Total text units	1,243	2,455	1,125	914	261	1,193	7,191
	(100%)	(100%)	(100%)	(100%)	(100%)	(100%)	(100%)

Percentages show keyword usage as a proportion of total text units, i.e. sentences, for each service area.

of Blair's use of community. It is much more than the locus of service delivery, it is about a particular kind of locality, with a distinctive value system.

Blair's expectations of the community are not fixed, however, but shifting over time. During Labour's first term, Blair discusses public services on the premise that all communities want the same thing, such as higher standards in maths and literacy, Sure Start centres or regeneration to tackle poverty. In the second term, Blair begins to talk more of individual communities themselves taking action to achieve certain policy goals. In the case of children's centres, for example, 'This shouldn't be looked at as something we're handing down to people, it is part of what the community is doing itself' (18 September 2002). He says, 'But most of all we want to give all of you the tools to tackle the scourge of anti-social behaviour in every neighbourhood and community in the country' (14 October 2003). There is an apparent shift here away from standardisation in the first term towards differentiation and coproduction.

It is in the context of law and order that Blair talks most about citizens. As discussed above, one feature of law and order is that it applies to everyone as a condition of being in a country, and therefore can be expected to have resonance for the citizenry as a whole. In relation to law and order, Blair believes that crime breaks the 'covenant between citizens'; former criminals are expected to become 'productive citizens'; 'law-abiding citizens' must be put first. In other services, he appears to want to bind the citizen – configured as the 'individual citizen' – into a differentiated model of public service reform. As he puts it: 'Personalised provision, tailored to the needs of each individual citizen, is our objective across the public services' (12 February 2004). Citizens, alongside consumers, are to be given more choice: 'Choice puts the levers in the hands of parents and patients so that they as citizens and consumers can be a driving force for improvement in their public services' (24 June 2004).

Although Blair talks less about the taxpayer than the citizen, the language that he uses when talking about services for the citizen and for the taxpayer is very similar, as the following two extracts illustrate:

> And as for taxpayer funded services, they want public services that are no longer monolithic in their provision but diverse; no longer dictate to their users but give them power and choice over the service; no longer hidebound by rigid demarcations but with staff that work flexibly and have the real chance for professional development.
>
> 3 December 2004

> ...so that what were often monolithic services, with only limited capacity to respond to individual circumstances in an individualized fashion, become far better-funded, better staffed and more diverse services, able to serve the needs of each individual citizen whether as a patient in the NHS, a pupil going through the school system, an unemployed person in search of a job or training, or an elderly person in need of long-term care and support.
>
> 22 March 2005

The themes of the consumerist solution set are evident here: an emphasis on remaking services around the choices and needs of their users, with flexible systems of delivery – here in contrast to the 'monolithic', 'limited' and 'hidebound' services of the past. Consistent with the consequentialist outcome orientation of consumerism, Blair also talks about the barriers between public and private providers being dismantled as part of a new partnership between state and citizen:

> Come on: this isn't the betrayal of public services. It's their renewal. All that is happening is that here, as round the rest of the world, we are dividing means and ends. The ends, universal provision remain the same. The means of delivery, partnership between public, private and voluntary sectors and between state and citizen, change.
>
> 3 October 2002

The reference to the rest of the world highlights the extent to which a distinctive view of globalisation underpins Blair's public service reforms, as various authors have noted (Hay, 1999, 2004; Moss and O'Loughlin, 2005; Finlayson, 2007).

Aside from rejecting monolithic services, Blair has little to say about the taxpayer. Given that the tension between taxpayers and consumers was an important theme of public services under the Conservatives – and of neo-liberalism more generally (Clarke, 2004) – it is interesting to see how little Blair talks about public services from the perspective of the taxpayer. The gap between those using and those paying for services, central to the rationale for the poll tax as discussed in Chapter 4, is de-emphasised here.

The terms used by Blair to refer to service users in general – client, consumer, customer – are all used more in the second term than the first. Blair uses the term consumer in relation to public services for the first time in December 1999 in a speech on the health service, in which he talks about the NHS providing a new range of 'consumer-focused services'. The term is used most in Labour's second term in office, with 24 hits in speeches between June 2001 and May 2005. There are three senses in which Blair uses the term consumer. The first is as a noun referring to users of public services: the patient, parent, passenger, etc, as consumer. The second is as an adverb or adjective to clarify what sort of reform is proposed: consumer choice, consumer-focused services, consumer power. Seven of the 27 hits refer to the need to expand consumer choice. Alongside choice consumers are to have 'minimum standards', 'instant access' to services that are 'prompt, convenient, responsive and of the highest quality'. The third usage is in the context of social change: Blair talks of living in 'a consumer age' and 'a consumer society'. He attributes certain characteristics to public service 'consumers'. They are 'demanding' and 'self interested', and he talks of their high and rising expectations. Discussing a PFI project for school building in Glasgow, for example, he asserts:

> In all areas, what counts is what provides a better public service for the consumer... All of this change amounts to the biggest reform programme in public services for half a century. All of it driven not by out-dated or even new-fangled ideology but by a sense of mission: to renew our public services for the 21st century consumer age in which we live.
>
> *Consumer age* 16 July 2001

Thus there is an inevitability to consumer-oriented services. Blair's opposition to ideology is apparent in this quote. Overall in the speeches the term ideology or ideological is used 36 times by Blair, of which all but three are negative. Ideology is 'irrelevant', 'old', 'confused', 'fatal', 'distrusted', 'narrow', 'chained', 'dogmatic', 'misjudged', 'outdated', even 'insane'. Pragmatism is in favour – four out of the five mentions are favourable – and flexibility is particularly prized; with 66 mentions, all of them positive. Opponents of Labour's reforms are the forces of 'dogma and vested interests' (16 October 2001) and 'cosy elitism' (12 July 2002). New Labour's assumption that 'what counts is what works' (Labour Party, 1997, p. 4), affirms the consequentialism that is characteristic of consumerism.

Blair rarely talks about the customer, the service specific and payment-based subset of consumer. When it occurs, the term customer is generally used by Blair in the context of transport or welfare. Its use in relation to public transport, as a service paid for, in part at least, at the point of use, is unsurprising. It is harder to configure the welfare user as a customer, given the lack of payment. Blair clarifies his meaning of the term in a speech on welfare reform in June 2002, when he says, 'Instead of the old benefit mentality, individuals are treated as customers and potential employees – given high quality advice and support by professional advisers in a business-like environment' (10 June 2002). Thus he suggests that the term customer forms two purposes: first, marking an obvious break with the past, and second, making the service more closely analogous to a business.

Analysis of some of these general service terms is limited by the small data set. Within the service specific category – patient, pupil, parent – the high number of hits for some of these terms allows the tracing of patterns over time. Shifts from the standardisation to the differentiation narrative of consumerism can be traced, for example. Compare the following two quotes:

'The people of Britain – whether they are parents, pupils, patients or passengers – rightly expect modern, fast and convenient public services' (2 December 1999).

'The key to reform is re-designing the system round the user – the patient, the pupil, the passenger, the victim of crime' (16 October 2001).

Between these two speeches, Blair's emphasis shifts, moving from a first term focus on making services as accessible as possible for users, and a second term orientation towards personalising the service around the users.

In specific services the differences are sometimes stark. For example, in health, Blair's first term emphasis is on quality and access in the NHS: 'All patients wherever they live are entitled to prompt, convenient quality when they need' (29 February 2000). The term 'choice' does not feature at all. It is after the 2001 election that the language shifts to a more patient-oriented model of knowledge, in which patients make choices about their healthcare. The NHS in the past is criticised for showing, 'lack of responsiveness to patients' (6 December 2001). Patients are to be able to choose their GP, the hospital and date of their hospital operation (16 October 2001, 12 July 2002, 6 May 2003). Blair talks of the importance of 'the patient experience' (16 July 2001). The result by 2004 is: 'a step change to a decentralised, non-monolithic consumer and patient driven NHS' (19 June 2004).

In schools, Blair's early speeches place emphasis on improving standards: 'As a Government we acknowledge our duty, on behalf of parents and children, to secure acceptable minimum standards in schools – all schools – something that should have been done decades ago' (2 December 1999). Parents must have better access to help and advice (23 March 1999). Over time there is more emphasis on a differentiated service: pupils must have 'personalised lessons' (24 October 2005). Parents too are to have more choices in Labour's second term: 'the more choice there is for parents, the more pressure for change and improvement within the system' (26 November 2002). In the third term: '...[C]hoices, now exercised only by the fortunate and the well off, can be given to all parents' (24 October 2005).

A recurrent assumption in Blair's speeches, consistent with the consumerist model, is that changes are driven by the expectations of users. In schools, for example, government must meet 'the expectations of parents that all children should be up to standard by the time they leave primary school' (16 March 1999). 'Expectations of pupils are rising steadily' (12 February 2001). Information technology plays a role in increasing user expectations in health: 'Fulfilling consumers' expectations is different now for doctors whose patients have discussed their symptoms in internet chatrooms or called NHS Direct' (25 January 2002).

The consumerist emphasis on outcomes is evident in relation to bringing in new providers of services. In health, 'I say: if PCTs or regional health directors want to use spare private sector capacity or do innovative deals with private or voluntary sectors to help patients, they should be free to do so' (16 October 2001). In education, a diversity of providers will improve services: 'The best local authorities already increasingly see their primary role as championing parents and pupils rather than being a direct provider of education' (24 October 2005).

Although similar themes run across the keywords, parents play a distinctive role in Blair's speeches. As well as being the most utilised keyword, parents have expectations placed upon them that are not given to other service users. Whereas the term responsibility is only applied once to patients and to pupils – and not at all to clients, consumers and customers – the term occurs 16 times in connection to parents. Parents are responsible for the actions of their children (20 January 1998); for rooting out failure and improving standards in schools (8 February 1998); for making sure their children attend school and do not commit crimes (7 June 2000); for disciplining their children (24 October 2005). Parents who do not comply may be subject to court orders (22 March 2002; 14 October 2003; 3 May 2004). Given this emphasis on responsibility, it is worth noting that the term parent is used proportionally more in the context of welfare than education – and that a third of the hits in the welfare category are for lone parents.

As well as behaving responsibly, parents are expected to play an active role in their child's education: 'So turning around schools doesn't just depend on motivated teachers and pupils; it also depends on parents, on local people willing to give time as governors or mentoring children' (14 February 1999). Parent groups are encouraged to get involved in education action zones (15 January 1999). Blair talks of the importance of having motivated parents and pupils in improving schools, and indeed the possibility of parents setting up schools themselves (24 October 2005). Additional rights that parents will get over areas such as curriculum, school meals and uniform are to be conditional: 'with these rights comes an expectation that parents become much more engaged and interested in their children's education' (24 October 2005).

Analysis of these nine keywords cannot reveal all the ways that Blair talks about the users and beneficiaries of public services, but they do help to reveal the patterns that span the 193 speeches, across the eight year period. In particular, they show Blair's preference for service specific terms when talking about public services, and the dominance of (responsible) parents and communities to his vision of public service reforms. Support for the consumerist solution set is shown in the way that Blair draws on preference accommodation and consequentialism to justify service reforms: rising public expectations necessitate choice and a wider choice of providers. The narratives of consumerism are present in the extracts used here, with an apparent shift towards choice and personalisation in the second term, although coproduction is also important.

Narratives of consumerism

To trace the three narratives more systematically in Blair's speeches, it is possible to use the narrative keywords developed earlier in the chapter. Table 6.5 shows the findings of the quantitative keyword analysis. Again, the column percentages in brackets indicate in what proportion of overall text units and speeches the word occurs to allow comparability between terms of different length.

When talking about public services, Blair positions them most often in terms of the standardised keywords (7.4 per cent of text units) and least often in relation to differentiation (5 per cent). Thus overall Blair emphasises a standardised and accessible service, although the balance shifts over time. Standardisation is used most in the first term, and its usage declines relative to the other narratives in the second and third terms. Blair's solution set appears to shift from one in which all users must get the same, high quality service, to one based on services being more differentiated and coproduced. The increase in prevalence of both the differentiation and coproduction narratives in the second term suggests that for Blair personalisation and coproduction are not contradictory pulls. Rather, users are to become more involved in service delivery assisting providers in fitting the service to their individual needs.

The themes of differentiation in public service reform start to emerge in late 1999 when Blair makes reference to the need for 'public services

Table 6.5 The three narratives over time in Blair's speeches

		First term		Second term		Third term		Total	
		Units	Speeches	Units	Speeches	Units	Speeches	Units	Speeches
Standardisation	Right	45 (1.3%)	28 (44.4%)	48 (1.5%)	24 (60.0%)	13 (2.3%)	5 (62.5%)	106 (1.5%)	57 (51.4%)
	Access	21 (0.6%)	16 (25.4%)	23 (0.7%)	14 (35.0%)	3 (0.5%)	2 (25.0%)	47 (0.7%)	32 (28.8%)
	Inform	9 (0.3%)	8 (12.7%)	13 (0.4%)	9 (22.5%)	3 (0.5%)	3 (37.5%)	25 (0.3%)	20 (18.0%)
	Standard	135 (4.0%)	40 (63.5%)	101 (3.2%)	23 (57.5%)	17 (3.0%)	6 (75.0%)	253 (3.5%)	69 (62.2%)
	Target	44 (1.3%)	19 (30.2%)	31 (1.0%)	19 (47.5%)	2 (0.4%)	1 (12.5%)	77 (1.1%)	39 (35.1%)
	Convenience	19 (0.6%)	7 (11.1%)	4 (0.1%)	3 (7.5%)	0 (0.0%)	0 (0.0%)	23 (0.3%)	10 (9.0%)
	Sub-total	273 (8.2%)	52 (82.5%)	220 (6.9%)	37 (92.5%)	38 (6.7%)	7 (87.5%)	531 (7.4%)	96 (86.5%)
Differentiation	Choice/choose	34 (1.0%)	14 (22.2%)	87 (2.7%)	28 (70.0%)	22 (3.9%)	3 (37.5%)	143 (2.0%)	45 (40.5%)
	Individual	38 (1.1%)	17 (27.0%)	51 (1.6%)	21 (52.5%)	3 (0.5%)	2 (25.0%)	92 (1.3%)	40 (36.0%)
	Personal	12 (0.4%)	9 (14.3%)	27 (0.8%)	12 (30.0%)	7 (1.2%)	4 (50.0%)	46 (0.6%)	25 (22.5%)
	Responsive	3 (0.1%)	3 (4.8%)	11 (0.3%)	6 (15.0%)	1 (0.2%)	1 (12.5%)	15 (0.2%)	10 (9.0%)
	Diverse	18 (0.5%)	4 (6.3%)	27 (0.8%)	15 (37.5%)	5 (0.9%)	3 (37.5%)	50 (0.7%)	22 (19.8%)
	Tailor	5 (0.2%)	4 (6.3%)	7 (0.2%)	7 (17.5%)	0 (0.0%)	0 (0.0%)	12 (0.2%)	11 (9.9%)
	Sub-total	110 (3.3%)	39 (61.9%)	210 (6.6%)	37 (92.5%)	38 (6.7%)	6 (75.0%)	358 (5.0%)	75 (67.6%)
Coproduction	Opportunity	71 (2.1%)	29 (46.0%)	93 (2.9%)	27 (67.5%)	18 (3.2%)	4 (50.0%)	182 (2.5%)	60 (54.1%)
	Engage	3 (0.1%)	3 (4.8%)	22 (0.7%)	15 (37.5%)	3 (0.5%)	2 (25.0%)	28 (0.4%)	20 (18.0%)
	Involve	27 (0.8%)	18 (28.6%)	26 (0.8%)	16 (40.0%)	7 (1.2%)	5 (62.5%)	60 (0.8%)	39 (35.1%)
	Empower	7 (0.2%)	4 (6.3%)	6 (0.2%)	4 (10.0%)	1 (0.2%)	1 (12.5%)	14 (0.2%)	9 (8.1%)
	Participate	5 (0.2%)	5 (7.9%)	7 (0.2%)	6 (15.0%)	0 (0.0%)	0 (0.0%)	12 (0.2%)	11 (9.9%)
	Responsible	82 (2.5%)	29 (46.0%)	70 (2.2%)	22 (55.0%)	6 (1.1%)	2 (25.0%)	158 (2.2%)	49 (44.1%)
	Sub-total	195 (5.8%)	42 (66.7%)	224 (7.0%)	33 (82.5%)	35 (6.2%)	8 (100%)	454 (6.3%)	80 (72.1%)
	Total hits	578 (17.3%)	63 (100%)	654 (20.5%)	40 (100%)	111 (19.5%)	8 (100%)	1,343 (18.7%)	111 (100%)
	Total text units	3,340 (100%)	63 (100%)	3,192 (100%)	40 (100%)	569 (100%)	8 (100%)	7,191 (100%)	111 (100%)

Percentages show keyword usage as a proportion of total public service text units, i.e. sentences, for each term.

that feel tailor-made – not uniform, "one size fits all"' (2 December 1999). Once Labour enters its second term, the theme of personalising services around their users intensifies. As discussed above, individual user choice is integral to this notion of consumerism, and to New Labour's second and third term policy agenda for public services. As Blair says in January 2005, 'Our experience of NHS and education reform tells us the more diversity of supply and patient and parent choice, the higher the standards of service, and the satisfaction of the consumer' (15 Jan 2005).

In Blair's early speeches there is an emphasis on the needs and convenience of users, whereas later speeches emphasise choice. For example, in a speech in January 1999 he says reform requires 'organising services around the needs of users, not the convenience of producers' (26 January 1999). In a later speech, he says, providers should 'no longer dictate to their users but give them power and choice over the service' (3 December 2004). In both cases it is the user's perspective that must come first, with the providers' views delegitimised, however user power is operationalised in different ways in the two extracts, indicative of a shift in narratives.

Blair is also clear that boundaries between the public and private sectors must be dismantled: 'The point, very simply, is this: the user comes first; if the service they are offered is failing, they should be able to change provider; and if partnership with other sectors can improve a service, the public sector should be able to do it' (16 October 2001). New initiatives such as academy schools, which bring private sponsors into school ownership and management, are cited as enhancing 'parent power' (12 September 2005). Blair's apparent pragmatism is evident in his speeches: 'For the public what matters is what is achieved' (13 October 1998); and 'Long gone are rigid demarcations between public, private and voluntary sectors, at least in the public's mind' (24 February 2004).

The shift in narratives over time is something that Blair himself acknowledges. At a speech at a party event in June 2003 Blair explained Labour's approach as a series of stages. Although the speech is not included in the corpus it is quoted here for corroborative purposes:

In respect of public service reform, the first term was about introducing proper means of inspection and accountability for public services and about intervention where there was failure. Inevitably, it was driven from the centre...To turn waiting lists around – which had risen by over 400,000 under the Tories – to get the issue of access to GPs or to A & E departments taken seriously, we needed targets, again centrally set...But it only takes us so far. Now there is a sustained programme of investment, with public spending rising as a percentage of GDP every year, we need to use the opportunity of investment to engineer real and lasting systemic reform. I want to focus on health and education. Here, reform means putting power in the hands of the parent or patient so that the system works for them not for itself.

Blair, 2003

Whilst this may reflect a *post hoc* rationale rather than a predetermined plan, it is consistent with the quantitative and qualitative findings about the shift away from a first term focus on standardisation to a more differentiated and coproduced solution set in the second and third terms.

The content analysis shows that within each narrative Blair favours some of the keywords over others. In relation to standardisation, he puts particular emphasis on the term standards itself, and says very little about information or convenience. In the differentiation narrative, he uses choice and individual more than other terms. The notions of responsive and tailored services are rarely invoked. Within the coproduction narrative, Blair shows a clear preference for the language of opportunity and responsibility, which together account for three-quarters of the hits in this category. He says comparatively little about engagement, empowerment or participation. Opportunity and responsibility have a common emphasis on users becoming more involved in service production, and are part of the 'opportunity, community, responsibility' triumvirate. However, they also have distinct implications, with opportunity placing less of a burden on the user than responsibility. The table shows that Blair talks more and more about opportunity with each succeeding term, but less and less about responsibility. It is possible that there is a substitution effect here in the sense that opportunities are replacing responsibilities in Blair's vision of public services. This can also be understand as a rebranding process, where the responsibilities of those on welfare to find work, for example, are repositioned as opportunities to do so.

One question to explore is whether some service users are given opportunities whereas others have responsibilities. Breaking down the narratives by service area, as shown in Table 6.6 reveals the patterns of usage.

As the table shows, Blair talks about opportunity and responsibility in the same service areas – education, welfare and law and order – rather than emphasising only opportunities in some policy areas and

Table 6.6   The three narratives by service area in Blair's speeches

		General	Education	Health	Welfare	Transport	Law/order	Total
Standardisation	Right	15 (1.2%)	38 (1.5%)	13 (1.2%)	10 (1.1%)	4 (1.5%)	25 (2.1%)	105 (1.5%)
	Access	8 (0.6%)	15 (0.6%)	12 (1.1%)	9 (1.0%)	1 (0.4%)	1 (0.1%)	46 (0.6%)
	Inform	7 (0.6%)	8 (0.3%)	4 (0.4%)	4 (0.4%)	1 (0.4%)	1 (0.1%)	25 (0.3%)
	Standard	44 (3.5%)	170 (6.9%)	20 (1.8%)	9 (1.0%)	5 (1.9%)	4 (0.3%)	252 (3.5%)
	Target	10 (0.8%)	36 (1.5%)	9 (0.8%)	4 (0.4%)	6 (2.3%)	9 (0.8%)	74 (1.0%)
	Convenience	5 (0.4%)	0 (0.0%)	18 (1.6%)	0 (0.0%)	0 (0.0%)	0 (0.0%)	23 (0.3%)
	Sub-total	89 (7.2%)	267 (10.9%)	76 (6.8%)	36 (3.9%)	17 (6.5%)	40 (3.4%)	525 (7.3%)
Differentiation	Choice/choose	42 (3.4%)	55 (2.2%)	15 (1.3%)	23 (2.5%)	2 (0.8%)	5 (0.4%)	142 (2.0%)
	Individual	12 (1.0%)	43 (1.8%)	5 (0.4%)	12 (1.3%)	0 (0.0%)	18 (1.5%)	90 (1.3%)
	Personal	4 (0.3%)	17 (0.7%)	4 (0.4%)	10 (1.1%)	1 (0.4%)	9 (0.8%)	45 (0.6%)
	Responsive	6 (0.5%)	1 (0.0%)	5 (0.4%)	2 (0.2%)	0 (0.0%)	1 (0.1%)	15 (0.2%)
	Diverse	12 (1.0%)	33 (1.3%)	0 (0.0%)	2 (0.2%)	0 (0.0%)	0 (0.0%)	47 (0.7%)
	Tailor	2 (0.2%)	7 (0.3%)	0 (0.0%)	2 (0.2%)	0 (0.0%)	1 (0.1%)	12 (0.2%)
	Sub-total	78 (6.3%)	156 (6.4%)	29 (2.6%)	51 (5.6%)	3 (1.1%)	34 (2.8%)	351 (4.9%)
Coproduction	Opportunity	29 (2.3%)	82 (3.3%)	3 (0.3%)	47 (5.1%)	1 (0.4%)	17 (1.4%)	179 (2.5%)
	Engage	1 (0.1%)	14 (0.6%)	3 (0.3%)	5 (0.5%)	0 (0.0%)	5 (0.4%)	28 (0.4%)
	Involve	11 (0.9%)	20 (0.8%)	7 (0.6%)	10 (1.1%)	0 (0.0%)	10 (0.8%)	58 (0.8%)
	Empower	4 (0.3%)	3 (0.1%)	5 (0.4%)	2 (0.2%)	0 (0.0%)	0 (0.0%)	14 (0.2%)
	Participate	3 (0.2%)	5 (0.2%)	0 (0.0%)	1 (0.1%)	0 (0.0%)	2 (0.2%)	11 (0.2%)
	Responsible	15 (1.2%)	33 (1.3%)	4 (0.4%)	39 (4.3%)	1 (0.4%)	34 (2.8%)	126 (1.8%)
	Sub-total	63 (5.1%)	157 (6.4%)	22 (2.0%)	104 (11.4%)	2 (0.8%)	68 (5.7%)	416 (5.8%)
	Total hits	230 (18.5%)	580 (23.6%)	127 (11.3%)	191 (20.1%)	22 (8.4%)	142 (11.9%)	1,292 (18.0%)
	Total text units	1,243 (100%)	2,455 (100%)	1,125 (100%)	914 (100%)	261 (100%)	1,193 (100%)	7,191 (100%)

Percentages show keyword usage as a proportion of total public service text units, i.e. sentences, for each term.

responsibilities in others. Within education there is more emphasis placed on opportunity, although responsibility is still frequently used. In welfare the two are more evenly matched, with a small preference for opportunity. Within the law and order text units, responsibilities outnumber opportunities two to one. This finding is consistent with the discussion at the beginning of the chapter about the distinctive characteristics of criminal justice services, which have no obvious role for the active user other than that of responsible, law-abiding citizen. New Labour's distinctive use of opportunity and responsibility as part of a coproduction narrative is returned to in the next chapter.

Blair uses the standardisation narrative most often when he talks about education and health, and least in the context of welfare and law and order. Since both of the latter involve users with limited autonomy, it is surprising that keywords associated with an equitable and accessible service are not more heavily utilised. The differentiation narrative is used most in education and least often in transport. Choice and responsiveness are seen as most appropriate in the general service category, and also regularly applied to education and welfare, although less so to other services. Law and order has the lowest score for choice, as might be expected, given that its users rarely have options about how and where they receive the service.

The narrative keywords provide a metric for understanding how Blair utilises the three public service narratives across services and over time. The widely perceived ambiguities of the New Labour model, which set great store by targets in its first term, and then seemed to redirect attention towards choice and personalisation, are reflected in the patterns of change found here. Although Blair's main priority continues to be making services standardised and accessible, he becomes more and more interested over time in the parts that differentiation and coproduction can play in service improvement.

Conclusion

The analysis of Blair's speeches helps to illustrate the solution set that he constructs and contributes to an understanding of New Labour's citizenship regime. Overall, it is possible to see strong themes of consumerism running through the public service sections of Blair's speeches. There is a focus on remaking services around the individual user. Terms that are conditional on service use (particularly the service specific ones of parent, patient and pupil) are together used much more than the non-service conditional terms. Parent is the most commonly used term overall, with parents expected to fulfil a distinctive burden of responsibilities. Service reforms are justified in the name of the rising expectations of their users, with other perspectives, particularly producers, marginalised. More generally there is a call to move away from the 'monolithic', 'one size fits all' services of the past. User demands for more personalised services are used to justify the expansion of service provision by non-state organisations.

However, Blair's speeches cannot be slotted neatly into a consumerist citizenship regime, given the importance of community and coproduction. Community is used in more speeches than any other keyword, confirming existing accounts of its importance to New Labour. The community is the site for service provision, and many services are given the label of community. It is also a value. The speeches do not make clear, however, what this label means for service provision, other than providing a new locus for service delivery.

Blair favours a distinctive type of coproduction which emphasises opportunity and responsibility and de-emphasises empowerment and engagement. Services are to provide opportunities and demand responsibility. However, responsibility is not evenly distributed: communities and parents are expected to behave responsibly, whereas other actors – consumers, customers, clients, patients, pupils and passengers – are not.

The speeches of a Prime Minister are not the only indicator of a government's approach, although they play a key role in signalling priorities and setting agendas. Speeches take place on set piece occasions where the emphasis is on impressing an audience rather than discussing specifics of policy. To explore the New Labour solution set in more detail the following two chapters look at different levels of government. Chapter 7 focuses on white and green papers in public services, assessing how far the same consumer orientation, and shifting narratives found in Blair's speeches are present in those documents. It also discusses the ambiguity of New Labour's approach to coproduction, which encourages an active role for the user, but only within certain constraints. Chapter 8 looks at local government and undertakes content analysis of corporate documents in case study authorities. It also discusses the role of the customer in New Labour's citizenship regime, drawing on interviews with officers, councillors and civil servants to explore how the term customer is used.

7
The Consumer in Whitehall

A citizenship regime, an account of the roles and expectations of the citizen and the state, is forged not only in the elite accounts of government leaders. It must also penetrate the bureaucracy and the detail of policy-making. To be a regime, it must hold across a range of service areas and over time. In order to explore how New Labour's citizenship regime extends downwards from Blair, it is necessary to examine the policy documents emerging from central government departments in the period since 1997.

This chapter uses content analysis to look at the command papers that policy-makers use to set out their priorities in particular policy areas: including green and white papers and strategic documents such as five year plans. Through analysing the texts it is possible to probe how the citizenship regime is interpreted and framed in specific policy areas. Of particular interest is the extent to which the discourses used here are the same as in Blair's speeches, indicative therefore of an integrated approach to service reform based on a common solution set. Having examined the documents, the chapter goes on to look at the way that both Blair's speeches and the policy documents utilise the coproduction narrative, examining in detail New Labour's focus on responsibility and opportunity.

The documents are not, of course, an accurate guide to future legislation nor still less to the implementation of policy on the ground. As Chapter 2 explained, the focus of the research is on the construction of policy rather than its implementation. The documents are also not independent of Blair's speeches. They are drafted by civil servants and signed off by ministers, both of which operate under bonds of loyalty to the Prime Minister and government as a whole. However, governments are complex organisations, and Prime Ministers are only able to control selective parts of the structure at any one time. It is therefore important to explore how far the themes of Prime Ministerial speeches are reflected in the language used in the policy documents emanating from departments.

Command papers

To assess the ways that policy documents use the keywords it was first necessary to generate a manageable sample for quantitative and qualitative analysis. To create a sample of documents, a full list of public service white and green papers and major strategy documents from the 1997–2005 period was put together from government department websites. The total number of documents was 48. A quota sample was then developed that would cover Labour's time in office and allow comparison between service areas. It was decided to utilise five documents for each public service area in the codebook (education, health, welfare, law and order, transport), generating 25 documents overall – just over half of total documents.

The first two texts included in each category were the earliest and latest documents for that service area. Since most departments published five-year plans around the summer of 2004, it was decided to include these as the third document in the set, to maximise comparability across service areas. To ensure a full set of five-year plans, the law and order plan was included even though it was published just after the cut off date for the study, in February 2006. Its publication had been expected since the summer of 2004 but had been delayed by the sudden departure of David Blunkett.

The fourth and fifth documents for each service were selected from the remaining list for that service area on the basis of perceived importance. Expert collections of New Labour policy were mined to identify the most regularly cited papers (Powell, 1999; Savage and Atkinson, 2001; Ludlam and Smith, 2004; Dorey, 2005; Seldon and Kavanagh, 2005). Reference to a document in one or more collection was taken to indicate that it made an important contribution to policy in that area. Transport has published only three major documents since 1997, so it was not possible to generate the sample of five publications for this policy area. To keep the sample at 25 documents, housing (which had two major policy documents in the period) was disaggregated from the broader welfare category to explore distinctive themes in this service area. Comparability with Blair's speeches was not reduced since none of the welfare sentences in his speeches were primarily about housing.

Documents were downloaded from departmental websites as PDF files, converted into text files and imported into N6 for analysis. The sample of documents and the list of sponsoring departments are shown in Table 7.1. References to the documents in the text are by year and sponsoring department only. Although most of the papers were taken from the department with the relevant portfolio (for example all the health documents were produced by the Department of Health), in other service areas the name of the relevant department changed, or the policy crossed departmental boundaries, as in the case of welfare.

Together the documents set out the major direction of public service policy under New Labour, providing detailed accounts of service shortcomings and possible solutions, where Blair's speeches only provided broad-brush priorities. Unlike the speeches, the documents are designed to be read, and are primarily designed for an audience with a reasonable grasp of the policy area rather than the general public. For that reason, it can be expected that their positioning of policy would be different to that found in the speeches of the Prime Minister. Another difference between the Blair sample and the texts used here is that in Blair's speeches the balance between service areas was determined by Blair's own priorities; thus there were many more sentences about education in the corpus than there were about welfare. Here the sample is selected to give balance between service areas, although by comparing proportional rather than absolute findings between the speeches and documents it is still possible to draw valid comparisons.

Multiple publics

Using the content analysis template developed in Chapter 6, the policy documents were searched for the service conditional and non-service conditional keywords. Table 7.2 shows the findings.

Overall, the single most commonly used term was community, occurring 2688 times, and in 6.3 per cent of sentences. Parent and patient were the next most utilised, occurring in 2.7 per cent and 2.6 per cent of sentences respectively. These findings are broadly similar to those in the Blair speeches, although with less emphasis on parent here and more on community. The least frequently used terms were taxpayer and client, which were each used in 0.1 per cent of total sentences. These terms were also the least frequently used in Blair's speeches.

Looking at the findings by service area, it is possible to see how each of the departments talks about those who use and benefit from its

Table 7.1 Sample of command papers

Policy area	Department	Title	Date	Doc type
Education	Department for Education and Skills (DfES)	Excellence in Schools	1997	White
	Department for Education and Skills (DfES)	Schools Achieving Success	2001	White
	Department for Education and Skills (DfES)	Future of Higher Education White Paper	2003	White
	Department for Education and Skills (DfES)	A Five Year Strategy for Children and Learners	2004	Strategy
	Department for Education and Skills (DfES)	Higher Standards; Better Schools for All	2005	White
Health	Department of Health (DoH)	The New NHS – Modern and Dependable	1997	White
	Department of Health (DoH)	Saving Lives: Our Healthier Nation	1999	White
	Department of Health (DoH)	The NHS Plan: A Plan for Investment, A Plan for Reform	2000	Strategy
	Department of Health (DoH)	Choosing Health	2004a	White
	Department of Health (DoH)	The NHS Improvement Plan: Putting People at the Heart of Public Services	2004b	Strategy
Welfare	Department of Social Security (DSS)	New Ambitions for Our Country: A New Contract for Welfare	1998	Green
	Department of Health (DoH)	Modernising Social Services	1998	White
	Department of Health (DoH)	Valuing People – A New Strategy for Learning Disability in the Twenty-first century	2001	White
	Department of Health (DoH)	Independence, Well-being and Choice: Our Vision for the Future of Social Care for Adults in England	2005	Green
	Department of Work and Pensions (DWP)	Opportunity and Security throughout Life	2005	Strategy

Table 7.1 Sample of command papers – *continued*

Policy area	Department	Title	Date	Doc type
Law and order	Home Office	Tackling Drugs to Build a Better Britain	1998	White
	Home Office	Justice for All	2002	White
	Home Office	Respect and Responsibility: Taking a Stand Against Anti-Social Behaviour	2003	White
	Home Office	Building Communities, Beating Crime – A better policy service for the 21st Century	2004	White
	Home Office	A Five Year Plan for Protecting the Public and Reducing Reoffending	2006	Strategy
Transport	Department of the Environment, Transport and Rural Affairs (DETR)	A New Deal for Transport: Better for Everyone	1998	White
	Department of the Environment, Transport and Rural Affairs (DETR)	Ten Year Transport Plan	2000a	Consult
	Department for Transport (DfT)	The Future of Transport	2004	White
Housing	Department of the Environment, Transport and Rural Affairs (DETR)	Quality and Choice: A Decent Home for All	2000b	Green
	Office of the Deputy Prime Minister (ODPM)	Sustainable Communities: Homes for all	2005	Strategy

Table 7.2 Service conditional and non-service conditional keywords, by service area, in the command papers

Policy areas	Document	Text units	Comm (%)	Tax (%)	Citizen (%)	Client (%)	Cons (%)	Cust (%)	Patient (%)	Pupil (%)	Parent (%)	Total (%)
Education	Excellence in Schools	1,349	56 (4.2%)	0 (0.0%)	9 (0.7%)	0 (0.0%)	0 (0.0%)	0 (0.0%)	0 (0.0%)	98 (7.3%)	101 (7.5%)	264 (19.6%)
	Schools Achieving Success	1,327	35 (2.6%)	1 (0.1%)	3 (0.2%)	0 (0.0%)	1 (0.1%)	0 (0.0%)	0 (0.0%)	167 (12.6%)	53 (4.0%)	260 (19.6%)
	Future of HE	1,384	19 (1.4%)	8 (0.6%)	1 (0.1%)	0 (0.0%)	0 (0.0%)	2 (0.1%)	0 (0.0%)	3 (0.2%)	2 (0.1%)	35 (2.5%)
	Five Year Strategy	2,474	72 (2.9%)	0 (0.0%)	6 (0.2%)	0 (0.0%)	2 (0.1%)	2 (0.1%)	0 (0.0%)	119 (4.8%)	154 (6.2%)	355 (14.3%)
	Higher Standards	1,743	65 (3.7%)	0 (0.0%)	1 (0.1%)	0 (0.0%)	0 (0.0%)	0 (0.0%)	0 (0.0%)	209 (12.0%)	356 (20.4%)	631 (36.2%)
	Subtotal	8,277	247 (3.0%)	9 (0.1%)	20 (0.2%)	0 (0.0%)	3 (0.0%)	4 (0.0%)	0 (0.0%)	596 (7.2%)	666 (8.0%)	1,545 (18.7%)
Health	The New NHS	1,486	100 (6.7%)	0 (0.0%)	0 (0.0%)	0 (0.0%)	0 (0.0%)	0 (0.0%)	183 (12.3%)	0 (0.0%)	0 (0.0%)	283 (19%)
	Saving Lives	1,938	90 (4.6%)	0 (0.0%)	14 (0.7%)	0 (0.0%)	1 (0.1%)	0 (0.0%)	30 (1.5%)	2 (0.1%)	20 (1.0%)	157 (8.1%)
	NHS Plan	2,012	57 (2.8%)	5 (0.2%)	19 (0.9%)	2 (0.1%)	2 (0.1%)	3 (0.1%)	406 (20.2%)	0 (0.0%)	2 (0.1%)	496 (24.7%)
	NHS Improvement Plan	1,344	75 (5.6%)	2 (0.1%)	2 (0.2%)	0 (0.0%)	1 (0.1%)	0 (0.0%)	396 (29.5%)	0 (0.0%)	4 (0.3%)	480 (35.7%)
	Choosing Health	3,365	294 (8.7%)	0 (0.0%)	6 (0.2%)	12 (0.4%)	34 (1.0%)	6 (0.2%)	62 (1.8%)	27 (0.8%)	72 (2.1%)	513 (15.2%)
	Subtotal	10,145 (23.9%)	616 (6.1%)	7 (0.1%)	41 (0.4%)	14 (0.1%)	38 (0.4%)	9 (0.1%)	1,077 (10.6%)	29 (0.3%)	98 (1.0%)	1,929 (19%)

Table 7.2 Service conditional and non-service conditional keywords, by service area, in the command papers – *continued*

Policy areas	Document	Text units	Comm (%)	Tax (%)	Citizen (%)	Client (%)	Cons (%)	Cust (%)	Patient (%)	Pupil (%)	Parent (%)	Total (%)
Welfare	New Ambitions	1,669	25 (1.5%)	10 (0.6%)	13 (0.8%)	0 (0.0%)	3 (0.2%)	46 (2.8%)	1 (0.1%)	2 (0.1%)	54 (3.2%)	154 (9.2%)
	Modernising Social Services	1,857	51 (2.7%)	5 (0.3%)	7 (0.4%)	3 (0.2%)	0 (0.0%)	0 (0.0%)	2 (0.1%)	0 (0.0%)	16 (0.9%)	84 (4.5%)
	Valuing People	2,023	122 (6.0%)	0 (0.0%)	20 (1.0%)	3 (0.1%)	0 (0.0%)	0 (0.0%)	22 (1.1%)	4 (0.2%)	43 (2.1%)	214 (10.6%)
	Independence, Well-being	1,492	131 (8.8%)	0 (0.0%)	2 (0.1%)	0 (0.0%)	3 (0.2%)	5 (0.3%)	2 (0.1%)	0 (0.0%)	12 (0.8%)	155 (10.4%)
	Opportunity and Security	1,966	15 (0.8%)	8 (0.4%)	5 (0.3%)	15 (0.8%)	3 (0.2%)	76 (3.9%)	14 (0.7%)	1 (0.1%)	112 (5.7%)	249 (12.7%)
	Subtotal	9,007	344 (3.8%)	23 (0.3%)	47 (0.5%)	21 (0.2%)	9 (0.1%)	127 (1.4%)	41 (0.5%)	7 (0.1%)	237 (2.6%)	856 (9.5%)
Law and order	Tackling Drugs	597	31 (5.2%)	0 (0.0%)	0 (0.0%)	0 (0.0%)	0 (0.0%)	0 (0.0%)	0 (0.0%)	0 (0.0%)	5 (0.8%)	36 (6.0%)
	Justice for All	2,700	288 (10.7%)	0 (0.0%)	3 (0.1%)	1 (0.0%)	2 (0.1%)	4 (0.1%)	5 (0.2%)	6 (0.2%)	27 (1.0%)	336 (12.4%)
	Respect and Responsibility	1,251	196 (15.7%)	0 (0.0%)	2 (0.2%)	4 (0.3%)	0 (0.0%)	1 (0.1%)	0 (0.0%)	3 (0.2%)	75 (6.0%)	281 (22.5%)
	Building Communities	2,175	512 (23.5%)	3 (0.1%)	29 (1.3%)	0 (0.0%)	3 (0.1%)	51 (2.3%)	1 (0.0%)	2 (0.1%)	1 (0.0%)	602 (27.7%)
	Five Year Strategy	550	92 (16.7%)	2 (0.4%)	3 (0.6%)	0 (0.0%)	0 (0.0%)	0 (0.0%)	0 (0.0%)	0 (0.0%)	2 (0.4%)	99 (18.0%)
	Subtotal	7,273	1,119 (15.4%)	5 (0.1%)	37 (0.5%)	5 (0.1%)	5 (0.1%)	56 (0.8%)	6 (0.1%)	11 (0.2%)	110 (1.5%)	1,354 (18.6%)

Table 7.2 Service conditional and non-service conditional keywords, by service area, in the command papers – *continued*

Policy areas	Document	Text units	Comm (%)	Tax (%)	Citizen (%)	Client (%)	Cons (%)	Cust (%)	Patient (%)	Pupil (%)	Parent (%)	Total (%)
Transport	New Deal for Transport	2,668	59 (2.2%)	8 (0.3%)	0 (0.0%)	2 (0.1%)	9 (0.3%)	25 (0.9%)	0 (0.0%)	1 (0.0%)	12 (0.4%)	116 (4.3%)
	Ten Year Transport Plan	1,429	21 (1.5%)	1 (0.1%)	1 (0.1%)	0 (0.0%)	1 (0.1%)	10 (0.7%)	0 (0.0%)	0 (0.0%)	0 (0.0%)	34 (2.4%)
	Future of Transport	1,512	39 (2.6%)	6 (0.4%)	0 (0.0%)	1 (0.1%)	7 (0.5%)	10 (0.7%)	0 (0.0%)	0 (0.0%)	0 (0.0%)	63 (4.2%)
	Subtotal	**5,609**	**119 (2.1%)**	**15 (0.3%)**	**1 (0.0%)**	**3 (0.1%)**	**17 (0.3%)**	**45 (0.8%)**	**0 (0.0%)**	**1 (0.0%)**	**12 (0.2%)**	**213 (3.8%)**
Housing	Quality and Choice	1,026	49 (4.8%)	1 (0.1%)	0 (0.0%)	1 (0.1%)	5 (0.5%)	7 (0.7%)	0 (0.0%)	0 (0.0%)	2 (0.2%)	65 (6.3%)
	Sustainable Communities	1,170	194 (16.6%)	1 (0.1%)	0 (0.0%)	0 (0.0%)	1 (0.1%)	9 (0.8%)	0 (0.0%)	1 (0.1%)	4 (0.3%)	210 (17.9%)
	Subtotal	**2,196**	**243 (11.1%)**	**2 (0.1%)**	**0 (0.0%)**	**1 (0.0%)**	**6 (0.3%)**	**16 (0.7%)**	**0 (0.0%)**	**1 (0.0%)**	**6 (0.3%)**	**275 (12.5%)**
	Total	**42,507**	**2,688 (6.3%)**	**61 (0.1%)**	**146 (0.3%)**	**44 (0.1%)**	**78 (0.2%)**	**257 (0.6%)**	**1,124 (2.6%)**	**645 (1.5%)**	**1,129 (2.7%)**	**6,172 (14.5%)**

Percentages show keyword usage as a proportion of total text units, i.e. sentences, for each document.

services. In education, as would be expected, people are primarily positioned as parents and pupils. As in the Blair speeches, parents have the edge here (8.0 per cent for parents compared to 7.2 per cent for pupils). Community is also used in the education context (3.0 per cent of sentences). Emphasis is placed on schools being at the heart of the community, a 'community resource', for example through the extended schools initiative. Schools are charged with improving community cohesion, particularly in deprived communities. Universities too are expected to serve and provide leadership within their communities. However, the education policy documents have less than the other publications to say about the community. Education is not talked about in relation to the general service terms either (customers, consumers, clients), with fewer hits in these categories than other services: people are neither citizens nor consumers in relation to education services. As a service it is directed much more resolutely at its direct beneficiaries than the other services. This finding fits the point made about recent education policy by observers: Moss and O'Loughlin argue that under New Labour, 'Education in the information age becomes an individualised process, resting as much on the autonomous effort and sense of responsibility of the individual as on the efforts of the state' (2005, p. 176).

In order to trace the roles and expectations of parents and pupils in the education documents, it is necessary to look in more detail at how the keywords are used, as Box 7.1 does. The same patterns are evident here as in Blair's speeches: an emphasis on responsibility, a theory of rising user expectations, a preference-accommodating approach to policy change and a consequentialist position on structural reform.

In the health documents, people are primarily positioned as patients, as would be expected (10.6 per cent of sentences), although community is also important (6.1 per cent). Indeed, community is used twice as often in health as in education. In health the term community is primarily used in support of the principle that people should be able to access health services locally. Given the environmental factors that shape health outcomes, communities must be the focal point for health improvement, described as 'a shift in public health approaches from "advice from on high to support from next door"' (DoH, 2004a).

The health documents also use the language of client, consumer and customer much more than the education texts. Indeed, the health documents talk about the consumer more than any of the other policy texts. Health is being developed for the 'consumer age' (DoH, 2000)

Box 7.1   Parents and pupils

A key expectation of parents in all the documents is that they will be involved in the learning process. Parents are 'key partners in their children's learning' (DfES, 2001), and schools must 'find new ways to involve and respond to parents' (DfES, 2001). The DfES Five Year Plan envisages parents becoming more involved in their children's learning: 'And we will require schools to make both pupil and parent views part of their school self-evaluation' (DfES, 2004). There will be 'A closer relationship between parent and schools, with better information through a new "school profile" and more family learning' (DfES, 2004). According to the 2005 white paper, reforms are designed 'to ensure that every parent is fully engaged with their child's learning and is treated as a full partner in the education service' (DfES, 2005). Pupils too are to play a stronger role: 'Pupils can have a real say in how they learn and achieve and can be much more involved in how the school is run, for example helping to interview new members of staff or contributing to decisions on school meals' (DfES, 2005).

Yet this emphasis on involvement is coercive as much as voluntary: 'To help build even stronger partnerships, all schools should, in discussion with parents, develop a written home-school contract' (DfES, 1997). The 2001 white paper talks of, 'Legislating to require parents to take greater responsibility for their children's behaviour and give schools powers to deal with parents who are violent or abusive (DfES, 2001). In the 2005 white paper there will be 'fines for parents if excluded pupils are found unsupervised during school hours' (DfES, 2005) In relation to law and order, as well as education, emphasis is placed on the responsibilities of the parents: 'As parents we are responsible for setting acceptable standards of behaviour and ensuring our children adhere to these standards' (Home Office, 2003). The Home Office proposes introducing parenting contracts: 'We intend to build on acceptable behaviour contracts for children and parenting contracts, to ensure young offenders and their parents take responsibility for their actions...' (Home Office, 2002). Only in higher education are responsibilities to be removed from parents: 'no student need rely on their parents to pay for the cost of their tuition...' (DfES, 2003).

Box 7.1   Parents and pupils – *continued*

Service reforms need to be sensitive to the expectations of users: 'Learners expect the same choice and innovation in education as they have in other parts of their lives, and parents want more for their children' (DfES, 2004). Access to information is an important prerequisite for parents to make choices with education. 'Every parent should be able to access that information, so that they can work with teachers to enable their child to achieve their full potential (DfES, 2005). Differentiation is also important. The five-year plan calls for: 'Greater personalisation and choice, with the wishes and needs of children, parents and learners centre-stage' (DfES, 2004). There is a responsibility on schools to 'tailor or personalise what is taught to get the most from each pupil' (DfES, 2004).

The role of the public sector is to undergo a transformation: '... the local authority must move from being a provider of education to being its local commissioner and the champion of parent choice' (DfES, 2005). Indeed, parents will be able to play a much more direct role in schooling, becoming more active coproducers: 'parents are able to set up new schools supported by a dedicated capital pot' (DfES, 2005).

and 'consumer society' (DoH, 2004a) in which we live. To understand the way that health services develop in the documents, Box 7.2 outlines the way that the term patient – the most frequently used keyword in health – is used in the documents. The consumerist themes of meeting changed user expectations and prioritising quality over ideology are all evident here.

In welfare, the most frequently used keyword is community, although welfare also has more hits than any other policy area for the service conditional terms client and customer. Indeed, insofar as the term customer is used at all in the documents, it is primarily as a welfare user, with 127 hits in the five welfare policy documents. This finding is surprising given the definition of a customer discussed in Chapter 3 – someone with an exit right who pays for a service – since these attributes are weaker in welfare than in other services, particularly transport. The customer occurs most often in the 2005 DWP five-year plan. As it makes clear:

Box 7.2   The patient

The 1997 health white paper, *The New NHS: Modern and Dependable*, fits into the standardisation narrative with its calls for 'greater consistency in the availability and quality of services, right across the NHS' (DoH, 1997). By the time of the 2004 *NHS Improvement Plan* priorities have shifted closer to the differentiation narrative: 'The next stage in the NHS's journey is to ensure that a drive for responsive, convenient and personalised services takes root across the whole of the NHS and for all patients' (2004a). As well as delivering differentiated services, the NHS will involve patients more in their own health management. The 1999 *Saving Lives* white paper calls for 'Expert patients programmes to help people manage their own illnesses' (DoH, 1999). The NHS five-year plan sets out the patient role in more detail: 'Patients will be empowered to take an active role in maintaining their own health, choosing which provider treats them and controlling healthcare decisions' (DoH, 2004b).

The subjective preferences of users are to be accorded more weight as predicted by the consumerist model. The Patient's Charter of the Major era is criticised for having 'concentrated too much on narrow measures of process' (DoH, 1997). The NHS's success in meeting patient needs will now be determined in large part by patients themselves: 'And it must be the quality of the patient's experience as well as the clinical result – quality measured in terms of prompt access, good relationships and efficient administration' (DoH, 1997). This definition of quality is restated in the NHS Plan: 'Quality will not just be restricted to the clinical aspects of care, but include quality of life and the entire patient experience (DoH, 2000).

User expectations are a key driver of change: 'The NHS has been too slow to change its ways of working to meet modern patient expectations for fast, convenient, 24 hour, personalised care' (DoH, 2000). New definitions of success are to be introduced:

> With much shorter waiting times for treatment, 'how soon?' will cease to be a major issue. 'How?', 'where?' and 'how good?' will become increasingly important to patients. Patients' desire for high-quality personalised care will drive the new

Box 7.2   The patient – *continued*

system. Giving people greater personal choice will give them control over these issues, allowing patients to call the shots about the time and place of their care, and empowering them to personalise their care to ensure the quality and convenience that they want (DoH, 2004b).

Ideologically imposed barriers between public and private sectors are to be broken down:

For decades there has been a stand-off between the NHS and the private sector providers of healthcare. This has to end. Ideological boundaries or institutional barriers should not stand in the way of better care for NHS patients (DoH, 2000).

... we need to improve the quality of service we offer to customers, and reduce the complexity of claiming benefits. We will meet that challenge through: knowing our customers – this means that we can tailor our services to them, providing the right level of support for their needs...

DWP, 2005b

The consumer is also a term used in the welfare documents. As the DWP five-year plan puts it, 'People increasingly see themselves as consumers of public services' (DWP, 2005b). This self-conscious consumerism is significant because it suggests that to be a consumer involves distinct attitudes, rather than simply being a synonym for service user. Similarly, the document states that through the expansion of direct payments to those with social care needs, 'People who are currently the passive recipients of services become consumers with the ability to shape and control the services they are willing to buy and shift the culture of care planning' (DoH, 2005b). Thus a consumer is a particular kind of empowered user with an exit power.

Part of the reason that the terms customer, consumer and client are used frequently in welfare is the lack of a service specific term, equivalent to patient or pupil. It is interesting to note though that client, the term historically associated with welfare user, had only 21 hits across all the welfare documents. It is clear that the language of client has only a residual hold within welfare policy.

The community in welfare is a site of recognition and status as well as service delivery: people must be empowered to 'participate fully in the life of the community' (DoH, 2005b). Status is also linked to being a citizen. As the *Valuing People* document puts it: 'People with learning disabilities are citizens too,' and should have rights and equality as a citizen (DoH, 2001). Overall though, the term citizen is not used as often in the welfare context as community, customer or parent.

Community is used most in the law and order documents. In the calculus of crime, there is a call to 'rebalance the criminal justice system in favour of the victim and the community so as to reduce crime and bring more offenders to justice' (Home Office, 2002). The community is also the place for punishment and rehabilitation, through 'community sentences' and 'community prisons'. Crime reduction requires 'community policing', particularly through 'Community Support Officers' (Home Office, 2005). Reform cannot be bestowed from on high: 'It is not about waving a magic wand – it is about giving people the tools they need to claim back their communities for the decent law abiding majority' (Home Office, 2004). The vision here of community is an idealised one: 'Healthy communities are built on strong families. These are communities where people know their neighbours and can call on them in good times and in bad' (Home Office, 2003); 'The community sets clear standards of behaviour' (Home Office, 2003). The law and order documents become more community-oriented over time, jumping from 5.2 per cent of sentences in *Tackling Drugs* (1998) to 23.5 per cent in *Building Communities* (2004).

One of the features of law and order is that it does not have a distinctive user group. For that reason it would be expected that these documents had fewer hits for the service specific terms. However, the term customer is used proportionally as often in law and order as it is in transport, where the role of customer appears more appropriate. In particular, the 2005 *Building Communities* white paper uses the term customer 51 times (in 2.3 per cent of sentences), more than in any other document in the sample apart from the DWP five-year plan, *Opportunity and Security*. The Home Office five-year plan promises, 'We will embed a genuinely responsive customer-service culture and make the police and their partners more accessible, visible and accountable' (Home Office, 2006). Overall the law and order documents are oriented more towards customers (0.8 per cent of sentences) than citizens (0.5 per cent).

The term community is used less in transport than the other services (in 2.1 per cent of text units), although it is still the most utilised term in this category. The second most frequently used term is customer (0.8 per cent of sentences). The low proportions of keyword hits for transport are likely to be because passenger, the most obvious user role in transport, was not one of the keywords.

The two housing documents are more firmly oriented towards the community, with a higher proportion of hits for that keyword than any service except law and order (11.1 per cent of sentences). Since housing more than any other service is rooted in a particular locality, it is to be expected that community would be given a high profile. The Office of the Deputy Prime Minister (ODPM) makes clear that it seeks to create 'sustainable communities' which 'need their own identities – we need to move on from soulless estates and poorly laid out rows of housing' (ODPM, 2005a). Adequate and affordable housing provision is part of the government's vision of a fairer society, in which more vulnerable members of society are supported. The term customer is also important in housing, signalling a new approach to housing allocation. In housing, social letting services must become more customer-focused (DETR, 2000a). Under choice-based letting: 'This shift moves away from council officers making important decisions about who was housed where, to customers being empowered and respected to make their own decisions about which housing is most appropriate for them' (DETR, 2000a).

One of the features of Blair's speeches was the way in which he contrasted services in the past – which were monolithic and hidebound – with those that New Labour would deliver. The same contrasts are evident in the command papers. The *NHS Plan*, for example, describes the era of the creation of the NHS thus: 'In 1948, deference and hierarchy defined the relationships between citizens and services. In an era of mass production needs were regarded as identical and preferences were ignored,' (DoH, 2000). The Department for Work and Pensions (DWP) five-year plan implicitly premises its account of the citizen-state relationship on a contrast with the past:

> This approach is about a new relationship between the citizen and the welfare state: a relationship that is active not passive, about responsibilities not just rights, support not just benefit, and individual services not just lumping people together.
>
> DWP, 2005

Similarly the *Building Communities* white paper accords a new role to users: 'Our aim is to put an entirely different dynamic in place to drive public services: driven by the user – in the case of policing and community safety, by the law-abiding citizen' (Home Office, 2004). The desirability of new policies, therefore, is premised on their ability to avoid the limitations that dogged services in New Labour's vision of the past.

The rationale for service improvement is complicated by the introduction of changed service expectations: not only must service reforms tackle the failings of existing services, they must also take into account new user demands. The same consumerist rationale of preference accommodation that drove reform in Blair's speeches is evident in these documents. According to the 1998 welfare green paper: 'Voters and consumers have become more demanding, with rising expectations of quality services... Consumers expect ever higher levels of service and better value for money' (DSS, 1998). In criminal justice, 'a growing consumer culture has led to rising expectations of customer service... Providers of services across the public and private sectors are facing mounting external pressures from a more demanding consumer culture...' (Home Office, 2004). In the 2005 education white paper: 'To respond to parental demand, we need to expand choice, create real diversity of provision, and to ensure that the benefits of choice are available to all...' (DfES, 2005). The pressure of growing public expectations is felt in the Home Office as well:

> The public today has higher expectations; society is more open; family and community relationships have changed; we have instant global communications; crime and criminality continually reinvent themselves and the threats to the law-abiding citizen and to civil society change and grow. The police service can and must itself change and grow to meet the challenges of today's world.
>
> Home Office, 2004

In places there is an acknowledgement that government policies are pushing expectations higher rather than rising to meet them. Labour's *Five Year Strategy for Teachers and Learners* notes, 'The emphasis on personalisation and choice in this strategy – coupled with the rapidly changing pressures of society and the economy – will raise the bar of public expectations further' (DfES, 2004). Occasional reference is made to need to build services around the expectations that people should, rather than do have. In *Modernising Social Services*, for example: 'Despite some excellent services in many places, and a generally high appreciation of services by users, social services are often failing to provide the support that people should expect' (DoH, 1999). In some part of the documents there is also recognition of the limitations that government faces in delivering user-led services. According to the *Rights and Responsibilities* white paper, 'It is important that public services are accountable to the broader community as well as delivering services to the individual clients' (Home Office, 2003). In education, exclusion procedures have been reformed 'to strike a better balance between the interests of the individual and the school community as a whole' (DfES, 2005). In the 2004 *Choosing Health* white paper: 'While we respect individuals' rights to make their own choices, we need to respond to public concern that some people's choices can cause a nuisance and have a damaging impact on other people's health.'

Recognition that governments drive as well as respond to public expectations, and that trade offs must be made between different beneficiaries, suggests a more nuanced account of service delivery than that predicted by the consumerist model. Although these statements are made infrequently, they hint at the complexity of public services delivery. Elsewhere such sensitivities are rejected altogether. As the 2005 *Independence, Well-being and Choice* white paper states: 'It is not the job of public services to tell people that they want too much' (DoH, 2005b).

One of the indicators of the consumerist citizenship regime evident in Blair's speeches was a tendency to focus on service quality and reject other aspects of service provision – such as delivery mechanisms and public/private boundaries – as irrelevant. These same trends are evident in the policy documents. There is a repeated discussion of the need to involve 'public, private and voluntary organisations' in the provision of services. In relation to transport, 'We need a new approach, bringing together the public and private sectors in a partnership which benefits everyone' (DETR, 1998a). In housing, 'We now look to those in the private, public and voluntary sectors to join us over the next decade and beyond in implementing these policies and ensuring that everyone has the opportunity, and choice, of a decent home' (DETR, 2000a).

Differences between public and private are finessed, based on a consequentialist logic. In welfare: 'Customers and taxpayers want improved services; they do not want money wasted on artificial barriers and inefficient processes' (DSS, 1998). The rejection of ideology is contrasted with the Conservatives:

The last Government's devotion to privatisation of care provision put dogma before users' interests, and threatened a fragmentation of vital services. But it is also true that the near-monopoly local authority provision that used to be a feature of social care led to a 'one size fits all' approach where users were expected to accommodate themselves to the services that existed.

DoH, 1999

This faith in a multiplicity of providers appears to intensify over time. The 1999 *Modernising Social Services* white paper states:

We should not expect frail or vulnerable people to have to shop around for services, dealing separately with social services, housing, community health services and other agencies.

DSS, 1998

By the time of the 2005 white paper, direct payments are encouraging social care users to do just that, shop around for the deal that they want:

[W]e want to move from a system where people have to take what is offered to one where people have greater control over identifying the type of support or help they want, and more choice about and influence over the services on offer.

DoH, 2005b

This document goes on to make a statement which is wholly in keeping with the individualistic assumptions of the consumerist solution set: in social care, one of the challenges is, 'the increased public expectation that people should be able to live with their own risk' (DoH, 2005b). This individualising of risk has been central to the neo-liberal approach to welfare reform, as well as to Giddens' third way (Beck, 1992; Giddens, 1994). Here it is positioned as a user demand, to which government must defer. Whilst the document usefully highlights the role of risk management in achieving the right balance between independence and protection in social care, it also highlights how far services have moved from a view of risk as a collective to an individual phenomenon.

Breaking down the findings over time, it is possible to identify changing trends during New Labour's time in office. Table 7.3 shows keyword usage by term of office. It highlights the rise in significance

Table 7.3 Service conditional and non-service conditional keywords, over time, in the command papers

Document	Text units	Comm (%)	Tax (%)	Citizen (%)	Client (%)	Consumer (%)	Customer (%)	Patient (%)	Pupil (%)	Parent (%)	Total (%)
First term											
Excellence in Schools	1,349	56 (4.2%)	0 (0.0%)	9 (0.7%)	0 (0.0%)	0 (0.0%)	0 (0.0%)	0 (0.0%)	98 (7.3%)	101 (7.5%)	264 (19.6%)
The New NHS – Modern and Dependable	1,486	100 (6.7%)	0 (0.0%)	0 (0.0%)	0 (0.0%)	0 (0.0%)	0 (0.0%)	183 (12.3%)	0 (0.0%)	0 (0.0%)	283 (19.0%)
New Ambitions for Our Country: A New Contract for Welfare	1,669	25 (1.5%)	10 (0.6%)	13 (0.8%)	0 (0.0%)	3 (0.2%)	46 (2.8%)	1 (0.1%)	2 (0.1%)	54 (3.2%)	154 (9.2%)
Tackling Drugs to Build a Better Britain	597	31 (5.2%)	0 (0.0%)	0 (0.0%)	0 (0.0%)	0 (0.0%)	0 (0.0%)	0 (0.0%)	0 (0.0%)	5 (0.8%)	36 (6.0%)
A New Deal for Transport: Better for Everyone	2,668	59 (2.2%)	8 (0.3%)	0 (0.0%)	2 (0.1%)	9 (0.3%)	25 (0.9%)	0 (0.0%)	1 (0.0%)	12 (0.4%)	116 (4.3%)
Modernising Social Services	1,857	51 (2.7%)	5 (0.3%)	7 (0.4%)	3 (0.2%)	0 (0.0%)	0 (0.0%)	2 (0.1%)	0 (0.0%)	16 (0.9%)	84 (4.5%)
Saving Lives: Our Healthier Nation	1,938	90 (4.6%)	0 (0.0%)	14 (0.7%)	0 (0.0%)	1 (0.1%)	0 (0.0%)	30 (1.5%)	2 (0.1%)	20 (1.0%)	157 (8.1%)
Quality and Choice: A Decent Home for All	1,026	49 (4.8%)	1 (0.1%)	0 (0.0%)	1 (0.1%)	5 (0.5%)	7 (0.7%)	0 (0.0%)	0 (0.0%)	2 (0.2%)	65 (6.3%)
The NHS Plan: A Plan for Investment, A Plan for Reform	2,012	57 (2.8%)	5 (0.2%)	19 (0.9%)	2 (0.1%)	2 (0.1%)	3 (0.1%)	406 (20.2%)	0 (0.0%)	2 (0.1%)	496 (24.7%)
Ten Year Transport Plan	1,429	21 (1.5%)	1 (0.1%)	1 (0.1%)	0 (0.0%)	1 (0.1%)	10 (0.7%)	0 (0.0%)	0 (0.0%)	0 (0.0%)	34 (2.4%)
Valuing People – A New Strategy for Learning Disability in the Twenty-first century	2,023	122 (6.0%)	0 (0.0%)	20 (1.0%)	3 (0.1%)	0 (0.0%)	0 (0.0%)	22 (1.1%)	4 (0.2%)	43 (2.1%)	214 (10.6%)
Subtotal	18,054	661 (3.7%)	30 (0.2%)	83 (0.5%)	11 (0.1%)	21 (0.1%)	91 (0.5%)	644 (3.6%)	107 (0.6%)	225 (1.2%)	1903 (10.5%)

Table 7.3 Service conditional and non-service conditional keywords, over time, in the command papers – *continued*

Document	Text units	Comm (%)	Tax (%)	Citizen (%)	Client (%)	Consumer (%)	Customer (%)	Patient (%)	Pupil (%)	Parent (%)	Total (%)
Second term											
Schools Achieving Success	1,327	35 (2.6%)	1 (0.1%)	3 (0.2%)	0 (0.0%)	1 (0.1%)	0 (0.0%)	0 (0.0%)	167 (12.6%)	53 (4.0%)	260 (19.6%)
Justice for All	2,700	288 (10.7%)	0 (0.0%)	3 (0.1%)	1 (0.0%)	2 (0.1%)	4 (0.1%)	5 (0.2%)	6 (0.2%)	27 (1.0%)	336 (12.4%)
Future of Higher Education White Paper	1,384	19 (1.4%)	8 (0.6%)	1 (0.1%)	0 (0.0%)	0 (0.0%)	2 (0.1%)	0 (0.0%)	3 (0.2%)	2 (0.1%)	35 (2.5%)
Respect and Responsibility: Taking a Stand Against Anti-Social Behaviour	1,251	196 (15.7%)	0 (0.0%)	2 (0.2%)	4 (0.3%)	0 (0.0%)	1 (0.1%)	0 (0.0%)	3 (0.2%)	75 (6.0%)	281 (22.5%)
A Five Year Strategy for Children and Learners	2,474	72 (2.9%)	0 (0.0%)	6 (0.2%)	0 (0.0%)	2 (0.1%)	2 (0.1%)	0 (0.0%)	119 (4.8%)	154 (6.2%)	355 (14.3%)
The NHS Improvement Plan: Putting People at the Heart of Public Services	1,344	75 (5.6%)	2 (0.1%)	2 (0.2%)	0 (0.0%)	1 (0.1%)	0 (0.0%)	396 (29.5%)	0 (0.0%)	4 (0.3%)	480 (35.7%)
Choosing Health	3,365	294 (8.7%)	0 (0.0%)	6 (0.2%)	12 (0.4%)	34 (1.0%)	6 (0.2%)	62 (1.8%)	27 (0.8%)	72 (2.1%)	513 (15.2%)
Building Communities, Beating Crime – A better policy service for the 21st Century	2,175	512 (23.5%)	3 (0.1%)	29 (1.3%)	0 (0.0%)	3 (0.1%)	51 (2.3%)	1 (0.0%)	2 (0.1%)	1 (0.0%)	602 (27.7%)
The Future of Transport	1,512	39 (2.6%)	6 (0.4%)	0 (0.0%)	1 (0.1%)	7 (0.5%)	10 (0.7%)	0 (0.0%)	0 (0.0%)	0 (0.0%)	63 (4.2%)
Sustainable Communities: Homes for all	1,170	194 (16.6%)	1 (0.1%)	0 (0.0%)	0 (0.0%)	1 (0.1%)	9 (0.8%)	0 (0.0%)	1 (0.1%)	4 (0.3%)	210 (17.9%)

Table 7.3   Service conditional and non-service conditional keywords, over time, in the command papers – *continued*

Document	Text units	Comm (%)	Tax (%)	Citizen (%)	Client (%)	Consumer (%)	Customer (%)	Patient (%)	Pupil (%)	Parent (%)	Total (%)
Opportunity and Security throughout Life	1,966	15 (0.8%)	8 (0.4%)	5 (0.3%)	15 (0.8%)	3 (0.2%)	76 (3.9%)	14 (0.7%)	1 (0.1%)	112 (5.7%)	249 (12.7%)
Independence, Well-being and Choice: Our Vision for the Future of Social Care for Adults in England	1,492	131 (8.8%)	0 (0.0%)	2 (0.1%)	0 (0.0%)	3 (0.2%)	5 (0.3%)	2 (0.1%)	0 (0.0%)	12 (0.8%)	155 (10.4%)
Subtotal	22,160	1,870 (8.4%)	29 (0.1%)	59 (0.3%)	33 (0.2%)	57 (0.3%)	166 (0.8%)	480 (2.2%)	329 (1.5%)	516 (2.3%)	3,539 (16.0%)
Third term											
Higher Standards; Better Schools for All	1,743	65 (3.7%)	0 (0.0%)	1 (0.1%)	0 (0.0%)	0 (0.0%)	0 (0.0%)	0 (0.0%)	209 (12.0%)	356 (20.4%)	631 (36.2%)
A Five Year Strategy for Protecting the Public and Reducing Reoffending	550	92 (16.7%)	2 (0.4%)	3 (0.6%)	0 (0.0%)	0 (0.0%)	0 (0.0%)	0 (0.0%)	0 (0.0%)	2 (0.4%)	99 (18.0%)
Subtotal	2,293	157 (6.8%)	2 (0.1%)	4 (0.2%)	0 (0.0%)	0 (0.0%)	0 (0.0%)	0 (0.0%)	209 (9.1%)	358 (15.6%)	730 (31.8%)
Total	42,507	2,688 (6.3%)	61 (0.1%)	146 (0.3%)	44 (0.1%)	78 (0.2%)	257 (0.6%)	1,124 (2.6%)	645 (1.5%)	1,129 (2.7%)	6,172 (14.5%)

Percentages show keyword usage as a proportion of total text units, i.e. sentences, for each document for the term community from the first to the second term, dropping off again in the third term (from 3.7 per cent of text units in Labour's first term, to 8.4 per cent in the second term and 6.8 per cent in the third term). This jump from the first to the second term and subsequent decline is mirrored in Blair's speeches, signalling common patterns in New Labour's tendency to frame its policy around the community. The language of patient is used less and less over time, as it was in Blair's speeches, whereas the language of pupil and parent are used more and more, again similar to the pattern in the Blair texts. The rise in the significance of pupils and parents is particularly evident after the 2005 general election, a time when the government was launching its new education white paper.

The three narratives

Through the keyword searching it is possible to trace the use of the three public service narratives across services and over time. Table 7.4 shows the results of the keyword searches. The table is abbreviated, showing narrative categories rather than individual search terms, because of its large size. The full table is given in Appendix 3. As the table shows, narrative terms were used in over a quarter of the sentences overall (28.5 per cent). They were used most in health (in 32.0 per cent of health sentences), and least in transport (22.3 per cent of transport sentences). However, even in transport, narrative terms were used in over one fifth of total sentences, suggesting that the narratives together are an important component of public service positioning.

The standardisation narrative is used the most overall, occurring in 11.8 per cent of sentences. The differentiation narrative is the second most frequently used – 9.0 per cent – and the coproduction narrative is used in 7.7 per cent of total sentences. These findings differ slightly from those found in Blair's speeches. Although Blair also used the standardisation keywords more frequently than any other, his second more utilised narrative was coproduction, with the differentiation keywords getting the least attention. Thus the policy documents put more emphasis than Blair on developing services that are tailored to the needs of their users, and less emphasis than the Prime Minister on what users themselves must contribute to the service.

Disaggregating the command paper data by service area, it is possible to see that the first narrative is the most frequently used in education, health and transport, suggesting that these are the most standardised services – the same pattern as in Blair's speeches. In welfare and

Table 7.4 The three narratives by service area in the command papers
(See Appendix 3 for a full version of this table)

Document	Text Units	Standardisation (%)	Differentiation (%)	Coproduction (%)	Total (%)
Education					
Excellence in Schools	1,349	233 (17.3%)	39 (2.9%)	80 (5.9%)	352 (26.1%)
Schools Achieving Success	1,327	200 (15.1%)	108 (8.1%)	125 (9.4%)	433 (32.6%)
Future of HE	1,384	170 (12.3%)	100 (7.2%)	87 (6.3%)	357 (25.8%)
Five Year Strategy	2,474	193 (7.8%)	273 (11.0%)	212 (8.6%)	678 (27.4%)
Higher Standards	1,743	271 (15.5%)	260 (14.9%)	192 (11.0%)	723 (41.5%)
Subtotal	**8,277**	**1,067 (12.9%)**	**780 (9.4%)**	**696 (8.4%)**	**2,543 (30.7%)**
Health					
The New NHS	1,486	138 (9.3%)	60 (4.0%)	118 (7.9%)	316 (21.3%)
Saving Lives	1,938	219 (11.3%)	107 (5.5%)	108 (5.6%)	434 (22.4%)
NHS Plan	2,012	298 (14.8%)	151 (7.5%)	72 (3.6%)	521 (25.9%)
NHS Improvement Plan	1,344	223 (16.6%)	265 (19.7%)	80 (6.0%)	568 (42.3%)
Choosing Health	3,365	510 (15.2%)	556 (16.5%)	338 (10.0%)	1404 (41.7%)
Subtotal	**10,145**	**1,388 (13.7%)**	**1,139 (11.2%)**	**716 (7.1%)**	**3,243 (32.0%)**

Table 7.4　The three narratives by service area in the command papers – *continued*
(See Appendix 3 for a full version of this table)

Document	Text Units	Standardisation (%)	Differentiation (%)	Coproduction (%)	Total (%)
Welfare					
New Ambitions	1,669	97 (5.8%)	101 (6.1%)	55 (3.3%)	253 (15.2%)
Mod Social Services	1,857	243 (13.1%)	110 (5.9%)	142 (7.6%)	495 (26.7%)
Valuing People	2,023	246 (12.2%)	170 (8.4%)	170 (8.4%)	586 (29.0%)
Independence, Well-being	1,492	105 (7.0%)	329 (22.1%)	128 (8.6%)	562 (37.7%)
Opportunity and Security	1,966	175 (8.9%)	193 (9.8%)	172 (8.7%)	540 (27.5%)
Subtotal	**9,007**	**866 (9.6%)**	**903 (10.0%)**	**692 (7.7%)**	**2,461 (27.3%)**
Law and order					
Tackling Drugs	597	46 (7.7%)	21 (3.5%)	40 (6.7%)	107 (17.9%)
Justice for All	2,700	306 (11.3%)	117 (4.3%)	230 (8.5%)	653 (24.2%)
Respect/Responsibility	1,251	105 (8.4%)	76 (6.1%)	154 (12.3%)	335 (26.8%)
Building Communities	550	34 (6.2%)	22 (4.0%)	27 (4.9%)	83 (15.1%)
Five Year Strategy	2,175	274 (12.6%)	213 (9.8%)	317 (14.6%)	804 (37.0%)
Subtotal	**7,273**	**765 (10.5%)**	**449 (6.2%)**	**768 (10.6%)**	**1,982 (27.3%)**

Table 7.4 The three narratives by service area in the command papers – *continued*
(See Appendix 3 for a full version of this table)

Document	Text Units	Standardisation (%)	Differentiation (%)	Coproduction (%)	Total (%)
Transport					
New Deal for Transport	2,668	382 (14.3%)	131 (4.9%)	136 (5.1%)	649 (24.3%)
Ten Year Transport Plan	1,429	161 (11.3%)	47 (3.3%)	17 (1.2%)	225 (15.7%)
Future of Transport	1,512	185 (12.2%)	116 (7.7%)	76 (5.0%)	377 (24.9%)
Subtotal	**5,609**	**728 (13.0%)**	**294 (5.2%)**	**229 (4.1%)**	**1,251 (22.3%)**
Housing					
Quality and Choice	1,026	91 (8.9%)	151 (14.7%)	51 (5.0%)	293 (28.6%)
Sustainable Communities	1,170	130 (11.1%)	97 (8.3%)	101 (8.6%)	328 (28.0%)
Subtotal	**2,196**	**221 (10.1%)**	**248 (11.3%)**	**152 (6.9%)**	**621 (28.3%)**
Total	**42,507**	**5,035 (11.8%)**	**3,813 (9.0%)**	**3,253 (7.7%)**	**12,101 (28.5%)**

Percentages show keyword usage as a proportion of total text units, i.e. sentences, for each document.

housing the second narrative, emphasising differentiation, is used most, as it was also by Blair. It is only in law and order that emphasis is placed primarily on terms that suggest user involvement and responsibility, the third narrative. This finding is not consistent with Blair's speeches, where law and order was in the main a standardised service. In the policy documents, discussion of crime is linked to public involvement in crime prevention, whereas Blair focuses more on a consistent response to crimes committed.

Looking at the way that the keywords are used within the standardisation narrative, it is welfare and housing where the texts make most reference to rights. Access is most commonly invoked in the context of transport, and inform is most often connected to health. As in Blair's speeches, education and standards are most commonly linked together, as are transport and targets. Convenience is mentioned little in these documents. The findings suggest that although standardisation is important in all these services, it takes on a different dimension within each service: transport must be accessible and health users must be kept informed, whereas education must emphasise high standards.

Similarly in the differentiation narrative certain keywords are applied more to some service areas than others. Choice – often seen as central to Labour's education and health agendas – is used most often in transport. Welfare is the most 'individual' service, whereas health is the most 'personal'. Whilst housing is to be 'responsive', education is to be 'diverse' and 'tailored'.

Within the coproduction narrative, opportunity and responsibility are used much more than the other keywords. Education and housing provide the most 'opportunities' (3.2 per cent of sentences in each service area). Perhaps surprisingly, it is law and order that calls for most engagement, involvement and empowerment (2.0 per cent, 2.3 per cent and 0.5 per cent of sentences respectively). Since the users of law and order services are likely to be unwilling users – as victims, defendants or criminals – this finding suggests that the documents refer to crime prevention rather than prosecution. Law and order also calls for the most responsibility (4.2 per cent of sentences), suggesting that the documents require people to behave responsibly in avoiding criminality and anti-social behaviour. Education calls most for participation (0.9 per cent).

Table 7.5 shows the findings of the narrative keyword searches broken down by New Labour's three terms of office. Again, the full table is abbreviated here, and reproduced in full in Appendix 3. In the analysis of Blair's speeches it was found that the Prime Minister talked

Table 7.5 The three narratives over time, in the command papers
(See Appendix 3 for a full version of this table)

Document	Text Units	Standardisation (%)	Differentiation (%)	Coproduction (%)	Total (%)
First term					
Excellence in Schools	1,349	233 (17.3%)	39 (2.9%)	80 (5.9%)	352 (26.1%)
The New NHS – Modern and Dependable	1,486	138 (9.3%)	60 (4.0%)	118 (7.9%)	316 (21.3%)
New Ambitions for Our Country	1,669	97 (5.8%)	101 (6.1%)	55 (3.3%)	253 (15.2%)
Tackling Drugs to Build a Better Britain	597	46 (7.7%)	21 (3.5%)	40 (6.7%)	107 (17.9%)
A New Deal for Transport: Better for Everyone	2,668	382 (14.3%)	131 (4.9%)	136 (5.1%)	649 (24.3%)
Modernising Social Services	1,857	243 (13.1%)	110 (5.9%)	142 (7.6%)	495 (26.7%)
Saving Lives: Our Healthier Nation	1,938	219 (11.3%)	107 (5.5%)	108 (5.6%)	434 (22.4%)
Quality and Choice: A Decent Home for All	1,026	91 (8.9%)	151 (14.7%)	51 (5.0%)	293 (28.6%)
The NHS Plan	2,012	298 (14.8%)	151 (7.5%)	72 (3.6%)	521 (25.9%)
Ten Year Transport Plan	1,429	161 (11.3%)	47 (3.3%)	17 (1.2%)	225 (15.7%)

Table 7.5 The three narratives over time, in the command papers – *continued*
(See Appendix 3 for a full version of this table)

Document	Text Units	Standardisation (%)	Differentiation (%)	Coproduction (%)	Total (%)
Valuing People – A New Strategy	2,023	246 (12.2%)	170 (8.4%)	170 (8.4%)	586 (29.0%)
Subtotal	**18,054**	**2,154 (11.9%)**	**1,088 (6.0%)**	**989 (5.5%)**	**4,231 (23.4%)**
Second term					
Schools Achieving Success	1,327	200 (15.1%)	108 (8.1%)	125 (9.4%)	433 (32.6%)
Justice for All	2,700	306 (11.3%)	117 (4.3%)	230 (8.5%)	653 (24.2%)
Future of Higher Education White Paper	1,384	170 (12.3%)	100 (7.2%)	87 (6.3%)	357 (25.8%)
Respect and Responsibility	1,251	105 (8.4%)	76 (6.1%)	154 1(2.3%)	335 (26.8%)
A Five Year Strategy for Children and Learners	2,474	193 (7.8%)	273 (11.0%)	212 (8.6%)	678 (27.4%)
The NHS Improvement Plan	1,344	223 (16.6%)	265 (19.7%)	80 (6.0%)	568 (42.3%)
Choosing Health	3,365	510 (15.2%)	556 (16.5%)	338 (10.0%)	1,404 (41.7%)
Building Communities, Beating Crime	2,175	274 (12.6%)	213 (9.8%)	317 (14.6%)	804 (37.0%)

Table 7.5 **The three narratives over time, in the command papers** – *continued*
(See Appendix 3 for a full version of this table)

Document	Text Units	Standardisation (%)	Differentiation (%)	Coproduction (%)	Total (%)
The Future of Transport	1,512	185 (12.2%)	116 (7.7%)	76 (5.0%)	377 (24.9%)
Sustainable Communities: Homes for all	1,170	130 (11.1%)	97 (8.3%)	101 (8.6%)	328 (28.0%)
Opportunity and Security throughout Life	1,966	175 (8.9%)	193 (9.8%)	172 (8.7%)	540 (27.5%)
Independence, Well-being and Choice	1,492	105 (7.0%)	329 (22.1%)	128 (8.6%)	562 (37.7%)
Subtotal	22,160	2,576 (11.6%)	2,443 (11.0%)	2,020 (9.1%)	7,039 (31.8%)
Third term					
Higher Standards; Better Schools for All	1,743	271 (15.5%)	260 (14.9%)	192 (11.0%)	723 (41.5%)
A Five Year Strategy for Protecting the Public	550	34 (6.2%)	22 (4.0%)	27 (4.9%)	83 (15.1%)
Subtotal	2,293	305 (13.3%)	282 (12.3%)	219 (9.6%)	806 (35.2%)
Total	42,507	5,035 (11.8%)	3,813 (9.0%)	3,253 (7.7%)	12,101 (28.5%)

Percentages show keyword usage as a proportion of total text units, i.e. sentences, for each document about differentiation and coproduction more in the speeches from the second and third terms than the first, suggesting that these narratives were becoming more important and standardisation was becoming less important. This table shows a similar pattern. The frequency of the standardisation keywords remained about the same between the first and second terms (11.9 and 11.6 per cent respectively), rising slightly in Labour's third term (13.8 per cent). Differentiation became much more significant after the 2001 election, rising from 6.0 per cent of text units in the first term to 11 per cent in the second term, and again to 12.3 per cent in the third term. Coproduction follows a similar pattern, rising from 5.5 per cent of text units in the first term to 9.1 per cent in the second term, and 9.6 per cent after the 2005 election. Here, consistent with Blair's speeches, is an overall preference for standardisation, with the relative importance of standardisation becoming challenged over time, as the government becomes more interested in the differentiation and coproduction approaches.

New Labour and coproduction

Given the emphasis on opportunity and responsibility in these documents, as well as Blair's speeches, it is worth looking at New Labour's approach to coproduction in more detail. One of the non-consumerist features of New Labour's approach has been its emphasis on the delivery of services in ways that are coproductive. Across Blair's speeches and the command papers, the themes of opportunity and responsibility are particularly dominant. These terms have different, and in some ways contradictory, emphases. Opportunity is associated with capacity-building and taking something from government; responsibility is associated with obligation and giving something back. However, it is these two terms, much more than engagement, empowerment, participation or involvement that are applied to public services in Blair's speeches and the policy documents.

Looking at the ways in which opportunity is used in these documents, emphasis is placed on individuals and families making the most of the opportunities that government provides. Training and employment opportunities are particularly important in the welfare documents, although transport reforms are also discussed in relation to the opportunities they create for people to access work. In housing people are to be guaranteed the 'opportunity of a decent home' (DETR, 2000b), suggesting that users who do not make the most of the opportunities given will not be able to access the service. Similarly, in education, parents are required to make the most of good educational opportunities. In health there will be opportunities for patients to have more of a say in the service.

Responsibilities are often assumed to be twinned with rights in the New Labour discourse, and it is possible to see that link made in some of these documents. This juxtaposition is particularly important in law and order. 'Our aim is a society where we have an understanding that the rights we all enjoy are based in turn on the respect and responsibilities we have to other people and to our community' (Home Office, 2003). Policing involves rights and responsibilities. 'Local policing, for example, is at its most effective when performed as a shared undertaking: policing being done with the public. This is about individuals recognising their own responsibilities in terms of helping to prevent and reduce crime, not just their right to live in safer communities' (Home Office, 2004). Overall in the command papers, responsibilities are emphasised much more than rights (2.3 per cent to 0.8 per cent of sentences): rights and responsibilities, which occur 339 and 978 times respectively separately, only co-occur in 42 sentences. The same bias towards responsibilities is evident in Blair's speeches: they are mentioned 158 times, whereas rights feature 106 times, and the terms only co-occur in 38 sentences. The findings of the speeches and policy documents combined support the point made by Fairclough, in an earlier analysis of Blair's speeches: 'the close relationship between "rights" and "responsibilities" in New Labour's language is absent, and we have rather the divorcing of rights from responsibilities...' (2000, p. 41).

Again as in Blair's speeches, responsibilities in the policy documents are not evenly distributed. The taxpayer, for example, is only invoked in relation to the affordability of services, with no balancing responsibilities. Whereas responsibility and community are used together in 109 sentences, citizen and responsibility are used in only 11 sentences, customer and responsibility in 6 sentences and consumer and responsibility in 4 sentences. Customers and consumers are expected to bear few responsibilities in relation to public services.

Under-utilised in the policy documents and Blair's speeches are terms which relate to the engagement and empowerment of users. Engage, empower and participate are among the least used of the keywords in the policy documents and the speeches. The sorts of coproduction envisaged by New Labour involve risk transfer and the relocating of burdens, rather than empowerment of users. Through expert patient schemes, direct payments and parenting orders public services are produced by users in the home, privatising problems and increasing pressure on family carers (Clarke *et al*, 2000, p. 3). Under this approach, coproduction becomes a form of DIY welfare, analogous to the co-productive activities of the consumer of flatpack furniture (Wikström, 1996). As Aldridge puts it: '[McDonalds] are indeed fast, but the speed is achieved by getting the customer to do a lot of the work: to stand in a queue, pay immediately, carry his food to the table, and dispose of the remains afterwards' (Aldridge, 2003, p. 113). There are analogies here with the New Labour variant of coproduction, in which users manage their own conditions and the risks associated with them. The scope for more collective conceptions of coproduction to be the basis of remaking public services is discussed in the concluding chapter.

Conclusion

The discussion here points to diversity rather than homogeneity in the public service solution set put forward by central government command papers: the keywords are utilised differently in relation to different public services. It is unsurprising that varying accounts of provision and diverse vocabularies pervade these services: given the complexity and evolutionary nature of social production in a modern state it is unlikely to be otherwise. However some important cross-cutting themes do emerge which help to clarify the citizenship regime under New Labour.

The documentary analysis suggests that policy is being revised in a consumerist direction: individual service-oriented terms are used more than the non-service conditional terms. There is an emphasis on responding to user expectations, and to breaking down public-private boundaries in the name of better service quality, an example of consumerist consequentialism.

The standardisation keywords are the most commonly used overall, although both differentiation and coproduction narratives are also well used in the documents. Services are being differentiated and co-produced more in Labour's second and third terms than in first. In all services, users are to be given more choice of provider and more personalisation of provision. Similarly in all cases the coalition of producers is increasingly assumed to include the private and voluntary sectors, as well as service users themselves, who exercise a productive role either as expert patients, recipients of direct payments, or as parents signed up to home-school contracts. Although emphasis is placed upon coproduction, it is often an involuntary form of coproduction in which certain people are forced to take on new responsibilities.

Community continues to be an important term, and there is recognition in some documents of the need to trade off the needs of users against broader priorities. The community emphasis is the same as in Blair's speeches, and is clearly an important focus of service delivery, particularly in relation to law and order and housing. Thus the New Labour solution set is not only oriented towards individual users, and in that sense does not appear to have fully endorsed a consumerist citizenship regime. The relationship between a distinctively New Labour view of community and a consumerist model is returned to in the concluding chapter.

That public service command papers should echo the priorities of Blair's speeches so closely is unsurprising. They are presented to Parliament by ministers who serve in Blair's government, and are written by civil servants who must have no constitutional identity separate from the government of the day. Local government stands in a different relationship to the Prime Minister. Local authorities have their own electoral mandate, and most are not run by New Labour. Thus it is illuminating to compare how far narratives of service delivery in local government are constructed in the same way as in the national speeches and policy documents. The local citizenship regime is the focus of the next chapter.

8
Local Government: The Customer in the Community

Local government has been the key institution in the delivery of public services since the 1601 Poor Law made it incumbent on parishes to provide for the destitute, a division of powers institutionalised by the 1834 Poor Law Amendment Act (Birch, 1974, p. 12). The story of UK local government is usually told as one of decline in autonomy and status since a Victorian 'hey day' (Gyford, 1991, p. 28). The Beveridge-inspired reforms of the immediate postwar period saw local authorities stripped of much of their autonomy (Birch, 1974, p. 59), becoming 'very much the local arm of a national welfare state' (Gyford, 1991, p. 28). The erosion of local government powers during the 1980s limited the financial autonomy of councils, and restricted their discretion in key areas of service delivery including education and housing (Whitty *et al*, 1993; Cairncross *et al*, 1997).

Despite this loss of autonomy, local government remains an important political institution for its physical proximity to the citizen. John Stuart Mill and others talked of the importance of local government in inculcating the habits of democracy (Mill, 1966, ch. 15. See also Tocqueville, 1994, ch. 14). The scope for 'localism' to be the basis for community renewal and democratic engagement has recently caught the attention of major figures across the political spectrum (Letwin, 2005; Brown, 2006; Campbell, 2006; Miliband, 2006). Clarke *et al*'s claim 20 years ago is just as relevant now: '[I]t would be difficult to find any writer or politician in the field of social welfare who would argue (fundamentally) against decentralisation. It has become an unchallengeable "good thing", even though its precise implications remain unclear...' (Clarke *et al*, 1987, pp. 184–5).

Chapters 6 and 7 showed that aspects of the consumerist citizenship regime were evident in national speeches and policies, including an emphasis on the subjective preferences of individual users and a conse-quentialist approach to service reform, although community-oriented and coproductive approaches were also important. To assess how far these patterns are replicated within local government it is necessary to understand the roles and expectations of citizens in local public service delivery. Often the debate about citizenship and participation at the local level is separated off from discussions about the consumption of local public services. However, people's experience of local government is unlikely to be defined primarily by the opportunities it affords for political participation – given low levels of turnout and political knowledge (MORI, 2002) – but by its delivery of education, social and environmental services. Writing in 1920, Sidney and Beatrice Webb reflected this service orientation in their description of local govern-ment as 'an association of consumers' created to satisfy their needs, and talked of how municipalities allowed democratic control by 'Citizen-Consumers' (Webb and Webb, 1920, pp. 8, 224). Studying public services therefore helps to illustrate broader themes in the citi-zenship regime.

In opposition, Labour attacked much of the Conservative govern-ments' reform agenda for local authorities, and positioned itself as the defender of local government against the marauding centre (Gyford, 1991, p. 18). In office it has overhauled the structures and functions of local government, and instituted elaborate performance measures, overseen by the Audit Commission. Local government has been given new community renewal powers, although firmly placed within a framework of national targets (DETR, 1998b). Freedoms are premised on improved performance. In local government, as Orr argues, 'New Labour has operated along a number of discursive continua. These include freedom–prescription; decentralisation–centralisation; net-works–hierarchy; faith–scepticism; charismatic–bureaucratic power; and so on' (2005, p. 377).

The extent to which consumerism has become the dominant para-digm within local service delivery can be evaluated at two levels. The first is the framework that central government has set for local govern-ment. The second is the extent of consumerism within local authorities themselves. These two levels are considered in turn.

The framework for local government

In its *Modern Local Government* white paper, published in July 1998, Labour announced its proposals for local government, which included reform of the political decision-making structure, a new role as community leader, and a 'Best Value' regime for local services (DETR, 1998b). It was clear from the white paper however that there would be no return to the 'hey day' of local service delivery. In the introduction to the white paper the Deputy Prime Minister John Prescott stated, 'There is no future in the old model of councils trying to plan and run most services. It does not provide the services which people want, and cannot do so in today's world' (DETR, 1998b, p. 5). Based on the four Cs – challenge, compare, compete, consult – the Best Value regime ended the requirement that local services be outsourced, but insisted that if services remained in-house they be able to show that they were delivering 'best value' for their users. The Audit Commission measured how far councils were meeting national targets across hundreds of PIs, and league tables were published ranking councils according to their performance across these indicators (See www.audit-commission.gov.uk).

In 2001 the government published a second white paper: *Strong Local Leadership, Quality Public Services* (DTLR, 2001). Here there was an effort to recognise the burden that the Best Value regime imposed on local authorities and to move to a less intensive model of performance assessment. A new Comprehensive Performance Assessment (CPA) was developed, with reduced inspection for high performers and more punitive measures for 'failing' councils (Kelly, 2003, p. 462).

Content analysis of these two local government white papers, using the same keywords as in previous chapters, reveals a change of emphasis over the period. Table 8.1 shows the findings of keyword counts.

In these white papers the most frequently used term is community (5.8 per cent), registering much more than the second highest, taxpayer (1.5 per cent). In the first document, councils are to play a role of community leader, promoting community well-being, and meeting the needs and aspirations of the community. In the second white paper, councils are to lead and empower their communities in order to develop 'thriving communities'. The balance of keywords shifts between the documents. The term community features proportionally less in the second white paper than the first, whereas all the individual terms are used proportionally more. In particular, the taxpayer, the consumer and the pupil are more important roles in the second white paper than the first. This suggests that local government is being encouraged to become more oriented towards the individual over time. The taxpayer features more in these documents than in Blair's speeches or the other national policy documents, framing the future direction of local government around the needs of taxpayers in a way that is not done at

Table 8.1   Service conditional and non-service conditional keywords in the local government white papers

	Modern Local Government	Strong Local Leadership	Total
Community (%)	131 (9.6%)	108 (3.9%)	239 (5.8%)
Taxpayer (%)	15 (1.1%)	49 (1.8%)	64 (1.5%)
Citizen (%)	2 (0.1%)	7 (0.3%)	9 (0.2%)
Client (%)	0 (0.0%)	0 (0.0%)	0 (0.0%)
Consumer (%)	0 (0.0%)	4 (0.1%)	4 (0.1%)
Customer (%)	1 (0.0%)	3 (0.0%)	4 (0.1%)
Patient (%)	0 (0.0%)	1 (0.0%)	1 (0.0%)
Pupil (%)	0 (0.0%)	12 (0.4%)	12 (0.3%)
Parent (%)	2 (0.2%)	5 (0.9%)	7 (0.2%)
Total hits (%)	**151 (11.1%)**	**189 (6.8%)**	**340 (8.2%)**
Total text units (%)	**1,358 (100.0%)**	**2,791 (100.0%)**	**4,149 (100.0%)**

Percentages show keyword usage as a proportion of total text units, i.e. sentences, for each document.

central government level. Councils are required to set taxes 'at the levels needed to deliver local services according to local priorities, of a quality and at a price local taxpayers demand and are willing to pay for' (DETR, 1998b). The second white paper has a chapter on council tax, setting out proposals for reform (DTLR, 2001).

The balance between the three narratives in each of the white papers is shown in Table 8.2. The table indicates that the standardisation narrative is the most frequently used across the two papers (10.3 per cent of text units), with the coproduction narrative rated second (6.0 per cent) and differentiation talked about the least (3.3 per cent). Whereas standardisation and coproduction are talked about most in the first document, differentiation is talked about slightly more in the second (up from 3.2 per cent to 3.3 per cent). The biggest difference is for the standardisation narrative, which accounts for 13.7 per cent of text units in the first document and 8.7 per cent in the second. Co-production drops from 6.7 per cent to 5.7 per cent. Thus in the second document differentiation becomes more important relative to other two narratives.

The *Strong Local Leadership* document has more to say on choice than the first white paper, whereas *Modern Local Government* has much more

Table 8.2 The three narratives in the local government white papers

		Modern Local Government	Strong Local Leadership	Total
Standardisation	Right	18 (1.3%)	15 (0.5%)	33 (0.8%)
	Access	6 (0.4%)	33 (1.2%)	39 (0.8%)
	Inform	20 (1.5%)	70 (2.5%)	90 (2.2%)
	Standard	98 (7.2%)	55 (2.0%)	153 (3.7%)
	Target	44 (3.2%)	69 (2.5%)	113 (2.7%)
	Convenience	0 (0.0%)	1 (0.0%)	1 (0.0%)
	Subtotal	**186 (13.7%)**	**243 (8.7%)**	**429 (10.3%)**
Differentiation	Choice/choose	16 (1.2%)	48 (1.7%)	64 (1.5%)
	Individual	1 (0.1%)	6 (0.2%)	7 (0.2%)
	Personal	1 (0.1%)	0 (0.0%)	1 (0.0%)
	Responsive	13 (1.0%)	25 (0.9%)	38 (0.9%)
	Diverse	12 (0.9%)	9 (0.3%)	21 (0.5%)
	Tailor	0 (0.0%)	5 (0.2%)	5 (0.1%)
	Subtotal	**43 (3.2%)**	**93 (3.3%)**	**136 (3.3%)**
Coproduction	Opportunity	9 (0.7%)	14 (0.5%)	23 (0.6%)
	Engage	10 (0.7%)	17 (0.6%)	27 (0.7%)
	Involve	9 (0.7%)	13 (0.5%)	22 (0.5%)
	Empower	0 (0.0%)	8 (0.3%)	8 (0.2%)
	Participate	13 (1.0%)	8 (0.3%)	21 (0.5%)
	Responsible	50 (3.7%)	99 (3.5%)	149 (3.6%)
	Subtotal	**91 (6.7%)**	**159 (5.7%)**	**250 (6.0%)**
	Total	**320 (23.6%)**	**495 (17.7%)**	**815 (19.6%)**
	Total text units	**1,358 (100.0%)**	**2,791 (100.0%)**	**4,149 (100.0%)**

Percentages show keyword usage as a proportion of total text units, i.e. sentences, for each document.

to say on standards. The foreword to the first white paper, written by John Prescott, begins with a statement which fits well into the standardisation narrative:

People everywhere deserve and rightly expect a pleasant and safe environment in which they can live and work. We all want good quality public services, with rising standards in our schools and in our health care. We want local communities where everyone can participate in society, and effective care is available to those who need it.

DETR, 1998b

Keywords from the second narrative – emphasising the differentiated needs of the individual user – are used little in this white paper. This finding contrasts with the 2001 white paper, which begins with a fore-word from Blair in which he promises 'flexibility at the front-lines' and 'more choice for customers' (DTLR, 2001). Later in the document, in a discussion of service improvement the *Strong Local Leadership* white paper states:

One of our key principles of public service reform is more choice for the consumer including the ability, particularly where quality falls below acceptable standards, to have an alternative provider. We believe that rising expectations amongst the public, together with significant advances in the way in which services can be delivered, make it essential that there is real variety in the way in which ser-vices are delivered, genuine choice of service providers and genuine choice for service users.

DTLR, 2001

The same themes evident within Blair's speeches and the other central government policy documents are apparent here: the assumption that public expectations are rising, and that choice is the best way to respond to those expectations. At the policy level, therefore, there is evidence of national institutions pushing local government in the direction of a consumerist solution set, initially focused around stan-dards and later oriented towards choice and an explicit customer focus.

That central government's prescription for local government should be similar to its own national agenda for public services is not surpris-ing. To explore the citizenship regime within local government it is important to consider how far these central priorities are adopted at local level. Local authorities can develop their own language and approach to interaction with their citizens, although they must do so in a context that is constrained by national priorities and audit mech-anisms. Within local government itself it is possible to measure the penetration of consumer-oriented attitudes in various ways. One is by looking at local government documents; the other is by reviewing the attitudes and perceptions of those working in local government. The remainder of the chapter explores documentary and interview data in a sample of local authorities selected for analysis.

Providing services to the customer

Chapter 4 discussed how, during the 1980s, when national policy was focusing on marketisation and consumer oriented reforms, some local authorities were adopting a distinctive Public Service Orientation (PSO). PSO shared the focus on improving services for users but claimed a 'values' dimension, emphasising the importance and distinctiveness of public service, which was absent from the private sector-infused Conservative agenda (Rhodes, 1987, p. 63; Stewart and Clarke, 1987, p. 161). Exploring the extent to which nationally derived narratives of consumerism are utilised within local government therefore fits into long-standing debates about the extent to which local authorities copy, inherit or reject public management narratives developed nationally.

Primary local authorities are required to produce a corporate plan (CP) each year, setting out their strategic goals. The CP is therefore a useful document through which to analyse the roles and expectations attributed to local people. CPs lay out the council's corporate goals, its vision for specific service areas and its performance over various national and local indicators. In some councils this document is called the Performance Plan or the Strategic Plan; here they will be included in the category of corporate plan. Since most local authorities only make their most recent corporate plan available, in this case the 2005–2006 version, they represent a single data point rather than giving a picture of change over time, unlike Blair's speeches and the command papers.

A quota sample of local authorities was used to identify 18 councils, a manageable number for analysis. Although accounting for a small proportion of the 388 primary local authorities in England, the sample was designed to be large enough to limit the distortion of one or two outlier cases, whilst being small enough to allow detailed analysis of the documentation. The quota sample was broadly proportional of total councils by authority type and across England's regions. It also provided a proportional balance of councils controlled by the Labour Party, the Conservatives, the Liberal Democrats or that had no overall control. The quota included councils that scored high, medium and low on the comprehensive performance assessments conducted by the Audit Commission. Excel was used to generate lists of councils accord-

Table 8.3   Sample of local authorities

Council	Type	Control*	Region**	CPA***
1	Borough	Con	EEM	Good
2	Borough	Con	NW	Fair
3	Borough	Con	SE	Excellent
4	District	Lab	WM	Weak
5	District	Con	SW	Good
6	District	LD	NW	Weak
7	District	NOC	SW	Fair
8	District	NOC	SE	Weak
9	County	Con	EEM	2 star
10	County	Con	SE	4 star
11	County	Lab	WM	2 star
12	London (south)	Con	L	3 star
13	London (north)	Lab	L	4 star
14	Metropolitan	Lab	WM	1 star
15	Metropolitan	NOC	YHNE	4 star
16	Unitary	Lab	NW	4 star
17	Unitary	NOC	YHNE	1 star
18	Unitary	Con	SW	3 star

*   Political control as at February 2006. Con – Conservative; Lab – Labour; LD – Liberal Democrats; NOC – No Overall Control
** Regions are the standard ones used by the then Office of the Deputy Prime Minister. SE – South East, EEM – East, East Midlands, SW – South West, WM – West Midlands, NW – North West, YHNE – Yorkshire, Humberside and the North East.
*** District and Borough councils are scored on a scale of Weak-Fair-Good-Excellent. The other council types have undergone CPA more recently and are scored on new a scale from one to four stars.

ing to the four variables: council type, political control, region and CPA score. Corporate plans from the sample of 18 authorities were downloaded from websites as PDFs, converted into text files and imported into N6 for analysis. More details of the sampling process can be found in Appendix 4. The anonymised list of local authorities is provided in Table 8.3.

Quantitative and qualitative analyses of the corporate plans were undertaken to assess the frequency with which the keywords were used, as in the previous two chapters. Again, attention focused on how far terms linked to consumerism were used in preference to non-consumerist terms.

As Table 8.4 shows, community is the most commonly used word overall (981 hits, in 7.5 per cent of text units) and by every individual council. The emphasis on community clearly fits with patterns in the

Table 8.4 Service conditional and non-service conditional keywords, by service area, in the corporate plans

Council	Text units	Community (%)	Taxpayer (%)	Citizen (%)	Client (%)	Consumer (%)	Customer (%)	Patient (%)	Pupil (%)	Parent (%)	TOTAL (%)
1. Borough, EEM, Con	399	55 (13.8%)	3 (0.8%)	1 (0.3%)	0 (0.0%)	0 (0.0%)	8 (2.0%)	0 (0.0%)	0 (0.0%)	2 (0.5%)	69 (17.3%)
2. Borough, NW, Con	493	26 (5.3%)	0 (0.0%)	11 (2.2%)	0 (0.0%)	1 (0.2%)	12 (2.4%)	0 (0.0%)	6 (1.2%)	0 (0.0%)	56 (11.4%)
3. Borough, SE, Con	384	55 (14.3%)	0 (0.0%)	3 (0.8%)	0 (0.0%)	0 (0.0%)	4 (1.0%)	0 (0.0%)	0 (0.0%)	0 (0.0%)	62 (16.1%)
4. District, WM, Lab	117	30 (25.6%)	0 (0.0%)	0 (0.0%)	0 (0.0%)	0 (0.0%)	0 (0.0%)	0 (0.0%)	0 (0.0%)	0 (0.0%)	30 (25.6%)
5. District, SW, Con	1,075	91 (8.5%)	0 (0.0%)	7 (0.7%)	2 (0.2%)	0 (0.0%)	41 (3.8%)	1 (0.1%)	1 (0.1%)	1 (0.1%)	144 (13.4%)
6. District, NW, LD	534	47 (8.8%)	0 (0.0%)	1 (0.2%)	2 (0.4%)	1 (0.2%)	6 (1.1%)	0 (0.0%)	0 (0.0%)	0 (0.0%)	57 (10.7%)
7. District, SW, NOC	1,246	23 (1.8%)	0 (0.0%)	2 (0.2%)	0 (0.0%)	0 (0.0%)	18 (1.4%)	0 (0.0%)	0 (0.0%)	0 (0.0%)	43 (3.5%)
8. District, SE, NOC	747	74 (9.9%)	1 (0.1%)	4 (0.5%)	0 (0.0%)	0 (0.0%)	19 (2.5%)	0 (0.0%)	0 (0.0%)	0 (0.0%)	98 (13.1%)
9. County, EEM, Con	1,953	40 (2.0%)	0 (0.0%)	1 (0.1%)	1 (0.1%)	2 (0.1%)	17 (0.9%)	0 (0.0%)	6 (0.3%)	1 (0.1%)	68 (3.5%)
10. County, SE, Con	383	19 (5.0%)	0 (0.0%)	3 (0.8%)	4 (1.0%)	0 (0.0%)	6 (1.6%)	0 (0.0%)	0 (0.0%)	0 (0.0%)	32 (8.4%)

Table 8.4 Service conditional and non-service conditional keywords, by service area, in the corporate plans – *continued*

Council	Text units	Community (%)	Taxpayer (%)	Citizen (%)	Client (%)	Consumer (%)	Customer (%)	Patient (%)	Pupil (%)	Parent (%)	TOTAL (%)
11. County, WM, Lab	385	70 (18.2%)	1 (0.3%)	0 (0.0%)	2 (0.5%)	0 (0.0%)	24 (6.2%)	0 (0.0%)	0 (0.0%)	3 (0.8%)	100 (26.0%)
12. London, south, Con	1,850	102 (5.5%)	0 (0.0%)	8 (0.4%)	11 (0.6%)	5 (0.3%)	18 (1.0%)	3 (0.2%)	53 (2.9%)	33 (1.8%)	233 (12.6%)
13. London, north, Lab	443	31 (7.0%)	0 (0.0%)	1 (0.2%)	3 (0.7%)	0 (0.0%)	24 (5.4%)	0 (0.0%)	9 (2.0%)	1 (0.2%)	69 (15.6%)
14. Metropolitan, WM, Lab	647	70 (10.8%)	0 (0.0%)	12 (1.9%)	0 (0.0%)	0 (0.0%)	24 (3.7%)	0 (0.0%)	2 (0.3%)	4 (0.6%)	112 (17.3%)
15. Metropolitan, YHNE, NOC	515	45 (8.7%)	0 (0.0%)	2 (0.4%)	0 (0.0%)	0 (0.0%)	27 (5.2%)	0 (0.0%)	7 (1.4%)	7 (1.4%)	88 (17.1%)
16. Unitary, NW, Lab	1,491	133 (8.9%)	1 (0.1%)	20 (1.3%)	0 (0.0%)	3 (0.2%)	11 (0.7%)	0 (0.0%)	6 (0.4%)	4 (0.3%)	178 (11.9%)
17. Unitary, YHNE, NOC	275	44 (16.0%)	0 (0.0%)	9 (3.3%)	1 (0.4%)	0 (0.0%)	24 (8.7%)	0 (0.0%)	7 (2.5%)	3 (1.1%)	88 (32.0%)
18. Unitary, SW, Con	121	26 (21.5%)	0 (0.0%)	1 (0.8%)	1 (0.8%)	0 (0.0%)	25 (20.7%)	0 (0.0%)	3 (2.5%)	7 (5.8%)	63 (52.1%)
Total	13,058	981 (7.5%)	6 (0.0%)	86 (0.7%)	27 (0.2%)	12 (0.1%)	308 (2.4%)	4 (0.0%)	100 (0.8%)	66 (0.5%)	1,590 (12.2%)

Percentages show keyword usage as a proportion of total text units, i.e. sentences, for each document.

texts found in other chapters, as well as the local government white papers discussed above. Analysis of the context of the hits shows that the term community is most commonly used as an adjective, and in particular in the context of community strategy. All local authorities have a statutory requirement under the Local Government Act 2000 to produce a community strategy, setting out their approach to promoting or improving the economic, social and environmental well-being of their areas. Other common collocations were community safety and community plan. Here community is not used as a value or an ethical category, as it was by Blair, so much as a descriptor of services incorporating everyone in the area.

The second most frequently used term here, unlike in the national documents, is customer, occurring 308 times, in 2.4 per cent of text units. 'Customer service' is the most common collocation. Customer satisfaction, customer needs and improving customer access are also discussed frequently. One of the unitary councils uses the word customer in one in five of its sentences (20.7 per cent of text units). This is a council with a 'Customer First' commitment, a team of Customer Service Advisors and a Customer Service Centre. The consumer and the client get very little attention from the local authorities, with a sizeable proportion of hits in both categories coming from one London borough. In this borough, the term client is still a term applied to users of social care services, a usage that has largely been dropped elsewhere. Consumer was used in the context of consumer protection, a statutory duty for the counties, unitary authorities and London boroughs in the sample.

Taxpayer is used very little (6 hits across all the documents). It is interesting to note that whereas the local government white papers discuss the future of local authorities in terms of taxpayers, the councils themselves pay little attention to this role in their own strategic documentation. They are much more likely to refer to citizens (86 hits overall). The service-specific terms – patient, pupil and parent – are also used relatively little by these local authorities, compared with the national government texts. Since local authorities do not have direct responsibility for health provision, lack of attention to the patient is to be expected. However local authorities do retain direct responsibility for providing state education, so it is surprising that pupil and parent get relatively little attention when compared with Blair's speeches and the command papers.

The local authority findings show that, as in the Blair speeches and the central government policy documents, many reforms and initiatives are done in the name of the community. Services are delivered to the community and within the community, and councils signal their priorities through community strategies and plans. Whereas Chapters 7 and 8 revealed that individual service specific terms (patient, parent, pupil) outnumbered the other categories, this was not the case for the local corporate plans, where the service specific terms overall were the least commonly used. The corporate plans used the language of community and customer much more than any of the other keywords. The findings were tested to assess whether there was any difference between local authorities, based on council type, political control, region and CPA score; however there were no statistically significant differences in keyword usage on these criteria. The Labour-led councils for example were no more likely than other councils for example to use the term community or talk about services from the perspective of the customer.

The three narratives of consumerism

The balance between the narratives in the 18 councils can be explored in more detail by undertaking the same keyword searches for each of the narratives as in previous chapters. Table 8.5 shows the overall score for each of the narratives in the corporate plans. A longer version of the table is provided in Appendix 3.

It is evident from the table that the first narrative – that of standardising services and improving information and access – is dominant in the local government documents, occurring in 13.8 per cent of the total text units. All the councils had far more hits in this category than in any other. The coproduction narrative was second overall in terms of number of hits, accounting for 5.7 per cent of the total. It was the second most popular in all but two of the councils. The differentiation narrative accounted for 2.5 per cent of total hits, making it the least popular overall, and in 16 of the 18 individual councils. Again, there was no pattern by council type, political control or CPA score.

Box 8.1 gives examples of how each of the terms in the first narrative is used in the documents. It shows that local authorities are concerned to ensure that they are providing good quality and consistent services to local people. The emphasis is added by the author to highlight the use of the keywords.

The second narrative, shown in Box 8.2, emphasises the need to differentiate services according to the diverse preferences of local people. Although these terms were used much less than those in the

Table 8.5   The three narratives in the corporate plans (See Appendix 3 for a full version of this table)

Council	Text units	Standardisation (%)	Differentiation (%)	Coproduction (%)	Total (%)
1. Borough, EEM, Con	399	85 (21.3%)	21 (5.3%)	29 (7.3%)	135 (33.8%)
2. Borough, NW, Con	493	120 (24.3%)	14 (2.8%)	17 (3.4%)	151 (30.6%)
3. Borough, SE, Con	384	80 (20.8%)	12 (3.1%)	57 (14.8%)	149 (38.8%)
4. District, WM, Lab	117	22 (18.8%)	2 (1.7%)	11 (9.4%)	35 (29.9%)
5. District, SW, Con	1,075	114 (10.6%)	15 (1.4%)	48 (4.5%)	177 (16.5%)
6. District, NW, LD	534	57 (10.7%)	19 (3.6%)	17 (3.2%)	93 (17.4%)
7. District, SW, NOC	1,246	41 (3.3%)	4 (0.3%)	8 (0.6%)	53 (4.3%)
8. District, SE, NOC	747	122 (16.3%)	34 (4.6%)	50 (6.7%)	206 (27.6%)
9. County, EEM, Con	1,953	153 (7.8%)	6 (0.3%)	59 (3.0%)	218 (11.2%)
10. County, SE, Con	383	43 (11.2%)	11 (2.9%)	23 (6.0%)	77 (20.1%)
11. County, WM, Lab	385	43 (11.2%)	33 (8.6%)	32 (8.3%)	108 (28.1%)
12. London, south, Con	1,850	407 (22.0%)	56 (3.0%)	173 (9.4%)	636 (34.4%)
13. London, north, Lab	443	83 (18.7%)	8 (1.8%)	20 (4.5%)	111 (25.1%)
14. Metropolitan, WM, Lab	647	102 (15.8%)	24 (3.7%)	83 (12.8%)	209 (32.3%)
15. Metropolitan, YHNE, NOC	515	76 (14.8%)	21 (4.1%)	24 (4.7%)	121 (23.5%)
16. Unitary, NW, Lab	1,491	163 (10.9%)	23 (1.5%)	51 (3.4%)	237 (15.9%)
17. Unitary, YHNE, NOC	275	54 (19.6%)	14 (5.1%)	23 (8.4%)	91 (33.1%)
18. Unitary, SW, Con	121	40 (33.1%)	11 (9.1%)	24 (19.8%)	75 (62.0%)
Total	**13,058**	**1,805 (13.8%)**	**328 (2.5%)**	**749 (5.7%)**	**2,882 (22.1%)**

Percentages show keyword usage as a proportion of total text units, i.e. sentences, for each document.

Box 8.1   Narratives of standardisation

'We believe that you have the <u>right</u> to influence and control your own lives...' (Unitary Council, NW, Lab)

'...improving the <u>accessibility</u> and service to our customers' (District Council, WM, Lab)

'...improving provision of <u>information</u> to customers and local people' (Borough Council, NW, Con)

'...to achieve greater consistency, ensuring <u>standards</u> overall match the best' (County Council, SE, Con)

'Actions to reach the <u>target</u> included a programme of radio broadcasts reminding the public to secure their homes and a project to attack distraction burglary' (County Council, EEM, Con)

'What customers can expect:

– <u>convenience</u> – easy to contact us at a time that suits' (Unitary Council, SW, Con)

---

first narrative, they highlight the extent to which councils do recognise the need to bring greater choice and responsiveness into service delivery. As before the emphasis is added by the author.

Councils were classified as utilising the third narrative where they used the keywords to indicate local people being actively involved in service production. Examples of this narrative are shown in Box 8.3.

As with the Blair speeches and the policy documents, the narratives overlap, with some sentences including keywords from two or three narratives. For example one Metropolitan council utilised all three in a single sentence when listing its priorities for service delivery: 'To provide <u>information</u> to enable customers to make service <u>choices</u> and to <u>engage</u> with service users during period of service redesign' (Metropolitan Council, WM, Lab). That the narratives can be overlapping rather than contradictory fits the discussion in Chapter 3, which highlighted scope for the narratives to be layered rather than conflicting.

Box 8.2   Narratives of differentiation

'Increasing the take up of direct payments to allow service users greater <u>choice</u> in employing their own carers' (London Borough, Lab).

'...provide seamless services that can respond to customers as unique <u>individuals</u>' (District Council, SW, NOC).

'Ensuring that 100% of children have care pathways in place and a nominated <u>personal</u> adviser' (London Borough, Con).

'Act promptly and <u>responsively</u> to peoples needs' (Borough Council, NW, LD).

'Identifying and addressing the needs of our <u>diverse</u> communities and customers through "Customer First" will impact significantly on the organization in this period' (County Council, WM, Lab).

'But the landscape is changing and we have to adapt...<u>tailoring</u> change to meet the needs of the [local] communities we serve' (District Council, SW, Con).

In these documents, as at the national level, rights were often twinned with responsibilities – although as elsewhere there are more responsibilities than rights (138 hits for responsibility compared to 17 mentions of rights). Overall, there was less discussion in the local government documents of the coercive aspects of coproduction. There was little talk of contracts or sanctions for those who did not fulfill their responsibilities. Only in the London boroughs was reference made to 'acceptable behaviour contracts'.

The standardisation narrative is more dominant within local government than it is within the national texts, scoring twice as many hits as any of the other narratives. This finding suggests that whilst Blair is increasingly talking of the need to get away from a uniform, one-size-fits-all welfare state, many local authorities are still striving to get there. There appears to be little sense among the councils that their services are monolithic or have gone too far down the path of treating all

---

Box 8.3   Narratives of coproduction

'Core values: Being responsive to changing aspirations, priorities and <u>opportunities</u>' (Unitary, YHNE, NOC).

'We <u>engage</u> older people as all service users are reviewed on a regular basis when in receipt of services and service users views are collated through the comments and complaints procedures' (Metropolitan Council, WM, Lab).

'We will create a sense of belonging for all communities and encourage active <u>involvement</u> in community life' (Metropolitan Council, YHNE, NOC).

'<u>Empower</u> local people to have a greater voice and influence over decision making and delivery of services' (Borough Council, EEM, Con).

'Encourage communities to identify their needs, issues and sustainable solutions, and to <u>participate</u> in civic life' (District Council, SE, Con).

'Promote a greater sense of belonging, of pride in the borough and of the rights and <u>responsibilities</u> of citizenship' (Unitary Council, NW, Lab).

---

people alike. Opportunity is the most important of the coproduction keywords, as it was in Blair's speeches, although the term engagement is used more than responsibility, and the other coproduction keywords such as involve and participate are more heavily utilised here than at the centre. This finding fits the sense that local government is closer to the people than central government and provides more scope for direct involvement and participation in services. Coercive aspects of coproduction, linked to enforcing people to take on responsibilities, are underplayed in the local documents.

The customer in local government

The keyword searches highlighted the importance of the term customer, as the second most commonly used term in local government after community, playing a much stronger role than in Blair's speeches or the command papers. Qualitative interviews with officers and councillors in eight of the 18 local authorities, undertaken by the author during 2002 and 2003, shed light on how the term customer was used in local government. By focusing on eight authorities it was possible to undertake multiple interviewing across the case studies whilst avoiding potential distortions from one or two cases. The eight were selected to give a range of regions and council types. Twenty officers and eight councillors were interviewed, across the sample. To access personnel within the local authorities, websites were used to identify people with outward-facing policy responsibilities (service delivery, consultation and communication). Details of the interview design are given in Appendix 2.

In the first part of the interview respondents were asked general questions about their job to assess how far they spontaneously talked about local people as customers. In the 28 interviews, eight referred to people as customers of the council before the interviewer used the term: two councillors and six officers. Other respondents used more general terms like residents and the public. Among officers, those interviewees with a service delivery remit were the most likely to use the language of customer spontaneously.

When respondents were asked by the interviewer whether they felt it was helpful to see local people as customers, 19 of the 28 said that they did see the language as helpful. Officers were particularly in favour of customer language. 16 of the 19 officers expressed support for using the term customer, believing that referring to people as customers helped to instil a certain 'mindset' or 'culture'. One emphasised the importance of the language for internal change: 'I think that the reason we started to call them customers was to improve, it was to change our internal culture' (Head of Customer Services, London Borough, N).

None of the officers rejected the customer language. The three officers (all from different councils) who did not endorse use of the term customer felt that language wasn't significant, and that alternative terms were just as appropriate. As one put it, '[P]eople call them customers, clients whatever, service user. It depends, what's in a word? They're people who need or require a service from the council' (Head of Corporate Policy, Borough Council, EEM).

The councillors interviewed were more sceptical about the word customer, with five of the nine expressing reservations about customer terminology. Councillors tended to see customer language as an erosion of the role of citizen and the democratic linkages between themselves and local people. One said: 'No, they're citizens. We work for them, they elect us, they put us there, they can chuck us out' (Councillor, London Borough, N). Another said, 'They're more important than customers – we're their servants' (Councillor, Borough Council, NW).

To explore how they interpreted and applied the term customer, interviewees were asked 'What do you think it means to treat local people as customers?' Five conceptions of customer care emerged from the responses: personalising services around the user; giving users a choice of services; users paying for services; treating users with courtesy and respect; and improving user access to services. The most common response, favoured by 11 of the 28 local government respondents (ten officers and one councillor), was that to treat people as customers was to personalise local services and information around the needs of the individual user. As one put it, 'I think what we'd be trying to say is to think of the individual and each one as being individual rather than thinking of 800,000 people at a time' (Director of Policy, County Council, WM). Another said, 'We would as near as we could provide a tailored service' (Head of Customer Services, London Borough, N). According to a third, 'the important thing about customers and customer terminology is that hopefully it creates a different mindset among the people providing the service so that hopefully you are thinking about what people want rather than just what is most convenient for us to do' (Head of Best Value Review Team, District Council, SE). Emphasis was placed on being responsive to needs as defined by the customer, consistent with the differentiation narrative, rather than imposing assumptions about needs onto the user.

A second group of respondents (five of the 28) saw being a customer in terms of having choice. This response was particularly favoured by councillors, who made up four of the five who used this definition. According to one councillor, 'I was going to call them customers, which isn't bad, because in a sense it's different in the 21st century because people can tend to shop around for some of the things they want to do and so we've got to be slicker and more on the ball about things' (Councillor, Unitary Authority, NW). As one officer put it: 'Yes, there is a real move to looking at anyone who receives our services as customers, and there's obviously a lot more being done to actually enable them to choose what kind of services they want rather than the old idea of the local authority just systematically providing services' (Head of Communications, Metropolitan Council, YHNE). For these respondents, responsiveness to customers went beyond personalising services around people's needs to giving users themselves the choice of service, again consistent with the differentiation narrative.

The customer as payee response was given by three officers and two councillors, and drew on the assumption that a customer is one who provides financial payment for a service – part of the definition of customer given in Chapter 3. For these respondents the language of customer implied that public service users were paying taxes to fund services and so should receive good quality treatment. As one put it, 'Yes, they are our customers; they pay for the service. They are all taxpayers, and we're the service providers' (Head of Communications, Rural Borough Council, NW). Another described the language of customer as underlining the duty owed by the council to its taxpayers (Councillor, Rural Borough Council, E).

A fourth variant of customer responsiveness, invoked by four of the 28 respondents (three officers and one councillor), was that being a customer implied courtesy and respect. As one respondent said when asked what it meant to treat people as customers, 'We will be polite at all times; we will ensure that everyone is treated fairly and with respect' (Head of Customer Services, London Borough). One respondent linked this notion of customer to her council's customer charter. As she explained, 'There is a customer charter which is a set of ten promises, but they are more about style and respect than they are about a measurable service standard' (Head of Customer Services, London Borough). One officer talked of the council's 'Customer First Promise', which set out what customers could expect from the council, such as a timely and respectful service (Head of Communications, Metropolitan Council, YHNE). For these respondents treating people as customers was about the quality of personal interaction between service user and provider rather than broader aspects of service provision. This definition fits most closely with the standardisation narrative of consumerism.

Making services and council staff more accessible to the public was what a fifth group of interviewees (all officers) understood by the term customer (3/28). As one officer put it, 'If it's a direct service relationship with us in terms of trying to access something about the planning service then the term customer is appropriate' (Chief Executive, Unitary Authority, NW). Another said, 'We're looking at treating people more like customers rather than saying "we're open 9 till 5 Monday to Friday – like it or lump it"' (Head of Communications, Urban Borough Council, SW). Here the emphasis was not on the type of service provided but on the ease with which users could get access to services and information, part of a standardisation narrative. Respondents highlighted innovations that had improved accessibility such as 'one stop shops', email and websites.

Endorsement of one of the five conceptions of the customer did not follow local authority demarcations: it was not possible to trace a common approach to customer care within individual local authorities. Respondents appeared to be applying their own understandings of customer care rather than offering a corporate response. This inconsistency suggests that whilst local authorities are using the language of customer in their documents, they have work to do internally to develop coherent approaches to the user as customer.

When asked directly whether there was a council policy on calling people customers, ten of the respondents said that they were encouraged at a policy level by the council to use it. One councillor remarked, 'I prefer the word citizen really, but customer is always the word we use' (Councillor, Metropolitan Council, YHNE). One officer said the language was widespread although not mandated by policy: 'I don't think there's a policy. But you will find that that's what people call them' (Head of Policy, County Council, WM). There was little coherence even within councils about whether the language of customer had official endorsement. The head of customer services at the north London Borough believed that the language had been adopted at a corporate level – as her job title would suggest – whereas the officer with primary responsibility for consultation did not. Another officer highlighted differences within her own council:

> People with the tourist side of the business, they're certainly happy with customers. People in the leisure services line, they'll all have customers. People in the filling pot-holes in the road sector just laugh at the concept of having customers so there's still strands of old local government that will take a long, long while before they change.
>
> Head of Communications, Borough Council, EEM

In some cases a customer focus had prompted internal change within the council. Three of the councils had set up Customer Service divisions in their authorities, and all the councils had introduced 'one stop shops' to enhance access. A new set of staff were being appointed, trained in customer care rather than a specific service area, whose role was to respond as effectively as possible to a whole range of customer issues:

> We'll have people drawn in from the various departments with a generic training and the appropriate high-tech kit so that they have

the information in front of them, to be able to give people the information with the first person they contact.

Chief Executive, Unitary Council, NW

All of the councils had introduced or were introducing Customer Relationship Management (CRM) software. CRM packages, adapted from the private sector, compile data about service users' dealings with the authority onto a database, which staff across different departments can access to allow a quicker and personalised response.

Customer language was used by these councils in their recruitment strategies. As one respondent indicated, 'I was recruited just over a year ago to bring some of the customer care concepts and service performance with me from another authority' (Director of Corporate Policy, District Council, SW). Another interviewee reported that her authority used the term customer in job advertisements, which brought new types of employee to the council:

> It certainly has attracted people from outside the public sector to the jobs here, and so we have people with a different approach who see our customers as the centre of their world rather than an intrusion into their world.
>
> Head of Communications, County Council, WM

Within central government there was an assumption that people's private sector experiences were driving up their public sector expectations. Interviewees at local level were asked how far they felt that this was the case. Twenty of the 28 respondents felt that private sector experiences did shape people's public sector expectations, and that better standards of private sector customer care had an impact. As one councillor put it:

> I think that people expect more 24/7 working then they ever used to. You used to accept that a shop was closed on a Sunday, and now that's changed. So people think that services should be seven days a week.
>
> Councillor, District Council, SW

Other respondents thought that local people's private sector experiences did not shape their expectations of the council, although there was a difference of opinion on whether this attitude was a sign of high or low expectations. One respondent said, 'I certainly hope not. A lot of my experiences with the private sector are awful' (Head of Policy, County Council, WM). Another felt that the council could not match services provided in the private sector, and that local people recognised that, adjusting their expectations accordingly (Head of Customer Services, London Borough, N).

Interviewees indicated that it was relatively recently that the language of customer had become popular – originating in the last two or three years. When asked whether the language had originated locally or had come from central government, most respondents were unsure. There was a presumption that local initiatives had combined with national priorities to give prominence to the 'customer focused' approach. Whereas some respondents expressed resentment towards elements of Best Value and Comprehensive Performance Assessment, none of the respondents reported that they had been forced by central government to orient themselves towards their 'customers'. Rather there was a willingness amongst most of the respondents to take ownership of the customer language, and acknowledge its importance to the improvement of services.

Participants were asked whether they felt there were any problems with calling people customers. All the respondents could identify limitations with using the language of customer in relation to service users. Responses fitted into one of two categories. For some respondents (12 of 28) the problem with customer language was that the council could never provide services in the range and quantity that a customer would want. In the case of social services support, for example, one respondent noted that he might have to tell an applicant for a carer:

> What we're saying is there are actually other people who have greater difficulty and at this moment in time in terms of resource allocation what we're saying is you have to wait until you become worse.
>
> Head of Policy, County Council, WM

For a larger category of respondent (16 of the 28) the customer language was limited because it did not capture the democratic role of the citizen. Councillors in particular (7 of the 9) were keen to emphasis the citizen dimension to being a local service user. One councillor raised concerns about the extent to which the language of customer 'privatised' the relationship with local people (Councillor, County Council, WM). Officers appeared to see the role of customer as compatible with that of citizen, the former reflecting the role of service user, the latter indicating the democratic role of voter. This split between politicians and bureaucrats is perhaps unsurprising, since bureaucrats engage with the citizen primarily as service user, whereas councillors are more oriented towards the citizen as voter.

The customer in central government

The analysis of corporate plans showed that the language of customer was more heavily utilised in the local government publications than in the central government speeches and policy documents. However, as Chapter 7 discussed, the term customer did also feature in the command papers, and was becoming widely used in some of the later documents. In a small number of interviews with civil servants in the Departments of Health and Education, it was possible to identify how far common patterns existed with the local government interviewees in terms of definitions and ambiguities surrounding the role of customer. Four interviews were conducted with middle-ranking civil servants from the Department of Health and the Department for Education and Skills. These departments were selected as having responsibility for key areas of public service delivery. Departmental websites were used to identify contacts within the departments.

Each of the four was keen to talk about the customer orientation of their service. A consultation manager at the Department of Health (DoH) stated, 'It's a bit of language that is extensively used. I was on an interview panel yesterday and one of the questions was what do you understand in the context of this job by the term customer care' (Interview, 3 April 2003). A civil servant in the Connexions Unit within the Department for Education and Skills (DfES) affirmed the wide usage of the term customer: 'One of the DfES behaviours is about involving customers, and it's about saying that everyone who works for the DfES should be driven by these behaviours' (Interview, 14 February 2003). A senior member of the Learning Disability Unit in the Department of Health said:

> In some ways I'm more comfortable with the idea of talking about customers than with talking about service users. It's much more helpful to think along those lines, to think what kind of service do you try to give to customers.
>
> Interview, 13 February 2003

A member of the Youth Participation Team in the DfES said, 'I think we see our work as being driven by our customers who are young people' (Interview, 14 February 2003).

As in the local government interviews, the civil servants endorsed the use of customer language to underpin changes to the internal culture. One said:

> The reality is that for some services that people need there is only going to be one provider. The best that the customer model can do is to keep everyone on their toes and make them think about the quality of service that they are providing and how far it's targeted at the needs of the individual.
>
> Learning Disability Unit, DoH, Interview, 13 February 2003

Another commented, 'In terms of an attitude of mind and the way that you put your services together, if you think of people as customers that does help' (Connexions Unit, DfES, Interview, 14 February 2003).

The same patterns were evident here as in the local authorities, in that the respondents did not believe that their departments had developed coherent models of customer care despite talk of establishing common 'behaviours'. As one put it:

> I think we're probably a bit confused really and not consistent about how we do approach people. So while I personally think it's helpful to think of people as customers, I couldn't say that if you look at the policy and how it's implemented that you would see that consistently throughout it.
>
> Learning Disability Unit, DoH, Interview, 13 February 2003

The respondents seemed to feel that the term customer was increasingly being used in their departments – in job interviews, in 'behaviours' – but without a clear departmental line on what it meant to be a customer.

Personalisation and choice were central to the definitions of customer put forward by the civil service interviewees, as they were for a majority of local government respondents. Treating someone as a customer involved developing services that were tailored to the needs of the user, defined as the direct users of the service – patients, the disabled, young people – rather than wider beneficiaries, such as parents or carers. The language of customer was seen as more 'person-centred' and 'active' whereas the 'lazy jargon' of service user implied 'passive' receipt of services (Learning Disability Unit, DoH, Interview, 13 February 2003). As this respondent said:

> [O]ne big change I'd really like to see that would really start to get us into the customer focus and change the relationship to one of

customer-provider would be to see a big shift to people receiving payments and starting to buy services in the patterns and shapes they wanted.

> Learning Disability Unit, DoH, Interview, 13 February 2003

Choice was seen as central: 'as customers they don't have to use the service if they don't want to, so you have to make sure your service is meeting their needs because they may go and choose something else' (Consultation Coordinator, DoH, Interview, 3 April 2003). One mechanism for achieving this expansion was the use of direct payments, enabling those with social care needs to 'buy in' their own care rather than accept local authority provision. However, the take up of direct payments had at this time been 'very very small', according to the interviewee in the Disabilities branch of the Department of Health. He explains their lack of popularity:

> It makes it a much, much more uncertain world if the person in need of care has got money and can buy whatever they want to meet their needs... It's a step into the unknown, it's a lot of hassle, it means you have to deal with a lot of things regarding finances, possibly employing people on some basis, or contracting with people to give you services which is all handled by someone else at the moment.
>
> Learning Disability Unit, DoH, Interview, 13 February 2003

The trade off between risk and choice – a trade off rarely made explicit in the texts – comes out clearly here.

Analysing the interview findings in the context of the three public service narratives, definitions of being a customer at local and national level were primarily focused around the differentiation narrative, emphasising choice and personalisation. A minority prioritised the standardisation narrative – enhanced access, convenience and respect for users. It is clear from these interviews and from the text searches that the customer is not a coproducer: customers are not engaged or empowered, nor do they have responsibilities. This finding has implications for service delivery. If local and central government are increasingly framing the service user as a customer, they may find that they are creating a user with demands but no counterbalancing sense of responsibilities or active participation.

Conclusion

The data presented here, derived from content analysis of strategic documents from 18 local authorities, as well as interviews with councillors and officers in eight authorities, provides an insight into the way that policy actors within local government construct a solution set for public services. The analysis shows that councils use the term 'community' more than any of the other keywords in the documents. The second most commonly used keyword was customer. Local authorities appear to be developing services for the customer in the community. These patterns hold across the sample of local authorities, with no evidence of differentiation according to political control, region, council type or CPA score.

Interviews with officers and councillors showed that the language of customer was widely used, and there was no sense that the orientation towards treating people as customers was centrally imposed. Rather officers indicated that they saw it as part of their objective of providing a high quality and responsive service to local people. However, interviewees did acknowledge that the customer role did not encompass all linkages between the council and local people, a feeling held particularly strongly by councillors. Interviews with civil servants highlighted similar patterns, with a customer-model, based around personalisation and choice, being endorsed by respondents, and shaping internal practices such as recruitment. However, there was also an awareness of the risks created by new user choices.

The analysis of narratives showed that all the councils had a marked preference for the first narrative emphasising service standardisation, which accounted for almost two-thirds of the total narrative keywords in the documents. Second in popularity was the coproduction narrative, whereas the differentiation narrative was used relatively little. Standardisation was also the most popular narrative overall in Blair's speeches and the command papers, however there it was increasingly being challenged by the other two narratives by the 2005 period from which the local government corporate plan data is taken.

There are a number of possible interpretations of this finding and three are presented here. The first is derived from the observations of the time-lag between agenda-setting and policy change. Labour's first term agenda of targets and standards took several years to be embedded in a structure of audits and incentives, which do not yet show signs of being dismantled. The structural incentives to move towards differentiation and coproduction may therefore not yet in place to push councils in that direction. The transition from ideational to institutional change can be slow, particularly to filter down to the local level (Hay, 1999, pp. 44–5). According to this explanation, and based on changing trends in the local government white papers, it is to be expected that local authorities will inherit a policy agenda of differentiation and coproduction once it has time to be more fully embedded in national policy.

The second explanation is that New Labour at the national level has misrepresented the welfare state. In its emphasis on differentiation it assumes a uniformity which has never existed, and therefore it is not surprising that local authorities still aspire to offer a standard service. This explanation suggests that Labour's diagnosis of problems in the welfare state is misplaced, and that local authorities may not move onto the differentiation and coproduction agendas because they will struggle to reach a point where standardisation is the norm. Here we may see the national debate being ignored as local authorities focus on their own priorities.

A third explanation is that councils of all political hues are resisting a trend towards marketisation at the national level, for which the language of choice and differentiation is seen as a cover. As discussed in Chapter 5, there is no shortage of commentators interpreting Blair and New Labour's approach in these terms (Crouch, 2003; Leys, 2003; Lawson, 2005; Whitfield, 2006), and it may be that local authorities in this analysis are resisting the differentiation model because of political differences with the national government. The parallel here would be in the efforts of local authorities in the 1980s to develop the Public Service Orientation as an alternative to the nationally directed new public management-type reforms. In this scenario it would be expected that local authorities will continue to resist the introduction of choice and differentiation in local service delivery, perhaps in the hope that in a post-Blair era, a new national leader might set out a different agenda for public services.

Chapters 6, 7 and 8 have shown that the battleground of public service reform has largely been fought over the question of what it is that people want from public services and how those expectations are changing. As the interviews here confirmed, there is no consensus on public expectations. Some councillors saw user demands as driven by a 24/7 consumer culture, others felt that people moderated their demands because of constraints on the public services. The next chapter moves away from looking at the ways in which central and local government represent the preferences of users, to exploring the evidence on what it is that people themselves want from public services.

9
The Citizen Perspective

At the heart of the consumerist citizenship regime is preference accommodation: public services are remade around the subjective preferences of users, and other perspectives are downgraded or delegitimised. The previous chapters show dominant themes of preference accommodation in the way that policy actors in central and local government talk about public services. The authenticity of individual experiences of service use is given primacy, and public service reformers have focused on adapting services to better meet the subjective needs of their users. Although earlier reformers such as the Fabians were unashamed preference-shapers (Clarke *et al*, 1987), such approaches are now rejected as paternalistic, and reformers debate what the preferences of the public actually *are*, not what they should be. As Chapters 6 and 7 show, the New Labour approach to public service reform is premised on the assumption that the public demand personalised public services, of a standard they experience in the private sector, leaving a democratic government with no alternative but to provide this as far as possible. Opponents of consumerised public services have responded by marshalling data to show that the public do not want the kinds of personalised, choice-based forms of social production that New Labour is offering – or at least do not want them if something else is on offer. Thus public attitudes to the consumerisation of public services have become the central battleground for reformers.

This chapter will explore how existing data on public attitudes to public services have shaped the terms of the debate, and have been utilised in support of and against consumer-oriented reforms in public services. Some of the ambiguities in existing data are then probed using new data from ten focus groups with members of the public, to explore what can be learned about apparently ambiguous public attitudes.

New Labour and preference accommodation

The tendency of New Labour to be *preference-accommodating* rather than *preference-shaping* in its policy has been highlighted by Hay (1999, p. 135). Two particular themes are important. The first, is retrospective, what Hay calls the 'neo-Downsian' nature of New Labour's approach (1999, p. 135. See also Downs, 1985). Hay argues that whereas the New Right sought to remake public attitudes according to their diagnoses of Britain's ills, New Labour developed 'a tendency to "reify" the attitudinal preferences of the electorate,' as a precondition of electability (Hay, 1999, pp. 67, 68). In developing a retrospective account of social change, New Labour strategists have relied heavily on the sociological theory of the rise of a self-confident and aspirational consumer, whose demands from public services are shaped by private sector service provision. Building in part on analyses developed by new left thinkers of the 1970s and 1980s, derived most directly from the 'New Times' thesis, New Labour endorsed an account of social change that emphasised the rise of the consumer in a post-Fordist society (Hall and Jacques, 1989; Mulgan, 1991; Zuboff and Maxmin, 2003). The work of Anthony Giddens informed New Labour of the need to adapt to 'reflexive modernity' (Giddens, 1994). Thus the Blairite project is premised on the need for New Labour to come into line with the 'individualism, consumerism and aspirations' of the "new middle class"' (Gould, 1998, pp. 124, 6). This account became the basis for understanding what is possible and desirable for public services in the late twentieth and early twenty-first centuries.

The second, forward-looking, strand in New Labour's approach is its call for policy to be 'evidence-based'. Social scientific research becomes an important source for policy-making. In the case of public service reform, consultative and evaluative data on public attitudes is given particular weight, with attention placed on surveys, although qualitative mechanisms such as citizen's forums and panels are also widely used, particularly at local level (Needham, 2004; Moss and O'Loughlin, 2005, p. 176). Thus research techniques are utilised to gather data on public preferences. The privileged place of public consultation in New Labour policy-making is highlighted by the then Cabinet Office minister Ian McCartney's comment to the Public Administration Select Committee (PASC):

> The most telling way of putting a case in government now internally is not the big stick, 'I am from the Treasury' or 'I am from the Cabinet Office'. The big stick is the evidence that you bring with you of the constituents, whether it is pensioners or postmasters or

postmistresses... Increasingly that is why some of the larger departments are extending the whole concept of consultation right down.

PASC, 2000, §494

Within public services, government has encouraged departments to
experiment with a range of consultative mechanisms, from traditional
written consultations to more experimental techniques such as citizen's
juries and visioning exercises (Needham, 2004). In particular, the New
Labour governments have been keen to develop new measures of user satisfaction with public services. In the first term, resources focused on a
5000-strong People's Panel, designed to consult 'customers' on a range of
issues including their priorities for public services and levels of satisfaction with different public services (CMPS, 2001). In Labour's second term,
the People's Panel was wound up and the Office of Public Service Reform
(OPSR) was created to improve the collection of customer satisfaction
data, as minister Douglas Alexander explained:

The Office for Public Services Reform works with and encourages
Government Departments and public agencies to conduct and act
upon customer satisfaction surveys to ensure that the voice of the
customer is central to service delivery.

Alexander, 2002a, Col. 388W

The OPSR worked on bringing customer satisfaction data more fully
into target-setting, particularly the Public Service Agreements signed
at national level between the Treasury and service departments. It
also signalled its intention to develop an index of customer satisfaction, based on indices used in Canada and the United States. As
John Hutton, then Chancellor of the Duchy of Lancaster and Minister
for the Cabinet Office, explained in a speech to the Social Market
Foundation,

It is by embracing customer satisfaction as the key driver for public
services – finding out what people actually want from their services
and using that information to drive change programmes – that we
can help public services catch up with the best on offer in wider
society...[M]aking the goal of customer satisfaction fundamental to
the ethos of public services is essential if we are to succeed in
moving from the paternalistic statism of the past to the progressive,
individual empowerment of the future.

Hutton, 2005

There is no doubt here of the priority that ministerial discourses give to the 'customer' experience in public services and to developing comparative mechanisms to generate data. Individual departments focus on measuring, comparing and increasing the satisfaction of individual service users, conceived as customers, embedding preference-accommodation in public service reform.

The government's evidence-based approach to policy-making has been criticised by a range of actors, however, highlighting a tendency to set aside evidence where it makes uncomfortable reading (See for example Whitfield, 2006). Even where data is not deliberately ignored, it remains the case that data gathering and analysis is highly interpretive. The New Labour governments have taken one reading of the available data, and it is one that fits into a consumerist solution set by assuming that the public wants its experiences of private sector consumption to be replicated in the public sector. The contested nature of the data and New Labour's reading of it requires more detailed attention.

Exploring public attitudes to public service reform

A large number of agencies have commissioned polls and qualitative research to find out what it is that the public wants from public services, including government departments, trade unions, professional associations, think tanks and newspapers. As a result there is a large amount of public attitude data available. The research agency MORI alone has conducted hundreds of services on this theme since 1997 (See http://www.ipsos-mori.com/sri/index.shtml). Research into public attitudes to public services has tended to focus on, first, assessing existing levels of customer satisfaction and, second, understanding levels of public demand for various mechanisms to improve services, such as the use of private sector providers and the expansion of user choice.

Looking first at the issue of existing levels of customer satisfaction, it is important to be clear what is meant by the term satisfaction and what issues need to be faced when measuring it. A 2001 report by the Performance and Innovation Unit (PIU) in the Cabinet Office explored the various ways of understanding satisfaction. They reported that the most widely used approach is to see it as an equation: expectations minus perception of service received (Donovan *et al*, 2001, p. 12). Alternative approaches to satisfaction have attempted to develop more objective measures of the performance of the product or service's perceived characteristics, or to use an equity measure, where the customer perceives that the outcome of a purchase is proportional to what she and/or the seller are putting in (Donovan *et al*, 2001, p. 12). However, none of these alternative approaches are widely used. The standard measure of satisfaction is to compare the perception gap between the expected and actual service received.

To understand satisfaction therefore it is first necessary to measure expectations. The PIU report stated, 'Expectations are formed by many factors including previous experience, word of mouth, service reputation, the media, communications by the service provider and, crucially, the needs and characteristics of the service user' (Donovan *et al*, 2001, p. 5). The speeches and documents discussed in previous chapters give an account of public expectations as rising and insatiable. Public expectations are believed to have been pushed up by a combination of private sector experience and rising wealth. Research for the National Consumer Council found support for this, with 69 per cent of survey respondents agreeing with the statement: 'It's not that the public services have declined over recent years, but that people now demand and expect more of them' (NCC, 2003, p. 8).

There are rival interpretations of the data on public expectations. The first is to see public expectations as not exogenous to government behaviour but created by it. Blair hints at this when he says: 'I know, too, that the more we talk about public services, the more the public expect of them' (16 October 2001), although elsewhere he positions government as at the whim of a restless public. According to this explanation, government policy is less preference-accommodating than it originally appears and is actually engaged in a more subtle process of preference-shaping, offering reforms based on a consumer solution set that does not itself derive in the first instance from consumer preferences. Schumpeter's point about producers dictating to rather than being directed by consumer preferences is important here (Schumpeter, 1976, p. 257). Finlayson argues, for example, that rather than responding to rising citizen demands, New Labour has lowered public expectations of public services. As he puts it:

> [P]ublic services have been undermined politically and organisationally, with the expectations of the public systematically lowered. It thus contributes to a declining sympathy for politics, which it is in the interests of politicians to foster, because it enables them to shift blame for policy failures onto executive agencies, quangos, private contractors and so on.
>
> Finlayson, 2003a, p. 23

Thus he sees it as part of a deliberate policy of depoliticisation in which government is able to avoid the blame when problems arise. The extent to which New Labour uses a discourse of preference accommo-dation whilst also directing public attitudes towards a particular model of public service reform is discussed more in the final chapter.

A recurring theme in New Labour accounts of public attitudes to public services is that the driver for rising public expectations is the experience of improved customer service in the private sector. The assumption that the public wants its experience of public service use to match private services as closely as possible accounts for the importing of language such as customer into public service delivery. A distinctive feature of this perspective is the high regard in which it holds private sector customer care. As Blair put it in a speech in 2001: 'Private com-panies can in many cases be more responsive [than the public sector] to the immediate needs of demanding consumers' (16 July 2001). Again in 2004, 'In public services, patients and parents are looking for the same responsiveness for their particular needs as they experience as a matter of course in the other parts of their lives' (3 December 2004). In a speech in 2005, the then Cabinet Minister John Hutton acknowl-edged that not all experiences with the private sector may be good, but argued that it still had a better record than the public sector in leaving the public feeling empowered:

> Of course, the private sector gets it wrong – frequently – and can offer poor value for money and quality of service. The public's frus-tration with private sector call-centres is just one example of that. But the key difference is that consumers in the wider economy feel empowered when they can exit from poor service providers – when they have choices.
>
> Hutton, 2005

The government's account of public service use is therefore premised on a desire to offer users the same sorts of exit powers in the public as the private sector in order to increase empowerment.

Whether or not people want public services to be more like private services is ambiguous, however. On the question of whether private services are better than public services, research for the Office for Public Management found that 41 per cent of survey respondents felt that services provided by private businesses were about the same as public services. Only 28 per cent said that private businesses were better, whereas 23 per cent said they were worse (Steele and Corrigan,

2001). British Social Attitudes data asked people whether government or business were best at providing a good quality service, and found that 51 per cent said a private company compared with 41 per cent for government. However respondents stated by a margin of 73 per cent to 21 per cent that government was better at ensuring that services go to people who need them most (Appleby and Alvarez-Rosete, 2005).

Rather than reading across from private sector experiences to public sector expectations, there is evidence that people value the distinctive features of public service use. Research for the National Consumer Council found that people valued what they saw as distinctively public services:

> We also ask people what marks out the best public services – what is that factor that differentiates them? People speak about empathy, compassion, warmth, the human touch, respect – taking the time to listen and respond to individual circumstances, and focusing help on people who need it most. So people don't want to throw away what public services can offer. In fact, they want whatever is provided, by whoever provides it, to be more like public services rather than less.
>
> NCC, 2005, p. 4

Research for the Open University found that users and staff in case study public services repeatedly used the phrase 'not like shopping' to describe public service use (Clarke, 2005).

It does appear that there is something in the concept of being a customer that people do like. A MORI poll in 2004 reported that 80 per cent of respondents agreed with the statement, 'Britain's public services need to start treating users and the public as customers in the same way that the private sector does'. However the questionnaire did not elaborate on what it meant to be treated as a customer, so it is unclear how respondents were interpreting the term (MORI, 2004). The discussion in Chapter 8 highlighted the ambiguity in the term customer, which can mean a variety of different things when applied to public services.

It is also possible to probe the assumption that users of public services are generally dissatisfied and disappointed. There are some indications that people are feeling more satisfied, although again much depends on the definition of key terms. Research on public services for the National Consumer Council found that 61 per cent of respondents agreed with the statement: 'Frontline staff have become more customer-focused over the last five years' (NCC, 2003, p. 18). In contrast, research for MORI's delivery index shows since the beginning of 2002, the percentage of people who disagree that Labour's reforms will improve public services has exceeded the proportion who agree (MORI, 2006). Julian Le Grand, Blair's advisor on public services in his second term, is critical of the claim that people are happy with the treatment they get in the public sector:

> It is worth noting that the view that the public services are staffed by helpful, welcoming knights is not one necessarily held by the public. When asked by MORI what words they think applied to public services in Britain today, the highest ranked adjectives were (in descending order) bureaucratic, infuriating, faceless, hardworking (a positive note there), unresponsive and unaccountable. The lowest ranked were friendly, efficient, honest and open.
>
> Le Grand, 2006a

Part of the ambiguity in the data may stem from not comparing like with like, for example by comparing generalised survey findings with surveys of service users. The widely observed 'I've been lucky' factor, suggests that actual service experiences are better than the general public perceptions of the service (Mattinson and Trayner, 2004). As the PIU report into user satisfaction puts it:

> Users of a service are almost always more satisfied than those who do not have first hand experience (for example, 80 per cent of users of local secondary schools are very or fairly satisfied but only 30 per cent of the general population are very or fairly satisfied with secondary schools.) Surveys of the general population which ask questions about satisfaction with, say, the NHS, are not useful guides to customer satisfaction and should be treated with caution.
>
> Donovan *et al*, 2001, p. 5

This 'I've been lucky' factor is often seen as a symptom of an age in which government is held in low esteem and levels of public trust are low, such that people assume services are worse than they actually are (Mattinson and Trayner, 2004). However it is not new. Poister and Henry cite a conclusion from Katz *et al*, in 1975 that 'client evaluations of specific services they receive tend to be more positive than ratings of these same services by the general public' (Poister and Henry, 1994, p. 156). Their own survey research comparing user attitudes to public and private services reached the same conclusion. The views of non-users about services are of course legitimate and politically important, but they are not necessarily an adequate measure of service quality.

A further contested area of public attitudes relates to the mechanisms of public service reform discussed in earlier chapters. It is clear that the government sees service improvement as fundamentally linked to a diversification of providers, and an expansion in user choice. On the question of how people feel about private companies providing public services, Unison research found that of a range of techniques to improve public services, allowing 'businesses and voluntary groups to run more services' was ranked lowest (Unison, 2006). A MORI poll for the GMB in July 2001 found that only 11 per cent believed bringing in private sector companies would be most likely to improve public services (MORI, 2001). Research for the Guardian by ICM in March 2003 found that 62 per cent of respondents agreed that the government was placing too much emphasis on bringing in private companies to deliver services' (Travis, 2003).

This ICM poll, however, highlights the ambiguity of public attitudes, since in the same survey, 80 per cent were in favour of allowing private companies to run public services if they could guarantee service improvement (Travis, 2003). It seems likely that the keyword here is 'guarantee'. Since much of the contested battleground in public services is whether or not private providers do improve services, it seems misleading to take this uncertainty out of the question. More tangible support for private involvement comes from a MORI poll in the Black Country, which found that 71 per cent of respondents reported being happy about the NHS paying for patients to have their operations in private hospitals, compared with 11 per cent who said they were unhappy (Le Grand, 2006a).

What these findings appear to show is that the public do not have a principled objection to private sector involvement in public services, and are willing to accept involvement in specific cases, but that they do not see private involvement as the key mechanism to improve services. The anxiety that the public sometimes feel about private involvement in public services has been explored by Clarke. He argues that we have seen continuity rather than change in public attitudes over the period of new right and New Labour dominance, with continued support for more resources in public services and resistance to privatisation:

> A central issue in this political terrain is the persistence of popular attachments to conceptions of the public and the social. These

attachments have been regenerated around a number of focal points: for example, the failures of privatisations (especially the railways), a concern for public transport, a refusal to see the National Health Service privatised (resulting in a variety of smaller corrosive reforms), and concern about market failures and public health (especially in food supply).

Clarke, 2004, pp. 41–2

Aside from private involvement in public services, the most high profile battle over public preferences is the extent to which service users want a choice of service provider. Although, as Lent and Arend highlight (2004), there are various sorts of ways in which choice can and has been extended in public services, attention has focused on provider choice, and it is here that most opinion data is available. Chapters 6 and 7 highlighted the importance of choice to public service reform, particularly in Labour's second and third terms. Setting out the anti-choice argument, Stuart Hall claims:

> Actually, there is no identified groundswell of public demand for more 'choice' in the abstract. Undoubtedly, many people would quite like to be able to choose a good secondary school for their children or an efficient hospital to be ill in, wherever they live and however rich or poor they may be – a quite different matter. However, repeating that 'choice' is a wide-spread demand is a way of making what is affirmed as a fact but is really only a prophecy, self-fulfilling.

Hall, 2003, p. 16

The debate over choice in public services has become emblematic of wider tensions over the direction of public service reform, given the close connection between choice and markets. Again, straightforward opinion poll data on choice is problematic because there are different types of choices in public services, and because choice needs to be compared with levels of support for other allocation mechanisms. Drawing on survey and focus group data, Clarke argues that choice in the abstract is popular with people – even if there is not a groundswell of demand for it, as Hall points out – but that people are much more wary of it in specific services: 'This ambivalence seems to centre on a positive disposition towards choice as an abstract principle and more negative responses or anxieties when choice becomes specified in more particular or precise ways' (2005, p. 55). Opinion polls have generally shown support for choice in public services if the public is asked 'Would you like to have a choice of school/hospital?' A YouGov poll for The Economist found that 66 per cent wanted hospital choice, and 76 per cent of parents with children at state school wanted school choice (*Economist*, 7 April 2004). An Audit Commission study looked at how survey respondents rated different kinds of choices and found that choice for special needs children was rated most highly (43 per cent). However, the report then noted: *no need for choice*

> The focus groups were able to suggest a small number of ideas for new areas of choice, but the overall impression was that they simply wanted better quality local services in the areas that were important to them.
>
> Audit Commission, 2004

MORI polling for the BBC similarly showed that public opinion was divided, with slightly more respondents in favour of a quality local service than of expanded choice (53 per cent to 43 per cent) (MORI, 2004). However, Le Grand argues that the trade off between choice and better local services is a false one, because choice is the best, and perhaps only, mechanism available to deliver better local services (2006a). Similarly in a speech to the NHS Confederation, Patricia Hewitt, indicated that the key aim of choice was to drive up standards in clinical care and provide incentives to providers to be more effective and efficient, rather than to empower users (Hewitt, 2005). Here then users become as much a means to an end as an end in themselves, in the same way that they were under Thatcherite health policies (Klein, 2001, p. 116).

On a different tack, Le Grand has argued that choice is a mechanism to rebalance public services away from the sharp-elbowed middle classes, and towards lower socio-economic groups who in surveys such as British Social Attitudes (BSA) have been particularly supportive of choice (Le Grand, 2006a). Supporting this finding, in 2004 the Audit Commission reported that those on lowest income (DEs) were most in favour of choice, leading the Commission to hypothesise that high income users were less concerned about choice in public services because they had more choices available to them in the market (Audit Commission, 2004).

Responding to Le Grand, John Appleby, author of the BSA report on attitudes to choice in the NHS, argued that although those with lower educational qualifications were more likely to be in favour of choice than those with higher qualifications, the differences by socio-economic group were not large. He goes on, 'Over and above surveys like the BSA, what we need is evidence of how the government's particular policy on choice (and competition) affects the key founding objective of the National Health Service: equality of access for those in need' (Appleby, 2006). Similarly, Frances Blunden of Which? (formerly the Consumers' Association), questioned Le Grand's presentation of the data, and highlighted the findings of a 2005 Which? survey: '[T]he public's appetite for choice is inconsistent and variable, often depending on their personal circumstances, state of health and the types of choice they are offered. For some choice is an unwanted and overwhelming burden at times of stress and vulnerability' (Blunden, 2006). In an exchange of letters in the *Financial* Times, Le Grand wrote back saying 'It is a little surprising to find a senior figure in Which? providing ammunition for the critics of empowering the less well-off in the NHS, even if that ammunition is faulty. Perhaps Which? needs to reflect precisely on which groups in society most need its help and advice' (Le Grand, 2006b). Such clashes are characteristic of the frustration of both sides in the choice debate.

Cabinet Office minister John Hutton justifies the government's choice-oriented reforms by pointing out that there has been high take-up of choice in services where it has been offered:

> When choice was offered to cataract patients waiting for operations in London, over 70 per cent exercised it. 60 per cent of patients waiting for heart operations did the same. Waiting lists in London fell by a substantial 19.4 per cent compared to a fall of 7.6 per cent in the rest of England – showing that our reforms can tackle the imbalance that has traditionally seen the wealthy get more from the NHS than the poor.   *Tackle Inequality*
>
> Hutton, 2005

As with the involvement of private companies in public services, apparently ambivalent public attitudes to choice in public services can be explained by different survey methodologies: respondents are likely to respond differently to choice in the abstract than the specific, and to questions that just ask about choice, compared to those that ask for choice to be ranked against other improvement mechanisms. NCC research into patient choice, for example, found that respondents (particularly less affluent ones) prioritised speed, efficiency and equity over choice. Part of the difficulty of understanding public attitudes to gov-

choice best important?

ernment policies on choice is that the government's rationale for choice shifts. In a Fabian pamphlet on public service reform written in 2002, for example, Tony Blair writes, 'Choice enhances quality of provision for the poorest, helping to tackle inequalities while it also strengthens middle class commitment to collective provision' (Blair, 2002, p. 28). More recently, the government has argued that the thrust behind public service reform has been to ensure that middle class advantages are reduced:

> The affluent have always had choices. In most parts of life, if they don't like what they are offered by state services they can buy themselves something better...Our challenge is firstly to offer everybody the chance to choose a better deal from public services regardless of wealth...
>
> Hutton, 2005

Similarly, the debate switches between a demand-led account of choice – people want the same choices in public services that they receive in other points of their life – to an instrumental account of public services, where the public may think they prefer a good local service but only because they do not realise that choice is the way to achieve just that (Le Grand, 2006a).

People are also seen as having got it wrong when they express concerns that private companies will not be able to channel resources to those that need them as effectively as government. Reflecting on this survey finding, Le Grand noted:

> This is presumably because [respondents] saw private companies following normal private markets in favouring the better off. But as we have seen, the funding policies under the choice and competition reforms can be designed to encourage providers to meet the needs of the less well off, and even to specialise in doing so.
>
> Le Grand, 2006a

However, it is unclear why public attitudes, so central to other aspects of New Labour reforms, should so easily dismissed here.

The discussion highlights the problem of preference accommodation in public services. If services are to be redesigned around the preferences of consumers, there must be accurate information about what those preferences are. In the private sector, purchasing patterns give fairly clear signals about user preferences, although they are also

Problem of Choice

supplemented by extensive use of market research techniques to under-stand underlying attitudes to brands and products. In the public sector, users usually have limited exit rights, and may continue to use service even though they find aspects of provision highly problematic. Survey data are highly sensitive to question wording, and reported findings often aggregate what may be important differences between respondents – such as users and non-users of the service. In using data selectively, politicians undertake preference-shaping whilst maintaining a claim to be responding to public demand. The way that the government shifts between preference-shaping and preference-accommodation is important and will be returned to in the conclusion.

Exploring public attitudes

To probe some of the ambiguities in the survey data on public services, particularly around the relationship between public and private providers, the role of choice, and what it means to be a customer and a citizen, the author conducted ten focus groups. The focus group methodology allowed an exploration of how public service users talked about and rationalised their experiences of public and private consumption. The groups were held in outer London, the West Midlands, Yorkshire, Wales and Scotland. The geographic spread of the groups allowed some spatial comparison and minimised the potential distortions of a single area study where an issue like a local hospital closure may have polarised opinion. Each group contained participants from three life-stages: pre-family, family and post-family, since life stages are likely to have a significant impact on private and public consumption patterns. Groups were recruited by a trained market researcher, through face-to-face recruitment. All members of the public in a local area were eligible to participate, excluding people with elected or senior positions in public services and those who sit on the boards of public agencies, to avoid 'expert' views distorting the discussion. Participants were paid a small incentive, consistent with good practice in qualitative research. A pilot group was moderated by a Market Research Society trained moderator, and observed by the author prior to moderating the groups in the main study. The groups were tape-recorded and transcribed, and then coded using N6. All groups followed the same topic guide and general format, utilising a combination of written and oral data gathering techniques.

The themes addressed – experiences and expectations of public and private service consumption – were central to people's lives, and emphasis was placed on discussing the topic using language and concepts that participants could understand. Focus groups are a tool to study what Wilkinson calls 'the person-in-context' (1998, p. 111). Following Kitzinger, emphasis was placed on understanding the discourses that are used in the 'public arena' (1994, p. 117) rather than attempting to see the groups as 'a cost-effective technique for interviewing several people at once' (Kitzinger, 1994, p. 104). Transcript analysis was sensitive to the interactions between participants rather than reporting comments as though there was never 'more than one person in the room at the same time' (Kitzinger, 1994, p. 104. On this see also Wilkinson, 1998, p. 112, Silverman, 1998a).

Expectations

The premise of the interpretive approach used here is that it is essential to study the narratives people use to understand and explain ideas and events. To begin to probe these narratives in relation to public and private services, participants were asked firstly to complete written exercises about what it meant to be a customer and a citizen. The written responses revealed three main versions of being a customer, with some respondents utilising more than one. The first was a functional, transaction account: a customer is one who pays for and receives goods or services. The second was linked to the quality of the service: a customer is someone given choice, value for money and courteous treatment. The third emphasised the customer experience and the importance of being made to feel valued by the provider. The first two of these tie in closely to the definitions of customer given by the central and local government interviewees, discussed in Chapter 8, although the third one is somewhat distinct. The following statements from the focus groups illustrate the difference between the three definitions:

I think being a customer is paying for a service, i.e. supermarkets, receiving a service such as gas and electric supplies (Bristol, female, written).

Having freedom of choice. Expecting a certain level of service and expertise. Having the final say on a transaction and being allowed to change one's mind (Winchmore Hill, male, written).

Companies exceeding my expectations. It is about excellent service that puts the customer first in all aspects of my contact with an organisation – from initial contact, through sale and aftercare and at all times in any communication. It is about making my shopping/ contact easy and a 'wow' experience (Leeds, female, written).

These three approaches suggest that the word raises varying expectations, ranging from the purely functional to the '"wow" experience'. Only three of the women and five of the men across all the groups used just the first, purely transactional, definition of being a customer. All the rest incorporated some notion of service quality, responsiveness or care into their definition.

Recurring themes connected to being a customer were respect and politeness – a minimum expectation for many respondents. Rights were also an important theme, including the right to complain and to return faulty items. Most participants' description of being a customer was positive or neutral, although two of the men linked being a customer to queuing and receiving poor quality of service.

In the written exercises, respondents from across different groups used a common set of words to convey what the term citizen meant to them. Respondents linked being a citizen to belonging to a collective (community, society, nation, majority), which brought with it certain rights, and also a requirement to follow the rules, be responsible and give and receive respect:

> Certain rights and responsibilities. Member of a community (Bristol, male, written).
> Knowing where your rights are. What your responsibilities are to other members of the general population (Bridgend, male, written).
> Responsibility. Respect for community as a whole. Playing a part, citizen to community and vice versa (Glasgow, female, written).

Comparing the written comments for 'customer' and 'citizen', responses differed between wanting the same and different things as customers and citizens:

> Citizens and customers could potentially be the same thing, because you're talking about rights, you've got expectations... As citizens we receive certain services as well, why should we receive different types of service to if you went in to Dixons or somewhere like that to buy a product? (Winchmore Hill, male, written)
> As a customer you're wanting service from other people and organisations, whereas as a citizen you have to put in your fair share (Leeds, female, written).
> As a customer you have no responsibility. It can be like a single transaction, whereas a citizen is an ongoing role that one plays (Winchmore Hill, female, written).

The respondents expected to be treated with respect as customers, and felt that they ought to treat others with respect as citizens. In relation to the rights of a citizen, respondents talked about the need for fairness and equality so that all had the same rights, themes that were not evident in relation to being a customer. Only one respondent commented on the need to be treated fairly as a customer (Leeds, female, written).

Participants were asked which term (customer or citizen) they had found easiest to define, and the majority said customer. It was a role familiar to them from everyday retail environments, whereas citizen was more theoretical. The following comment was typical of the response:

> You don't experience being a citizen everyday, I think you are overall a citizen, but you do experience being a customer every day, whether it be going to the shop or buying something online (Bridgend, male, spoken).

A minority of respondents took a different view. As one put it, 'You're a citizen all the time, you're not necessarily a customer all the time' (Winchmore Hill, male, spoken). Overall, the respondents were more comfortable with the role of customer and saw it as more clearly linked to a discourse of people getting what they want, whereas citizen was more closely linked to notions of fairness, although it was not a role which many respondents found easy to define.

Later in the groups, participants were asked to write two postcards, one to Tony Blair about what they wanted from public services, and one to the head of the Confederation of British Industry (then Digby Jones) for what they wanted from private services. These postcards aimed to highlight how far respondents had similar expectations and wish lists and formed the basis for a group discussion comparing public and private services. The exercise was done towards the end of the group, after participants had spent time looking at specific examples of services.

Participants did not want the same things from both sectors. Issues around consistency of service, accountability and the need to allow front-line providers to get on with the job were limited to the public sector. Concerns about cost, profit and competitiveness were used in relation to the private sector. Better services in the public sector would be quicker, cleaner and consistent, whereas in the private sector they would primarily be cheaper. In both public and private services users wanted better quality goods for the same or lower cost – although in relation to public services this was most often expressed in terms of efficiency, whereas in private services it was mostly expressed as value. People wanted to be valued, listened to and informed in both sectors.

In all the groups, participants reported higher expectations of private than public services. This was generally because people expected more for a service that they paid for at the point of use:

> You expect a certain standard when you are paying directly for a service. With private, you pay the money to get the service, with public you are lucky to have it (Bristol, male, spoken).
>
> My expectation of a private company is much higher, because I physically have to hand them money…When it comes down to a public body, yes I pay that in taxes or in council tax, but I also hear a lot of things around resources shortages, shortage of police officers, shortage of money given to them by the government (Bridgend, male, spoken).

Thus even though the respondents recognised that they did pay for public services through taxes, the indirect nature of the financial transaction and recognition of service rationing altered their expectations of public provision.

Experiences

The other element of the customer satisfaction equation, alongside expectation, is experience. To explore their consumption experiences, participants were asked to define what they saw as good customer service, although most responded with stories of their own experiences of *bad* service – particularly relating to call centres, staff with inadequate levels of training, hard-sell techniques or goods out of stock. As one said, 'I've been with [a high street bank] donkeys' years. I mean I'm not that satisfied – it's just inertia that's kept me there' (Winchmore Hill, male, spoken). Here respondents agreed with and picked up on stories told by other respondents, to tell their own stories.

> Moderator: Can you give me an example of good customer service?
> Speaker 1: A person answering the phone, not talking to a recorded message [general laughter]
> Speaker 2: That's very rare these days (Winchmore Hill, male, spoken)

Positive experiences of customer service often related not to the initial transaction but to getting a better than hoped for resolution of a problem. One talked of how a boiler engineer came out the same day to fix a fault: 'That is just so unusual' and 'He just really pulled out all the stops and it's unique when you get people like that' (Winchmore Hill, female, spoken). In another case, 'I've never heard of it...very rare...and I was really proud. It's the only thing I've ever had in my life which has really run smoothly in terms of a complaint' (Leeds, male, spoken).

In relation to public services, participants across the groups had a much higher perception of front-line workers and professionals than they did of the service as a whole. Front-line workers in health and education were depicted as heroic figures, struggling in a context of shortages and interference from political leaders and managers:

> The NHS generally – we think they do a good job with the resources that they've got (Winchmore Hill, male, spoken).
>
> Locally the schools are pretty good; the teachers do a good job. The only problem is funding (Bridgend, male, spoken).
>
> Bureaucracy in all services, e.g. health, education, etc, to be cut to minimum, thus allowing the 'foot soldiers' to do the jobs they're trained for (Bridgend, female, written).

Respondents were also resentful towards the gatekeepers of services, such as doctor's receptionists and council workers. They made a clear distinction between hardworking front-line professionals and lazy, demotivated clerical workers:

> Doctors, teachers, nurses, they go through years of training. Council worker you can go straight into that job tomorrow. There's no commitment to that job necessarily (Winchmore Hill, female, spoken).
>
> The staff [in the NHS] do the best that they can do. The cleaners may not do, but you can't really get decent cleaners (Bristol, female, spoken).

In the discussion, participants reported a lack of efficacy: a sense that there was nothing they could do to ensure that public services, and council services in particular, improved. Respondents reported frustration that they could not just go to another service provider as they would in a shop:

If I don't like Currys, I'll go to Comet. If I don't like my doctor's receptionist I've got no choice... That is the problem. I don't have any choice. I can't vote with my feet (Winchmore Hill, male, spoken).

You're stuck with the council basically. You're not going to move every five minutes to a different council to try to get a better service that way. It's almost like they know that, and think why should we offer a better service? (Winchmore Hill, male, spoken).

The monopolistic nature of public services was seen as a problem, although respondents were similarly opposed to private sector monopolies, and expressed particular frustration with the privatised rail and utility companies.

Participants were asked to work in groups to rate a range of public and private services as good, bad or in between, in order to highlight expectations and experiences. In discussing and justifying their choices, participants were often apologetic for their positive accounts of services ('I'm sorry but I have never had any problems'; 'personally, I think they are good'). This form of words was used particularly in services where participants felt that general perceptions were of poor services. One said, 'You keep hearing you can't get an NHS dentist, but we put it in the good pile because we've not had a problem' (Winchmore Hill, male, spoken). 'Everyone's going to have different experiences. My GPs always been brilliant' (Bristol, female, spoken). 'I had to deal with Enfield council last year, and I was really impressed with the building regulations department... I was expecting it to be drawn out, and red tape and all that, and it wasn't like that at all' (Winchmore, Hill, male, spoken). This analysis fits into the 'I've been lucky' explanation of public attitudes, and suggests that people report positive experiences of public service use with circumspection because of a feeling that it deviates from the norm.

The council as an organisation was almost universally unpopular: 'I think everyone's had a bad experience with the council', as one put it (Glasgow, male, spoken). It is interesting to compare the comments of one respondent at different points in a group. In the first comment he is talking about council tax and later education:

I pay two grand a year and I certainly don't get value for that at all.

[Later] I've got two grandchildren who go to a local church school round here and it's excellent (Winchmore Hill, male, spoken).

As these comments illustrate, respondents had no sense of what their council tax was spent on apart from waste services. Overall the responses indicate dualities in public attitudes: teachers are dedicated, council workers are lazy; doctors are hard-working, receptionists are rude. Recurring across the groups, these attitudes suggest that people are generally satisfied with the service outcomes that they get, but are less satisfied with aspects of the service 'experience', particularly at the entry point into services.

Improving public services

At a national level policy-makers have suggested various mechanisms to improve public services. Key themes looked at here included investment, user choice and greater use of private providers. Other themes raised within the groups are also considered: empowering front-line workers, fairness and accountability.

Investment

The financial resources of public services were mentioned by the majority of respondents, and there was awareness that New Labour had been putting additional money into public services. Generally, people were in favour of the increases – only a couple called for tax cuts or reduced spending on public services. However the vast majority wanted more efficiency and/or value for money in public service spending. As one put it, 'I want to know that my tax money is being used to provide a good service' (Bristol, female, written). Some reported seeing an improvement in service following the investment, particularly in the NHS, but more generally there was suspicion about where all the money had gone.

Choice

Given their frustration with monopolistic services in the public and private sectors, it might be expected that participants would favour a greater choice of provider as a way to improve services. Exactly the same divisions that have characterised the national debate, emerged in the groups:

> Moderator: Should we have more choice in public services, a choice of hospital to go to for example? Is that a useful way to improve services?
> Speaker 1: I must admit if I want to go into hospital I want to go to the one down the road, I want that to be as good a hospital as any

other. I don't want to think I can go to Aberdeen if that's the best hospital for a hip replacement. (Winchmore Hill, male, spoken).

If there was choice that would be fantastic (Bristol, female, spoken).

However, the latter view was articulated by only one participant in one of the groups. Most respondents expressed ambiguity about choice:

With private services I expect to have a choice, whereas with public, it's not something I would necessarily expect. With public services I just wanted to be treated fairly, and less corruption (Winchmore Hill, male, spoken).

Opposition to choice focused around three main factors. First, was the perception of the opportunity costs of choice, in terms of travel and risk. As one put it, 'if have a heart attack you just want to get to a hospital, any hospital quickly' (Leeds, male, spoken). Second was the sense that choice would lead to unfairness either between rich and poor or between areas:

It sounds nice in theory, but will it finish up with a two tier system?'(Leeds, male, spoken).

Choice only benefits those that can afford it (Bristol, male, spoken).

It gets very elitist doesn't it?...Everybody wants the best for their child, so if you've got half a dozen schools and school A is the best you are going to do your damnedest to get your child into school A (Bridgend, female, spoken).

I totally disagree with that, it just becomes a postcode lottery and you tend to get people...who are lucky enough to be living in that area who are going to be first in the queue to get that excellent service (Bridgend, male, spoken).

Third there was uncertainty about how choice would improve overall quality, beyond some flagship providers:

By saying you have a choice that school then gets better results and therefore better funding, therefore they can provide better teachers and the school down the other end...are getting less and less funding, that's not really giving people a choice is it? (Bristol, female, spoken)

As another said, 'Everyone wants to go to the best, what will happen to the rest of the schools?' (Leeds, male, spoken). The responses spoke to an anxiety around choice for themselves, but also a commitment to fairness in public services and a hostility to elitism.

Use of private providers

Although Blair has argued that users do not know or care whether public or private providers deliver public services, as reported in Chapter 6, participants in the groups were generally aware of which services were in the public and private domain, and sensitive to the differences. When asked to put cards showing different services into piles of public and private, people were able to put some cards in place easily, but recognised the ambiguous status of other services such as railways, waste collection and dentists. Participants were asked about whether private companies should be involved in running public services in order to improve them. Some participants reported that private companies were generally better at delivering services than the public sector, but this was immediately followed up by a sense of concern about the introduction of profit motives into public services.

> It's about time we had a government that looks after these things rather than giving it to a bloomin' supermarket (Leeds, female, spoken).
>
> It's two different things altogether. One is purely about making money, profit [private] and the other one is about providing services [public] (Glasgow, male, spoken).
>
> They're not doing it for nothing, if it's a business they've got to make a profit. So my fear would be because it's a public body it's taken out of our hands again, there's no control (Bridgend, female, spoken).

The following exchanges illustrate the way that participants interacted in the group discussions and are quoted at length:

> Speaker 1: Public companies were out there to provide a service, whereas a private one is out there to make money.
> Speaker 2: You take the Potters Bar rail crash and the one further up the line. The main reason for those crashes was the lack of maintenance and safety because it cost money, they cut back on that.
> Speaker 1: It wasn't in the budget was it? (Winchmore Hill, male, spoken)

Moderator: Should private companies get more involved in running schools and hospitals?
Speaker 1: No.
Speaker 2: No, it's totally different.
Speaker 3: It's about making money then isn't it?
Speaker 4: Profit.
Speaker 5: Those are profitable organisations. They've got a different agenda.
Speaker 3: I agree totally with that. What is their agenda? Their agenda is to make money. I wouldn't be able to trust them. At the doctors, they are trying their best for you. There is no motive behind what they're doing. If there was a private company involved I'd just be thinking –
Speaker 4: Which tests are you going to cut out?
Speaker 6: You couldn't possibly know if they were saying you need this operation because it was the most expensive one, just because they were going to get money out of you (Winchmore Hill, female, spoken).

Having largely rejected private provision and choice as mechanisms to improve services, participants were divided on what would improve public services. They were sceptical about targets because of fears of manipulation, but wanted fairness and consistency of service. Generally, they favoured giving more power to front-line workers, consulting users more, providing a single point of contact which could give a satisfactory and prompt response, and greater transparency about what money was spent on. A recurring theme was a call for a reduction in political interference and bureaucracy in front-line services, suggesting that people do not want centrally decided targets. Participants wanted 'professionals' or 'foot-soldiers' to have the freedom to deliver services without interference. In completing the phrase: 'What I want from public services is', the following responses emerged:

Consistent quality and equity of service (Bridgend, male, written).
Services that can be relied on and turn up on time (Glasgow, female, written).
High standards of service for all (Bristol, male, written).
Consistency (Glasgow, male, written).
Reliable services (Bristol, female, written).
Reliable (Winchmore Hill, male, written).

This recurrent commitment to consistency links into the first narrative of consumerism, based on standardisation and a good service for all. For respondents in the groups, consistency was linked to a principled commitment to fairness:

> Good schools for everyone – not choice (Bristol, female, written).
> More money to be spent fairly and in the right areas (Bridgend, female, written).
> Equality – same for everyone (Glasgow, female, written).
> Fair treatment...Consistency between council areas (Bristol, female, written).

Although people did talk about wanting to be treated as an individual, which is linked to the second narrative of consumerism, it was expressed as a desire to be listened to, rather than to have tailored services:

> They make me feel like an individual. They update me on what is happening (Winchmore Hill, female, written).
> 'Fair service, treated as an individual, listened to, efficient' (Winchmore Hill, female, written).

The importance of being listened to was raised by all groups. The following exchange was typical:

> Moderator: What sort of things are important to you when you contact the doctor and the local council?
> Speaker 1: You want to be cared for.
> Speaker 2: A compassionate person at the other end.
> Speaker 3: Or just a person at the other end.
> Speaker 4: And for them to see you as a person.
> Speaker 5: I think that's it. We want to feel we're being cared for, whatever we're wanting – in the shops or anywhere.
> Speaker 2: When you want help or advice they should be able to give it to you (Winchmore Hill, female, spoken).

Finally, respondents wanted to reinforce public accountability and responsibility. In public services, respondents were frustrated by the sense that there was no one to blame. Services were faceless, or run by politicians who refused to be accountable for failures.

No 'passing the buck', e.g. recent furore with Ruth Kelly (Bridgend, female, written).
More people to be held responsible for their actions, mainly finan-cially (Bridgend, male, written).
More accountability...Less passing 'the buck' (Winchmore Hill, female, written).
Accountability to the voter (Winchmore Hill, female, written).

Many of the accounts of how services could be improved, involved greater user consultation and participation, in ways that are consistent with the third, coproductive, narrative of consumerism.

To listen to the views of the people (Bristol, female, written)
To give people a voice, listen to what is being said by the ordinary person (Leeds, female, written).
They listen to what people want and not do just what they want (Winchmore Hill, female, written).
To be listened to and if necessary for any appropriate action to be taken (Winchmore Hill, male, written)

As these extracts make clear, being listened to is a vital precursor to service improvement, even if it is a fairly limited form of coproduction. For these respondents it was part of a broader commitment to fairness in public service provision and a resistance to reforms that would increase risk and compromise fairness. Although the participants found plenty to complain about in public services, their first-hand experiences were broadly of satisfaction with service outcomes, together with resent-ment at their treatment by service gatekeepers. They wanted better access, clearer information and to be listened to, but were wary of ini-tiatives such as choice and private sector provision that they felt would modify the core of the service.

Conclusion

The current debate on public service reform is conducted on the terri-tory of preference accommodation. Both advocates and critics of the government's approach offer an account of what it is that people want from public services – broadly reducible to 'choice' versus 'a good local service' – and rubbish any attempts to deviate from this. The authen-ticity of service users' accounts of the service trump other visions of service, which, as seen in other chapters, are rejected as paternalist.

New Labour has built preference-accommodation into its public service reform programme both retrospectively and prospectively. It draws on an account of social change in postwar Britain, highlighting the decline of deference and the rise of individualism and consumerism. It uses evidence-based policy to evaluate how new policies should be implemented and revised in the future, with particular emphasis on techniques to measure customer satisfaction.

Available data on public attitudes highlight the ambiguity of attitudes to public services. Surveys show high levels of enthusiasm for some kinds of choice in public services, and greater confidence in the ability of the private sector than the public sector to get things done. The public sector is felt to be bureaucratic and faceless. Yet, conversely, people do not value choice above certain other priorities in public service reform, and feel that the government is best at directing resources at those in need.

Some of the ambiguities that result from quantitative surveys can be probed in qualitative research. The ten focus groups discussed here were designed to explore how the expectations, experiences and requirements of public and private services were similar and different. Findings showed that the public are dissatisfied with many aspects of public service delivery, particularly with the council and clerical workers, and do not feel listened to or empowered as users. The role of customer was more familiar to them than that of citizen and they generally reported higher levels of satisfaction with private services. However, they did not want private companies to run public services, and the idea of choice was unpopular because it created risk and clashed with other priorities of consistency and fairness. They wanted public services to be more responsive and informative, with greater powers given to frontline professionals. People recognised that as a citizen they had more obligations, rights and responsibilities than as a customer.

Overall, there was a high degree of consensus over the need for fair and consistent public services that were responsive but not profit-driven. Dissatisfaction with public services did not lead participants to want them to be more like private services, but rather to want them to be more like they felt public services should be (a point made earlier in the chapter by the National Consumer Council): fair, consistent and needs- rather than profit-based. The findings suggest that policymakers should be wary of seeking to collapse the difference between public and private services, and recognise that service users do have different expectations of the two sectors. Better training for frontline providers and more integrated public services are more likely to produce satisfied users than the expansion of choice and service fragmentation.

The findings discussed here suggest that public preferences are more closely aligned to the standardisation and coproduction narratives of public services. They want better access to and information about services that are fair and consistent. They want services to listen to them as individuals but there is little support for differentiated services or for more choice. Relationships with frontline professionals are important – people want consistency and responsiveness, with less bureaucratic interference and more accountability. Thus New Labour's increased attention on the differentiation narrative, discussed in Chapters 6 and 7, appears out of step with public preferences. The overall implications of the empirical data, encompassing the focus groups, the content analysis and the interviews, for New Labour's citizenship regime are the focus of the final chapter.

1, little support for choice

10
Conclusion: Coproducing Public Services

The government-citizen relationship at a given point in time is constitutive of a particular kind of citizenship regime. Governments use narratives to develop a solution set containing assumptions about the roles that government and citizen should play in that regime. Content analysis offers one way to make sense of and compare these narratives. The approach taken here used keyword searching to assess the narratives of public services contained in Blair's speeches, central government command papers and local corporate plans. Interview data from central and local government were also used to highlight how policymakers engage with aspects of the solution set. Quantitative and qualitative public opinion data were examined to explore how members of the public perceive and compare expectations and experiences of public and private services.

This final chapter discusses what the data tells us about the New Labour solution set, and how far the citizenship regime created is consistent with the consumerist model developed earlier in the book. It explores how far divergent strands in the solution set are indicative of a lack of coherence in the government's approach. It goes on to look at the limitations of public service consumerism as a political project, and discusses how far the concept of coproduction can be reworked as a plausible and attractive model of responsive public services.

The individual and the collective

That there are differences of emphasis between the speeches, the command papers and the corporate plans is unsurprising given that they are different types of communication aimed at different audiences. There are however key themes running through all these sources that meet the criteria of consumerism developed in Chapter 3. The first is that the documents engage with people in service conditional roles (customer, consumer, client, parent, patient, pupil) more than in non-service conditional roles (community, citizen, taxpayer). In the texts from central government, service-specific roles – parent, patient, pupil – are utilised heavily. At local government level, greater emphasis is placed on the customer of public services, a more generic service role. However, this aggregative finding needs to be considered alongside the significance of the term community in all of the texts. Community is the most commonly used of all the keywords in the central and local documents and is Blair's second most used term after parent. This finding suggests that public services are not talked about only in service conditional terms. Nor are they focused wholly on individuals (the second criterion of consumerism) since community is a term that is explicitly collective.

The community performs many different functions in the texts: it is, most commonly, the site of provision. It is used as an adjective to indicate services based in a locality: community schools, community support officers, community nurses, community punishment. It is also the moral compass of an area: 'The community sets clear standards of behaviour' (Home Office, 2003). It is a victim – of crime and anti-social behaviour – but it also has responsibilities to work with government to tackle these scourges. Finally, it is a value: community is an alternative to 'selfish individualism' (Blair, 16 July 2001). These multiple uses of the term enhance what Levitas calls the 'promiscuous flexibility' and 'deep ambiguity of "community"' (2000, pp. 191, 196). She argues, 'What "community" does is to designate an alternative to both the untrammelled free market (of neo-liberalism) and the strong state (of social democracy)' (Levitas, 2000, p. 191). Its role is one of signalling rather than substantive content. Certainly what community is not in any of these texts is a site of discussion and contestation. It is a unitary actor with a single voice. There is a call to recognise the diverse needs of multicultural communities, but not the pluralism of ideas and life plans that can exist within any community (Bevir, 2005).

The most commonly used service specific term in all the texts is parent. Blair's emphasis on the parent rather than the pupil in education contrasts with the importance placed on the child in other parts of New Labour policy. Lister describes the child as having 'iconic status' in New Labour's 'social investment state' (Lister, 2003). However the role of the pupil in education is very much a subordinate one to the parent. The domain of the parent stretches into welfare as well as education, with a special emphasis on lone parents. These parents have rights and choices, but they are primarily coproducers, taking on responsibilities for service outcomes. Parents are expected to be willing coproducers of their own financial independence and their children's education, although if necessary coercive measures – parenting contracts, benefit withdrawal – will be imposed.

Customer is the most commonly used individual term in the local government documents, and is used frequently in the command papers, although less so in Blair's speeches. Given that definitions of the term customer often involve payment and a choice of provider, and thereby appear to limit the applicability of the term in public services, interviews in central and local government were used to understand better how the term customer was being applied. When Blair talked about the customer he indicated that it had two purposes: first, to signal a contrast with the past, when public service users were commonly known as clients; second, to make the environment in which services are delivered more business-like. In interviews with civil servants in the Department of Health and the Department for Education and Skills, respondents indicated that the term customer was widely used within their departments, and was a way of signalling a change of culture. However, there was inconsistency about what exactly the term meant.

Similarly in local government, definitions of the customer were varied, including someone paying for a service, someone treated with respect and someone who makes a choice. Some respondents, particularly councillors, were cautious about the term, concerned that it placed limits on the role of the citizen, although generally interviewees endorsed its usage. Officers and councillors talked of using the term customer in recruitment, and bringing in people with customer care skills from the private sector. Across the interviews and texts, the customer was rarely given responsibilities or expected to be involved in services as a coproducer. This assumption was shared by the focus group respondents who associated responsibilities with citizens but not customers. As one put it, 'As a customer you have no responsibility.'

A third criterion of the consumerist model – an emphasis on preference-accommodation rather than preference-shaping – was evident in the texts, particularly at central government level. A common theme in the texts and interviews was an account of sociological change in which people are becoming more demanding, with higher expectations. In Blair's speeches he talked of the way that in 'a consumer society', public services came under new pressures to deliver choice and personalisation. Rising public expectations created the context within which public services had to be reformed and improved. There was a difference of emphasis here with Conservative predecessors, for whom, as discussed in Chapter 4, the expectations of service users were as much an inflationary pressure on services as a useful benchmark for service improvement. Particularly important in the New Labour speeches and command papers was the assumption that people's experiences of services within the private sector created new expectations of public services. Although this trend was less pronounced in the local government corporate plans, local interviewees talked of how they were under pressure to provide the sorts of 24/7 services that local people experienced in other parts of their lives.

From the survey and focus group findings discussed in Chapter 9, it is clear that people's expectations of public and private services are highly varied, and cannot be cast into a private good/public bad mould. They expect to be treated well as customers in the private sector, paying for services up front, but often find that service levels are disappointing. In the public sector, they are generally happy with the service outcomes – NHS, schools, refuse collection – but are less satisfied with aspects of what might be called the service experience: the interaction with doctors' receptionists and council call centre operators. Here they feel disrespected and ignored by the frontline staff, although experiences of private sector call centres were no better. Not being listened to was the most common complaint about public services. There was little enthusiasm for increased choice of provider, because of the risks and inequalities it would bring, but some respondents did express frustration about their inability to use the threat of exit in public services.

The New Labour texts (i.e. those from Blair and central government departments) also showed strong evidence of the fourth criterion of consumerism: an emphasis on service outcomes for users and a downgrading of the importance of the structures or processes of delivery. The texts emphasised the need to expand the range of service providers into the private and voluntary sectors, in order to improve service quality. For Blair this was expressed as a rejection of ideology, in favour of flexibility and pragmatism and a commitment to doing what was required to make services better. As his advisors told the Guardian, '[Blair] is completely unideological about how services are delivered so long as they are delivered efficiently' (Wintour, 2003). However, the assumption that diversity of providers is key to service improvement has a strong ideological thread to it; it is as Clarke puts it, 'dogmatic pragmatism' (Clarke, 1999, p. 85 in Lister, 2003, p. 428). Various authors have noted the way in which New Labour's reforms use a circular logic, taking policy actions on the basis of contingent premises, which then 'propagate and reinforce the trends and understandings identified' (Moss and O'Loughlin, 2005, p. 171). Globalisation is particularly important here in creating the limitations within which New Labour believes itself to be operating (Hay, 1999, 2004; Moss and O'Loughlin, 2005).

In the focus groups, respondents were wary of private sector involvement in public services, concerned that profit motives would take precedence over issues such as safety and access. It may be that the public has got it wrong about the private sector, as Le Grand argues: that mechanisms can be introduced to ensure that private providers expand capacity and increase innovation without cherry-picking and cutting corners (Le Grand, 2006a). However, if customer satisfaction includes within it the sense of reassurance and trust felt by the users, then the anxiety created by profit-seeking cannot be discounted. Respondents wanted services to be accountable, but they saw a role here for improved performance by political leaders and managers, rather than the market. When one woman commented, 'It's about time we had a government that looks after these things rather than giving it to a bloomin' supermarket', she spoke of a feeling that government needs to have some of the answers.

The three narratives

The narratives used in relation to public services highlight different strands in New Labour's approach to service reform. The first one emphasises the development of standardised public services, the second focuses on the need to differentiate services around user preferences, and the third emphasises the importance of involving users in the production of services. In all the texts the standardisation narrative was the most frequently used. The themes of standards and targets, in particular, dominated all the documents. However, there was also a common trend of decline in the use of this narrative over time in the speeches and command papers. The standardisation narrative was strongest in Labour's first term, and less so after that, when differentiation and coproductive messages were increasingly being emphasised. In general the standardisation narrative is much stronger in local government than at the centre. The alternative narratives were underdeveloped here, particularly that of differentiation.

The relationship between these narratives can be constructed in different ways, as Chapter 3 outlined. For New Labour at the national level, the first and second narratives are presented as sequential – once targets have been achieved, differentiation of service must follow – with the third narrative running along in parallel to emphasise that users have responsibilities as well as rights to services. Thus standardisation becomes associated with early Blairism and differentiation with late Blairism.

This sequential account makes sense when comparing the Labour approach with that of its Conservative predecessors, discussed in Chapter 4. The Conservatives, despite a rhetorical focus on choice-based approaches, appeared to develop a mainly standardised model of consumerism based on charter rights to a guaranteed level of service. Labour's first priority on coming into office was to take further this standardisation model, and attempt to make it more effective than it had been in the charter era, as part of its commitment to managerialism. Over time, Labour developed its second narrative, becoming more interested in responding to the perceived needs of users rather than managerially driven standardisation. Rather than government taking on the role of devising a set of targets for all service users, emphasis was placed on users themselves expressing what they wanted from services. The professional assessment of need, which underpinned the traditional administrative approach, the charter initiative and, to some extent, target-driven systems, was downgraded.

The third narrative, focused on what users can put into services, sits alongside the other two and complements them in different ways. In the standardisation model, the role of the user is to accept the responsibilities that go along with rights and access to services. In the differentiation model, the user is expected to be actively involved in services, expressing needs and exercising choice. However, although users need to work with providers, user views have primacy.

The neat sequential account does not altogether satisfy, however. New Labour's attitude to consistency and differentiation is more pragmatic than this temporal process suggests. Policy actors are against consistent services when they attack the pre-1997 welfare state for its 'one size fits all' rigidity, but more favourable to it when they attack the traditional welfare state for its elitism and middle class bias. In education, for example, Blair makes clear that he is turning his back on the '"one size fits all" comprehensive era' (26 November 2002), whilst saying elsewhere: 'Yet as the post-war decades stretched into the Seventies, Eighties and Nineties, universal provision did not lead remotely to universal achievement, academic or vocational' (3 May 2004). In other words, the critique shifts, with the postwar welfare state being, at one moment, too elitist, at another too monolithic.

The sequential explanation also underplays ongoing tensions between the 'Blairites' and 'Brownites' within government, in which the demands of senior figures such as Milburn and Reid for more choice within public services can be interpreted as an attack on the target-oriented 'consolidators' at the Treasury (Peston, 2006, p. 303). Brown explicitly differentiated himself from markets in core public services in his 2003 Social Market Foundation speech and endorsed more sensitive and locally determined targets (Brown, 2003). Thus the tensions between the standardisation and differentiation narratives in public service reform can be interpreted as a symbol of New Labour's internecine struggles as much as a planned and evolutionary solutions to the problems besetting public services. Clearly this interpretation has implications for the future of public service delivery in the post-Blair Labour Party.

Certainly, the tensions between the narratives are obvious, despite efforts to elide them. Maintaining a standardised service whilst also differentiating and offering choice is problematic. Requiring, and indeed coercing, users to behave responsibly whilst also respecting their choices may be impossible. The tension between choice and equity has been a particular touchstone for critics of the New Labour agenda (Lawson, 2005; Appleby, 2006). As Bevir makes clear, choice is not simply a managerial device but is a new way of thinking about distributive justice:

> If individuals are free to choose things such as the schools their children go to or who is to manage their state-pensions, then we must accept the inequalities that result from some of them making good choices and others making bad ones. New Labour thus appears to be committed to allowing distribution to reflect the merits of the choices people make as well as their needs or welfare.
>
> Bevir, 2005, p. 65

It is this individualisation of risk that alarms the critics of New Labour. As Hood puts it, in defining the sovereign consumer: 'If you are foolish or gullible, you have to take the consequences' (1986, p. 171). Applying the same rubric to social production is highly problematic for those who remain wedded to a conception of public services based on the pooling of risk (Pollock, 2002).

The content analysis highlighted the way that the narratives were applied in different services, in some cases consistent with the properties of that service (for example rights were more important than choice in law and order), and in some cases in ways that do not fit the theoretical characteristics of that service (for example labelling welfare service users as customers). The differences between users of different services require more attention than catch-all terms such as public services and the welfare state allow. Greener has argued, for example, that education service users are much more familiar with and receptive to choice than the users of health services. Based on interviews with parents, he found that: 'Rationality appeared to be extremely contextual, with parents moving from almost passive recipients of healthcare to highly calculative, participative choosers of education within the space of a few seconds' (Greener, 2005, p. 238). Choice in education has been operational for much longer than in health, creating different user expectations, but it is also likely that users have different perceptions of risk and professional deference between education and health services. Thus in considering the way that public service delivery shapes the citizenship regime, it is important to be sensitive to the distinctive ways in which individual users and groups of users experience the service.

The consumer in the community

Paradox of New Labour

An apparent paradox of the New Labour approach is that it embraces many of the aspects of the consumerist solution set – an individualistic orientation towards user preferences, and an emphasis on quality over process – but does so whilst paying more attention to the notion of community than would be expected in the consumerist approach. In the juxtaposition of the terms consumer and community it is possible to highlight some of the key elements within the New Labour approach. The relationship between consumerism and community is a complex and contested one. Individualised, transactional definitions of the consumer jar with the organic and mutually supportive nature of the community. Aldridge argues, 'Within Western discourse on consumption there is a recurrent opposition between community and consumerism as ways of life' (Aldridge, 2003, p. 105).

Communities imply moral sanction and restraint, whereas consumerism is often linked to hedonism and excess (Bell, 1978). Davies highlights the paradox of communitarianism and consumerism as the moral agendas underpinning New Labour's policy agendas (2006). He argues that these are reconcilable in policy terms – ministers argue that people can participate in their local neighbourhoods and schools, but still want good customer service when they ring the Department of Work and Pensions call centre. However, in theoretical terms, '[T]hese two models of individual psychology point in radically different directions... Communitarianism reminds us of the enduring value of customs and heritage; consumerism revels in ephemera' (Davies, 2006, p. 69). The communitarians who have most influenced Blair, people like Macmurray and Etzioni themselves have little time for consumerism. Macmurray talks of the need for self control to resist the proliferation of desires in conditions of plenty (Macmurray, 1949, pp. 23–4 – cited in Bevir and O'Brien, 2003, p. 314). Etzioni calls for 'voluntary simplicity' in order to be 'freed from the culture of consumerism' (2004, p. 414).

There are ways of characterising community and consumerism, however, which find common threads rather than conflict. The 'arbitrariness and unevenness' that Crouch sees as a characteristic of community, can also be attributed to consumerism, and contrasted with the 'universalism of citizenship' (2001, p. 131). The irrationality that Davies sees in the consumer, is also discernible in some forms of community (2006). Both consumerism and community draw on romanticism, as Campbell argues. He traces how at certain periods 'an intense moral idealism went hand-in-hand with an unrestrained commercialism', for example in the 1890s, 1920s and 1960s (1989, p. 206). Thus community and consumerism may not pull in opposite directions.

Some have argued that New Labour's distinctive account of community is more easily reconciled with consumerism than alternative communitarian theories. Although Blair himself says: 'For myself I start from a simple belief that people are not separate economic actors competing in the marketplace of life', Driver and Martell are sceptical:

> The Left's traditional sense of community involving notions of co-operation, fellowship and solidarity and a shared experience of life, especially in terms of membership of the working class, has little place in the market-oriented, 'one nation' politics of New Labour.
>
> Driver and Martell, 1999, p. 30

Similarly, as Bevir puts it, 'New Labour...feeds hefty doses of individualism, competition, and materialism into the traditional social democratic ideal of community' (2005, p. 71).

If links between consumerism and community are contingent, community and coproduction appear easier to combine. The call on service users to become involved in shaping services, and to recognise responsibilities to do so, is more compatible with community than with some of the hedonistic versions of consumerism. Johnson points out the strong link between New Labour strands of communitarianism and self-help (2001, p. 185). There is a coercive element to the third narrative – a requirement on service users to take on responsibilities, even where they are unwilling to do so – that fits comfortably with communitarian calls to downgrade individual autonomy. As Rose argues, the freedoms granted by the state may simply facilitate ever more subtle forms of self-regulation (1999). Commenting on the expert patient scheme, Greener points out: 'There is something rather Foucaultian in attempting to convert chronically ill patients into self-managing self-carers' (Greener, 2005, p. 237). Coproduction can introduce conditionality into services, such that users who are not willing to play the role demanded of them by the community have services denied. Welfare-to-work is the most obvious conditionality in New Labour's policies (Moss and O'Loughlin, 2005, p. 170). Attempts to remove housing benefit from parents whose children do not attend school is another example.

These forms of coproduction do though share some consumerist features, as discussed in Chapter 7, privatising problems and requiring people to manage their own risks. The user becomes less rather than more empowered. Commenting on the emphasis on empowerment under New Labour, Hoggett notes, 'There seems to be a real contempt around for people who cannot or will not be "empowered" at the moment, especially if they are not obviously physically incapacitated in some way' (2001, p. 44). As Jenson and Phillips point out, there is a sense in which consumerist language individualises responsibility for one's life projects, and therefore for any failings that may occur (2001, p. 80). Thus coproduction can be co-opted by consumerism, becoming a mechanism for privatising and individualising aspects of public services that were previously about pooled risk and professional provision.

Through the promotion of narratives of standardisation and differentiation in public services alongside individualised variants of coproduction, New Labour offers a consumerist solution set for the problems that (it believes) beset public services. Ostensibly community-oriented services are to be remade around the choices and preferences of their users, utilising public and private providers without wasting time on debates about the distinctiveness of public provision. Given that public services form the only direct experience of government that most people have, this consumerist solution set shapes the New Labour citizenship regime: 'the institutional arrangements, rules and understandings that guide and shape concurrent policy decisions and expenditures of states, problem definitions by states and citizens, and claims-making by citizens' (Jenson and Phillips, 2001, p. 72).

What is wrong with a consumerist citizenship regime?

As discussed in earlier chapters of the book, critics of consumerism have been rebuffed with accusations of paternalism, producerism or nostalgia. All of these are emotive words to dismiss positions that are not without some merit. Although paternalism can be associated with elitism and deference, it also draws attention to the distributive inequalities that can result from leaving people to live with the consequences of their choices. Producerism is associated with the argument that unresponsive bureaucrats should be allowed to protect their perks and ignore the needs of their users. Rejection of this extreme view should not, however, lead to the dismissal of all claims about the need to protect the terms and conditions of the workforce and re-establish the principle of government as a 'model employer' (Sachdev, 2004). The nostalgia argument is based on an unsustainable golden age theory of public services, as Clarke *et al*, recognise, 'On one level, hardly anyone supported the welfare state as it stood in 1980, at least not until the Tories began to dismantle it' (1987, p. 193). However, it is not necessary to want to bring back the pre-Thatcher welfare state in order to be uncomfortable with the New Labour caricature of the welfare state as an insensitive, 'one-size-fits-all', monolith.

There are three further arguments that can be made against New Labour-style consumerism in public services and these are less susceptible to attack than paternalism, producerism or nostalgia. The first is that New Labour's solution set, despite having coproductive features, too often defines the interests of users as in conflict with those of producers. Service provision is conceived as an adversarial relationship, where consumers do battle with producers to get access to scarce resources. As Blair says, providers should 'no longer dictate to their users but give them power and choice over the service' (3 December 2004). However there is a failure to recognise that the interests of users and providers are often closely aligned. Successful delivery of public services requires high trust relationships between users and providers on the front line. This necessitates not only that NHS patients look after their own health and parents sign home-school contracts – as the New Labour version of coproduction demands – but also that service production be restructured to give users and providers the opportunity to build relationships. In social care, for example, this may mean taking steps to improve staff retention rates and ensure that vulnerable users see the same care assistant rather than having disjointed care from a range of agency staff. In education, it may involve encouraging parents to join governing bodies and parent-teacher associations so that they can contribute to the governance of the school rather than acting only as demanding customers or 'failed' consumers who must be coerced into home-school contracts.

The focus groups revealed that users themselves often do not perceive relationships with providers in mutually supportive, coproductive terms. They remain respectful and even deferential to some providers – teachers, doctors, nurses – but are resentful towards the clerical and manual staff that support them: receptionists, council workers, cleaners. It is necessary to develop mechanisms to break down the sorts of 'us and them' mentality that develops, and build the capacity of workers and users to shape services together –as joint work by the National Consumer Council and Unison is doing (NCC/Unison, 2006).

A second argument against New Labour's user focus is that it legitimises reforms which, when given an alternative reading, are not about user interests at all. The transfer of assets to the private and voluntary sectors can lead to a reduction in accountability to parents and communities, as for example in the academy schools initiative (Catalyst/ Public World, 2006). As Principal Policy Adviser at Which? Frances Blunden pointed out in the last chapter, initiatives such as choice do not necessarily improve services for their users (Blunden, 2006). There are at least three rationales that may underpin ostensibly consumer-oriented reforms in public service. First, such reforms may be about disciplining and controlling providers, in an effort to maintain cost control following service decentralisation. Hewitt has made clear that such intentions underpin the extension of patient choice in the NHS, as discussed in the last chapter (2005). Second, consumerism can be a legitimating tool for government attempts to depoliticise and disclaim difficult policy areas, passing responsibilities down to users or out to the private sector. It is a blame-shifting strategy, as Finlayson argued in the last chapter (2003a, p. 23). Third, as in the school academy example, consumerism can also provide a rationale for opening up the public sector to private investors, which may satisfy the broader political aims of a government intent on establishing its pro-business credentials (Catalyst/Public World, 2006). In all of these scenarios, service users are a means to an end, as they were for sections of the new right in the 1980s (Klein, 2001, p. 116), not the end in themselves that consumerism would suggest.

The third argument against the New Labour approach is that it delegitimises the accountability of public services to anyone *other than* their users. The authenticity of the customer's experience neutralises other forms of knowledge or political projects. It valorises the immediate responsiveness of providers to users in a marketplace, and sidelines or derides forms of accountability to other stakeholders or to political representatives. Even accepting the somewhat caricatured advantages of market responsiveness (and ignoring problems such as the market's tendency to cherry-pick desirable users), it is important to recognise that accountability in public services cannot end with accountability to users.

Since aggregated individual choices may lead to perverse outcomes – all parents wanting to go to the same school – and negative externalities – cancer contracted from passive smoking – there can be a need to enforce a collective line on service provision. Of course a collective orientation must supplement rather than replace good individual care in public services. Services do need to be sensitive and responsive to the needs of their users. However a 'user comes first' argument cannot be used to delegitimise all other perspectives. As Goss puts it, 'We need to value public services, not simply because they meet consumer needs, but because they offer something outside the consumer experience' (2005, p. 48). Occasionally in the New Labour texts there is recognition of a requirement to trade off the needs of the individual against the collective, or to recognise that one set of users might have different interests to another, but generally these are subordinate to the dominant consumer approach.

There is a resultant danger that citizenship becomes a fragmented rather than integrated identify, dislocated from the experience of using public services, in which people are parts of communities, or are consumers, customers, patients, parents, pupils, and sometimes taxpayers, but rarely citizens. Instructing people to think of themselves as consumers or customers when they use public services amounts to telling people that in as far as they get good quality service in the public sector, it is because they are customers. Being a citizen is not enough. It is hard to see why those same people will accept the collective responsibilities of citizenship – to participate in democratic structures, to contribute to redistributive taxation – when everything they get back from the state they get as customers not citizens. Some scholars argue that treating people well as customers of government is an essential pre-requisite to encouraging them to engage as citizens (Lowndes *et al*, 2001, p. 452). But it is not at all clear why high levels of customer satisfaction would stimulate political activity. If people are encouraged to think of themselves as customers of public services, then issues of democracy and the public good become as peripheral for the public sector as they are for the private.

The fourth and most profound argument against the New Labour approach is that it silences alternative narratives about public services. If people are aware only of the market, then the scope for them to explore the potential of the public realm is stunted. By embracing and legitimising marketisation, consumerist public service reforms deny the validity of non-market approaches. As McIvor puts it:

> The danger, then, of New Labour's new social democratic model is that an insistent marketisation of economic and social relations will dissolve the practical and epistemological resources needed to sustain and guide any progressive state action. If we are continually looking to 'strengthen markets in the public interest' we may find that there is no real 'public' left to serve or answer to, and that its 'interests' can only be defined abstractly by civil servants, anonymous regulators and public purchasing agencies, for whom it comes to mean little more than the maintenance of the market itself.
>
> McIvor, 2005, p. 87

Commenting on the 1980s, Ignatieff noted that 'most political rhetoric, whether of left or right, addresses the electorate not as citizens but as taxpayers or as consumers. It is as if the market were determining the very language of the political community' (Ignatieff, 1995, p. 72). This ownership of language is central to the setting out of alternative citizenship regimes. In a discussion of the rivalry between public and private activities, Hirschman points out that consumers can only turn to public life if they are conscious of being citizens. Otherwise rejection of consumerist accumulation can lead to a retreat into the private domain, the Buddhist ideal (1982, p. 63). There may be of course an advantage to politicians in encouraging people to see public services only as a reciprocation for the paying of taxes, since it shuts down alternative discourses and accounts of what politics is for. As Arendt argued, 'In Greece it was the ever-frustrated ambition of all tyrants to discourage the citizens from worrying about public affairs...and to transform the agora into an assemblage of shops like the bazaars of oriental despotism' (1958, p. 160).

Alternative discourses are not altogether silent, even at a governmental level, for example in the devolved regions of the UK. A large-scale research project into policy change following devolution found that Scotland and Wales had endorsed a more 'social democratic' agenda on public services that emphasised collaborative patterns of working and deemphasised the markets and targets used in English public service reform (Keating, 2005). The Welsh First Minister Rhodri Morgan, for example, told an interviewer, 'Greater consumer choice in public services does not fit in with Welsh values. What people want is a higher standard of community-based public services all round' (Hetherington, 2004). In Scotland in 2003, the then Health Minister Malcolm Chisholm was asked by the press whether the NHS in Scotland would follow the example set by John Reid in Westminster and refer to patients as consumers. He said: '"I won't personally do so. I don't use the word 'consumer' myself. I prefer to use the word 'patient'. When it comes to health, I think the word 'patient' is more appropriate"' (Templeton, 2003).

The success of Scotland and Wales in going their own way in public services is, as most elements of recent public service reforms, contested. Research comparing service outcomes in England, Scotland, Wales and Northern Ireland is ongoing under the Economic and Social Research Council's *Public Services Programme*. That England has performed much better on reducing NHS waiting lists is clear (Alvarez-Rosete 2005; Le Grand, 2006a), and criticism over waiting times led the Welsh Assembly to introduce patient choice in 2003. However policies such as free personal care for the elderly and the refusal to levy variable university tuition fees in Scotland indicate that devolution can offer a distinctive and attractive solution set for public services (Keating, 2005).

Setting out alternatives

The discussion of citizenship regimes at the beginning of the book highlighted some of the different ways in which the citizen-state relationship can be configured, including liberal, libertarian, communitarian and civic republican. Chapters 4 and 5 traced the way that this relationship has changed through the emergence and retrenchment of the welfare state in Britain. Both theoretical and historical approaches help to highlight the contingent nature of the citizenship regime in a state at any one time. Through studying the ways in which New Labour policy actors have interpreted and applied the different narratives to policy problems it has been possible to reveal the way they construct services, providers and users in a distinctive, and largely consumerist, way. This approach is crucial not only to the process of critique but also to moving forward. As Bevir points out:

> When we thus portray New Labour's beliefs and policies as contingent and contestable...[w]e challenge the self-understanding of those who expound these policies; we reveal to them the contingent, historical conditions of their beliefs, thereby undercutting their belief that these policies are necessary. What is more, we thereby open up the possibility of alternative narratives, policies, and practices.
>
> 2005, p. 128

Identifying alternatives is a crucial step in moving on from critique. Le Grand lays down an important challenge here:

> [If] the defenders of the public realm are to convince us that the government is on the wrong track, especially with respect to the usefulness of competitive pressures, then they must provide us with some evidence that their chosen path will do better... Until they do, their criticisms of current government policies cannot be taken seriously.
>
> Le Grand, 2003

In developing alternatives, many of New Labour's critics, such as Crouch (2003) have opted for voice, as a counter-weight to the governments' emphasis on choice and exit. Here public service users become involved in campaigning and complaining, speaking out through user groups, using complaint mechanisms and joining groups like parent-teacher associations. Shortcomings in public services can be highlighted in collective forums without the individualised risks and destabilisation of choice. Voice is clearly important to any civically imbued notion of public services, but it needs to operate under certain conditions. First, it must be dialogical rather than uni-directional. The organised voices of user organisations are an important stakeholder in service redesign but they are not the only legitimate voice, and their demands cannot be met without debate and reflection. In health, for example, the voice of patient groups can ally with the clout of pharmaceutical companies to pressure the NHS into making expensive and non-cost effective new treatments available. Mechanisms of voice need to be inclusive enough to consider the interests of non-users and a broader public interest.

If the public domain is to fulfil its potential to be a site of 'debate and contestation' (Marquand, 2004, p. 32), as well as engagement, then mechanisms of voice which encourage debate as well as claims-making must be utilised. A number of authors have suggested conceptual bases for greater citizen participation in decision-making, under headings including 'Strong Democracy' (Barber, 1984), 'Associative Democracy' (Hirst, 1994; Cohen and Rogers, 1995) and 'Empowered Participatory Governance' (Fung and Olin Wright, 2003, p. 15–39). Some authors have proposed specific mechanisms for increasing citizen involvement in governance including citizens' juries (Stewart *et al*, 1994; Coote and Lenaghan, 1997; Smith and Wales, 2000), deliberative opinion polls (Fishkin, 1991), 'deliberation days' (Ackerman and Fishkin, 2004) and online forums (Coleman, 1999). These mechanisms indicate ways in which the citizen role can become more participative and deliberative, involving a broad section of interests. Bevir calls, more generally, for an 'open community' which recognises and encourages pluralism, rather than the unitary community offered by New Labour (Bevir, 2005, ch. 6)

An alternative to voice and exit, although compatible with both, is to develop the non-consumerist variants of coproduction. Although coproduction can be a form of personalisation in public service delivery (Leadbeater, 2004), it can also be part of a more collective vision of service reform. Brudney and England argue that the individualistic forms of coproduction, which can be seen as characteristic of New Labour, should be placed at the bottom of a hierarchy of coproductive activity, and it is not until coproduction is undertaken at the group or collective level that it begins to transform services (1983, pp. 63–4). In a paper for the Downing Street Strategy Unit, Halpern *et al*, similarly locate 'individualised coproduction' as a transitional phase towards 'full coproduction' (2004, p. 67). Coproductive activities offer scope for citizens to be engaged and empowered in ways that are intimately connection to public services, rather than separating off the political citizen from the public service customer (Parks *et al*, 1981).

Non-individualistic forms of coproduction can take various forms. Group modes of coproduction may involve users coming together to shape or provide services, such as 'walking bus' initiatives for school children or neighbourhood watch schemes. Collective coproduction refers to programmes that benefit the whole community rather than groups of users. Current examples are lay magistrates and jurors. For Brudney and England these forms of collective involvement are at the top of the coproduction hierarchy: 'Inherent in the definition of collective coproduction is the notion of a redistribution of benefits from citizen activity. Regardless of which citizens participate in the service delivery process, the benefits accrue to the city as a collectivity' (Brudney and England, 1983, p. 64).

Services that are coproduced are likely to be more effective than those that are not. Coproduction can make service providers more sensitive to the needs and preferences of users, since the interaction feeds information about user preferences directly into the production process (Percy, 1984, p. 437). On the other side, 'citizens may become more knowledgeable of the content, costs and limitations of municipal services and their joint responsibility with service agents for their delivery' (Brudney and England, 1983, p. 62). Thus there are advantages to public officials in trying to develop coproductive relationships as much as possible. In particular coproduction can be a tool to diffuse tensions in front-line services such as housing and welfare payments, where user disempowerment and frustrated expectations can spill over into abuse. Whereas the consumer approach is premised on meeting continually rising user expectations, the coproduction model equips users with a clearer understanding of constraints and viable improvement mechanisms. Coproductive relationships, premised on credible commitments from both government agencies and citizens, can be the basis for more constructive interactions (Ostrom, 1996, p. 1082). Collaborative forms of coproduction accord value to continuity of care and the development of relationships based on trust rather than valorising the destabilising and fragmenting effects of competition between providers.

Although coproduction in public services is generally either taken for granted (as in jury service) or imposed in an individualised model (as in parenting orders), some research is indicating the potential for it to be developed as a tool of service improvement. Research for the Office of the Deputy Prime Minister (ODPM) highlighted the extent to which community involvement in service provision can improve service outcomes, particularly in deprived areas (ODPM, 2005b). The *Shared Solutions* project run by the National Consumer Council and Unison (2006) shows the potential of housing officers and tenants to work together to overcome mutual suspicion and agree service priorities if given the opportunity to do so.

Participation in such mechanisms will require government to be sensitive to the different needs and capabilities of citizens. Brudney and England argue that coproduction should include 'a willingness of authorities to work with residents to develop their capacities as potential coproducers of services' (Brudney and England, 1983, p. 62). Miller and Stirling highlight the importance of individual and social capital to effective coproduction and argue that users with less individual capital (physical and financial resources, health status, skills, knowledge) may not be able to participate effectively (2004, p. 5). Thus coproduction must work on developing individual and social capital rather than taking it for granted or punishing those with lower levels. Public employees must be willing to share power and to accept the greater complexity created by expanded citizen involvement (Brudney, 1984, p. 468, Percy, 1984, p. 441).

As discussed above, there are dangers in the coproductive model if it is used primarily as a device to cut costs, to penalise vulnerable users, or to individualise the public service experience. However, if it is conceived as a positive message of partnership between public service users and providers it has the potential to reveal new insights about how services should be developed. As Miller and Stirling put it:

> The usefulness of the coproduction analysis is that it provides the managerial legitimacy to accord a central role to service users in the production of outcomes... [I]t changes the concept of service users from customers who need a better service experience, to coproducers, who must be supported and treated as colleagues.
>
> 2004, p. 12

The potential for coproduction to underpin reform in specific service areas has been outlined by a number of authors, some of them using the vocabulary of coproduction and others describing reforms in recognisably coproductive ways. In public health, a number of authors have outlined the need to premise health reforms on better integration of patients into productive processes (Lupton, 1995; Cottam and Leadbeater, 2004; Hart, 2006). As Miller and Stirling, point out:

> Applying a coproduction analysis to existing or proposed services helps to highlight the balance of resources and raise questions about rights and responsibilities, equity and effectiveness. It does not in itself provide the answers. For these it relies on the continuing

creativity of staff and service users and their ability to learn from others and apply those lessons.

Miller and Stirling, 2004, p. 12

Coproduction offers a way of thinking about public services rather than a comprehensive policy agenda. It is oriented towards service users, and therefore cannot engage the full range of voices that have a legitimate say about what public services are for. It emphasises consensus building and therefore is a less appropriate channel than voice for the sorts of radical challenges that may be needed to public services, for example from marginalised groups of users. However, its account of how public services operate can be both more descriptively accurate and more normatively appealing than the neo-liberal alternative. It rejects the polarity of insensitive bureaucrats versus individualised consumers and recognises the potential for common interests. Whether or not coproduction is a radical proposal to improve public services depends on how it is utilised. It can be a bland description of the *status quo* in public services; it can be a legitimation for cost-cutting, stigmatisation of users and the substitution of self help for state action. To be a radical and progressive model of public service reform coproduction needs to be part of a broader programme of service remodelling. It needs to run alongside a commitment to the importance of public services for collective purposes as well as to meet the needs of users. This steers us towards the collective variant of coproduction and away from the state-less model that risks blaming people for their failure to be empowered.

Avoiding nostalgia in public service reform remains important. There was no prior tradition of active civic involvement in public services that is now in peril because of the triumph of the consumer. The post-war welfare state's discourses of solidarity and citizenship are important but they do not provide a toolkit of how to involve and empower users. Nor, as Clarke puts it, should one, 'romanticise the persistence of the public realm – it remains selective, unequal, differentiating, constraining and oppressive in many ways' (2004, p. 44). However it is vital to be alert to the way that narratives of consumerism close down alternative conceptions of public services, and justify patterns of ownership and delivery that disconnect public services from the public realm and the practice of citizenship.

Consumer-oriented public services may be attractive when compared with a passive clientelism in which people take what they are given from the state and are grateful for it, but this comparison is misleading.

If compared to coproductive relationships between service users and providers, consumerist approaches look narrow and one-sided. T.H. Marshall described societies as creating 'an image of an ideal citizenship against which achievement can be measured and towards which aspiration can be directed' (Marshall, 1992, p. 18). If New Labour discourses are measured against active, political and participatory narratives of citizenship they look meagre. If government aspirations of public service reform amount to no more than a desire to satisfy consumers, public services have lost their political core.

Appendix 1 – Content Analysis

Valid and reliable content analysis requires a full account of how searches were undertaken. This section explains how the texts were coded and how the keyword searches were designed.

Document coding

The sentence was used as the unit of analysis across all the documents. Sentences are 'the basic unit of meaning' in language (Budge *et al*, 2001: 217) and since they are separated out by full stops they are easier than parts of sentences or full paragraphs to identify consistently within and across documents by the coder and the computer software. Looking at sentences rather than words helps to deal with the problem of what Ray calls 'context dependence', whereby 'the meaning of a word will be altered by the presence or absence of other words...' (Ray, 2001, p. 152).

Blair's speeches were coded by policy area to allow disaggregation and comparison of the public service text units. A dictionary of policy categories was developed inductively by reading through the speeches to extract key themes. The speeches were then coded using the dictionary as a codebook, as shown in Box A.1.

Keywords such as 'health' and 'education' were used as a guide to coding, but the author was sensitive to context in assigning each sentence to a particular code. Each text unit was only coded once, according to its main theme, to facilitate comparison and analysis, as recommended by content analysts (Weber, 1990, p. 21; Neuendorf, 2002, p. 119). Since some sentences contained more than one theme, Weber's guidance on good practice in other coding dictionaries was followed: '...if an entry can be classified under more than one category it is classified in the category that seems most appropriate – most of the time – for most texts' (1990, p. 34).

Keyword searches

All the texts were searched to test the frequency of the service and non-service conditional and narrative keywords. Computer software was used for the counts to minimise problems of reliability. As Bara and Budge point out, 'Computers will always apply the same procedures to the same text in the same way' (2001, p. 13). In undertaking the word counts for the 16 terms, word roots were used, allowing a range of suffixes. Where necessary categories had be merged following two searches (e.g. choice and choose; respond and responsive). The search function in N6 counted the number of text units (sentences) in which the words occurred, rather than counting the overall number of hits. Although some hits may have been missed as a result (if a word was used twice in a sentence), the text unit search allowed thematic searching by service area which

Box A.1   Coding dictionary

Sentences in Blair's speeches were given one code, based on the dominant theme, selected from the following:

1. **Public services**

   1.1. **General** (text units covering more than one public service; public services in general; or services that do not fit into the categories below)

   1.2. **Education** (covering primary, secondary, FE, universities, skills, lifelong learning, pupils, students, teachers, teaching, GCSE, A-levels, degrees, class sizes, classrooms)

   1.3. **Health** (including NHS, hospitals, hospital departments, patients, doctors, GPs, consultants, nurses, other medical professionals, treatment, medical ailments, waiting lists)

   1.4. **Welfare** (including social care, social services, poverty, social exclusion, welfare, benefits, tax credits, New Deal, minimum wage, labour market, work, jobs, unemployment, pensions, child-care, housing)

   1.5. **Transport** (covering transport, trains, rail, buses, cars, bicycles, Tube, trams, congestion, speed, roads, motorways, passengers, cyclists, drivers)

   1.6. **Law and order** (including references to law and order, crime, types of crime, drugs, disorder, safety, police, prisons, jail, courts, law enforcement, anti-social behaviour, criminals, offenders, magistrates, prosecution, weapons and types of weapon, parole, probation, sentences)

2. **Europe and foreign affairs.** Text relating to the European Union (including Council of Europe, Presidency of Europe, European Court of Human Rights, Euro, single currency, EMU, single market, Common Agricultural Policy, expansion, Social Chapter, Constitution), defence and security (including Kosovo, Slobodan Milosevic, terrorism, Iraq, Saddam Hussein, Weapons of Mass Destruction, 9/11, Cold War, NATO, nuclear weapons, Sierra Leone), international development (including aid, AIDS and malaria prevention, debt relief), Britain's relationships with other states (including human rights abroad), international financial organisations (including G8, GATT, World Trade Organisation), cross-border crime (e.g. drugs), world history, the Commonwealth.

Box A.1   Coding dictionary – *continued*

3. **Constitution**. Entries relating to the civil service, devolution, human rights (domestic), Northern Ireland, multiculturalism, racism, Freedom of Information, monarchy, local government reform, House of Lords, immigration.

4. **Government-citizen relationship.** Indicates text units relating to role and expectations of government and citizen (e.g. rights and responsibilities), social change, political change, New Labour political project (including Third Way), internal party reform, trust, values, political culture, balance between state and private sector, modernisation, leadership, political history, ideology, ethics.

5. **Economy, industry and technology**. References to domestic economic matters (including tax, interest rates, exchange rates, Bank of England, budget, debt, surplus, inflation, industry, enterprise, competitiveness, productivity, small and medium enterprises, Confederation of British Industry, trade unions, Millennium Bug, regional development, inward investment and foreign trade, e-commerce, imports and exports, financial regulation) and energy; also science and technology (including the internet, mobile phones, biotechnology).

6. **Environment and agriculture.** Including the environment, sustainability, conservation, ecology, climate change, Kyoto, Rio, greenhouse gases, alternative energies, farming, food, BSE, food and mouth disease, waste.

7. **Culture, media and sport.** References to sports, individually and collectively, sporting events, Millennium celebrations, Millennium Dome, art, libraries, museums, fashion, theatre, music, newspapers, television, websites.

---

would not otherwise have been possible. Since the same method was used for all documents, the approach did not affect the comparability of the data.

Having generated the raw counts, rogue hits needed to be removed. Keyword-in-context (KWIC) lists were generated, showing the full sentence in which the term was used, to facilitate the identification of non-relevant usage of the terms. Removals were kept to a minimum to maximise the replicability of the findings. Inappropriate homographs, non-relevant suffixes and negatives were removed, including pupil as in part of the eye, patient as in willing to wait, right to mean correct, and the verb to target which has a different meaning to the noun and was not taken here to be indicative of standardisation. Non-relevant suffixes such as patiently, informal, targeted and targeting were also removed.

Two other sets of adjustment were considered but rejected to retain data reliability. First, it was necessary to decide whether or not to include the use of keywords as adjectives as well as nouns, for example 'customer service' or 'community centres'. It was decided to retain such hits since the choice of adjectives by policy actors was an indicator of the meaning and relative importance of the terminology. Second, it was considered whether to include hits from the contents page, index, header and footers since their purpose was only to flag up the use of the terminology elsewhere in the documents. However, it was decided that the use of terms in these contexts was a signal of their perceived importance, and that therefore such occurrences should be counted. The only exception to this was if the keyword was in a table that went over a page break and was therefore simply repeated as a column heading. Here the word was only counted once.

Although steps were taken during the process to ensure that coding and exclusions were done consistently, it is important to undertake additional reliability checks. Since all the research was done by a single author, the best available reliability test was for the author to recode the text units six months after the first coding, as a test of 'stability' (Weber, 1990, p. 17). Following Agasoster, five per cent of the speeches and documents were recoded six months after the original coding, and the total share of deviations was calculated: 'the share of content coded as category x the first time compared to the second time' (Agasoster, 2001, p. 87). N6 provides a function for testing inter-coder reliability, comparing text coded at different nodes, and this was used to test how far the sample data was coded in the same way at the later period. Overall, 93 per cent of units were coded the same between the first and second coding periods. Agasoster notes, although 'There is no absolute standards for what level of deviations should be accepted as reasonable...[r]esults with between 90 and 100 per cent correspondence are regarded as very good' (2001, p. 88).

The documents differed in length from short speeches to long policy documents. In the text findings are reported as a proportion of the text units in that document, facilitating comparison between longer and shorter documents. However, even by using text unit percentages to facilitate comparison, it is not possible to avoid entirely the problem of 'structural zeros' in short documents. As Volkens puts it in relation to analysis of party manifestos: 'If a party does not mention a specific issue, one can assume the saliency of the issue to be low. But one cannot assume the party is totally side-stepping it to the extent it would be with a longer programme' (2001, p. 102). Although caution is required with the short documents, the approach taken here generally assumed that 'higher relative counts (proportions, percentages or ranks) reflect higher concern with the category' (Weber, 1990, p. 56).

Appendix 2 – Interviews

Four anonymous civil servants, and 28 anonymous local authority officers and councillors were interviewed by the author, along with the following experts on aspects of the research:

- Mark Bunting, Research Manager, Opinion Leader Research (interviewed on 19 May 1999)
- Jane Steele, Head of Research, Public Management Foundation (interviewed on 19 May 1999)
- Sarah Hogg, former head of the Downing Street Policy Unit (interviewed on 8 March 2000)
- David Willetts, former Conservative minister (interviewed on 28 June 2000)
- Frank Dobson, former Labour minister (interviewed on 12 March 2003)
- David Hunt, former Conservative minister (interviewed on 9 June 2003)

The design of the interviews drew on the findings of Aberbach and Rockman about the best way to interview elite respondents (2002, p. 674). Interviews were face-to-face or by telephone, and were based on a semi-structured topic guide with open-ended questions, allowing flexibility in question ordering and responses. Except in the case of the expert interviews, interviewees were granted anonymity so that they did not feel that their comments could be traced back to them, encouraging frank responses. The problems of using interviews as a data source were recognised, including interviewer bias; question bias and informant bias (Brenner, 1985, pp. 157–8). The use of non-leading questions and the avoidance of questions that asked respondents to report particularly desirable or undesirable characteristics minimised this form of bias, although cannot remove it entirely (Benney and Hughes, 1984, p. 220).

Appendix 3 – Extended Versions of Tables

Table A.1 The three narratives by service area in the command papers – extended version of Table 7.4

Document	Text Units	Right (%)	Acc (%)	Inf (%)	Stand (%)	Tar (%)	Con (%)	Sub (%)	Cho (%)	Indiv (%)	Pers (%)	R'pond (%)	Div (%)	Tail (%)	Sub (%)	Opp (%)	Eng (%)	Inv (%)	Emp (%)	Part (%)	Resp (%)	Sub (%)	Total (%)
Excellence in Schools	1,349	3 (0.2%)	9 (0.7%)	43 (3.2%)	131 (9.7%)	46 (3.4%)	1 (0.1%)	233 (17.3%)	8 (0.6%)	21 (1.6%)	0 (0.0%)	4 (0.3%)	6 (0.4%)	0 (0.0%)	39 (2.9%)	28 (2.1%)	2 (0.1%)	23 (1.7%)	0 (0.0%)	4 (0.3%)	23 (1.7%)	80 (5.9%)	352 (26.1%)
Schools Achieving Success	1,327	5 (0.4%)	12 (0.9%)	23 (1.7%)	119 (9.0%)	41 (3.1%)	0 (0.0%)	200 (15.1%)	15 (1.1%)	44 (3.3%)	4 (0.3%)	12 (0.9%)	29 (2.2%)	4 (0.3%)	108 (8.1%)	63 (4.7%)	4 (0.3%)	17 (1.3%)	0 (0.0%)	11 (0.8%)	30 (2.3%)	125 (9.4%)	433 (32.6%)
Future of Higher Education	1,384	4 (0.3%)	75 (5.4%)	25 (1.8%)	61 (4.4%)	5 (0.4%)	0 (0.0%)	170 (12.3%)	27 (2.0%)	39 (2.8%)	8 (0.6%)	13 (0.9%)	11 (0.8%)	2 (0.1%)	100 (7.2%)	26 (1.9%)	11 (0.8%)	15 (1.1%)	1 (0.1%)	27 (2.0%)	7 (0.5%)	87 (6.3%)	357 (25.8%)
Children and Learners	2,474	9 (0.4%)	40 (1.6%)	44 (1.8%)	77 (3.1%)	22 (0.9%)	1 (0.0%)	193 (7.8%)	112 (4.5%)	43 (1.7%)	60 (2.4%)	24 (1.0%)	21 (0.8%)	13 (0.5%)	273 (11.0%)	79 (3.2%)	36 (1.5%)	37 (1.5%)	2 (0.1%)	26 (1.1%)	32 (1.3%)	212 (8.6%)	678 (27.4%)
Higher Standards	1,743 (4.1%)	29 (1.7%)	79 (4.5%)	78 (4.0%)	78 (4.5%)	16 (0.9%)	0 (0.0%)	271 (15.5%)	106 (6.1%)	36 (2.1%)	26 (1.5%)	26 (1.5%)	30 (1.7%)	36 (2.1%)	260 (14.9%)	66 (3.8%)	39 (2.2%)	40 (2.3%)	4 (0.2%)	10 (0.6%)	33 (1.9%)	192 (11.0%)	723 (41.5%)
Subtotal	**8,277**	**50 (0.6%)**	**215 (2.6%)**	**204 (2.5%)**	**466 (5.6%)**	**130 (1.6%)**	**2 (0.0%)**	**1067 (12.9%)**	**268 (3.2%)**	**183 (2.2%)**	**98 (1.2%)**	**79 (1.0%)**	**97 (1.2%)**	**55 (0.7%)**	**780 (9.4%)**	**262 (3.2%)**	**92 (1.1%)**	**132 (1.6%)**	**7 (0.1%)**	**78 (0.9%)**	**125 (1.5%)**	**696 (8.4%)**	**2543 (30.7%)**
The New NHS	1,486	3 (0.2%)	38 (2.6%)	33 (2.2%)	42 (2.8%)	22 (1.5%)	0 (0.0%)	138 (9.3%)	7 (0.5%)	25 (1.7%)	8 (0.5%)	19 (1.3%)	0 (0.0%)	1 (0.1%)	60 (4.0%)	13 (0.9%)	3 (0.2%)	28 (1.9%)	1 (0.1%)	7 (0.5%)	66 (4.4%)	118 (7.9%)	316 (21.3%)
Saving Lives	1,938	1 (0.1%)	36 (1.9%)	61 (3.1%)	51 (2.6%)	70 (3.6%)	0 (0.0%)	219 (11.3%)	4 (0.2%)	70 (3.6%)	19 (1.0%)	5 (0.3%)	6 (0.3%)	3 (0.2%)	107 (5.5%)	30 (1.5%)	4 (0.2%)	23 (1.2%)	2 (0.1%)	10 (0.5%)	39 (2.0%)	108 (5.6%)	434 (22.4%)
The NHS Plan	2,012	19 (0.9%)	72 (3.6%)	51 (2.5%)	92 (4.6%)	44 (2.2%)	20 (1.0%)	298 (14.8%)	28 (1.4%)	44 (2.2%)	39 (1.9%)	30 (1.5%)	4 (0.2%)	6 (0.3%)	151 (7.5%)	18 (0.9%)	4 (0.2%)	22 (1.1%)	4 (0.2%)	5 (0.2%)	19 (0.9%)	72 (3.6%)	521 (25.9%)
The NHS Improvement Plan	1,344	9 (0.7%)	73 (5.4%)	67 (5.0%)	48 (3.6%)	26 (1.9%)	0 (0.0%)	223 (16.6%)	109 (8.1%)	26 (1.9%)	67 (5.0%)	37 (2.8%)	16 (1.2%)	10 (0.7%)	265 (19.7%)	11 (0.8%)	12 (0.9%)	14 (1.0%)	21 (1.6%)	1 (0.1%)	21 (1.6%)	80 (6.0%)	568 (42.3%)
Choosing Health	3,365	8 (0.2%)	140 (4.2%)	204 (6.1%)	72 (2.1%)	70 (2.1%)	16 (0.5%)	510 (15.2%)	314 (9.3%)	121 (3.6%)	67 (2.0%)	33 (1.0%)	7 (0.2%)	14 (0.4%)	556 (16.5%)	131 (3.9%)	50 (1.5%)	46 (1.4%)	11 (0.3%)	25 (0.7%)	75 (2.2%)	338 (10.0%)	1404 (41.7%)
Subtotal	**10,145**	**40 (0.4%)**	**359 (3.5%)**	**416 (4.1%)**	**305 (3.0%)**	**232 (2.3%)**	**36 (0.4%)**	**1388 (13.7%)**	**462 (4.6%)**	**286 (2.8%)**	**200 (2.0%)**	**124 (1.2%)**	**33 (0.3%)**	**34 (0.3%)**	**1139 (11.2%)**	**203 (2.0%)**	**73 (0.7%)**	**133 (1.3%)**	**39 (0.4%)**	**48 (0.5%)**	**220 (2.2%)**	**716 (7.1%)**	**3243 (32.0%)**
New Ambitions	1,669	19 (1.1%)	30 (1.8%)	25 (1.5%)	16 (1.0%)	5 (0.3%)	2 (0.1%)	97 (5.8%)	8 (0.5%)	48 (2.9%)	30 (1.8%)	4 (0.2%)	0 (0.0%)	11 (0.7%)	101 (6.1%)	43 (2.6%)	2 (0.1%)	2 (0.1%)	3 (0.2%)	5 (0.3%)	25 (1.5%)	55 (3.3%)	253 (15.2%)

Table A.1 The three narratives by service area in the command papers – extended version of Table 7.4 – *continued*

Document	Text Units	Right (%)	Acc (%)	Inf (%)	Stand (%)	Tar (%)	Con (%)	Sub (%)	Cho (%)	Indiv (%)	Pers (%)	R'pond (%)	Div (%)	Tail (%)	Sub (%)	Opp (%)	Eng (%)	Inv (%)	Emp (%)	Part (%)	Resp (%)	Sub (%)	Total (%)
Modernising Social Services	1,857	15 (0.8%)	40 (2.2%)	42 (2.3%)	113 (6.1%)	23 (1.2%)	10 (0.5%)	243 (13.1%)	15 (0.8%)	60 (3.2%)	11 (0.6%)	16 (0.9%)	4 (0.2%)	4 (0.2%)	110 (5.9%)	25 (1.3%)	2 (0.1%)	26 (1.4%)	4 (0.2%)	8 (0.4%)	77 (4.1%)	142 (7.6%)	495 (26.7%)
Valuing People	2,023	25 (1.2%)	100 (4.9%)	58 (2.9%)	25 (1.2%)	34 (1.7%)	4 (0.2%)	246 (12.2%)	72 (3.6%)	62 (3.1%)	17 (0.8%)	13 (0.6%)	2 (0.1%)	4 (0.2%)	170 (8.4%)	65 (3.2%)	3 (0.1%)	44 (2.2%)	0 (0.0%)	21 (1.0%)	37 (1.8%)	170 (8.4%)	586 (29.0%)
Independence, Well-being	1,492	7 (0.5%)	52 (3.5%)	37 (2.5%)	2 (0.1%)	7 (0.5%)	0 (0.0%)	105 (7.0%)	128 (8.6%)	143 (9.6%)	21 (1.4%)	14 (0.9%)	19 (1.3%)	4 (0.3%)	329 (22.1%)	37 (2.5%)	8 (0.5%)	27 (1.8%)	9 (0.6%)	10 (0.7%)	37 (2.5%)	128 (8.6%)	562 (37.7%)
Opportunity and Security	1,966	56 (2.8%)	35 (1.8%)	51 (2.6%)	11 (0.6%)	21 (1.1%)	1 (0.1%)	175 (8.9%)	39 (2.0%)	75 (3.8%)	24 (1.2%)	7 (0.4%)	15 (0.8%)	33 (1.7%)	193 (9.8%)	69 (3.5%)	26 (1.3%)	10 (0.5%)	12 (0.6%)	9 (0.5%)	46 (2.3%)	172 (8.7%)	540 (27.5%)
Subtotal	9,007	122 (1.4%)	257 (2.9%)	213 (2.4%)	167 (1.9%)	90 (1.0%)	17 (0.2%)	866 (9.6%)	262 (2.9%)	388 (4.3%)	103 (1.1%)	54 (0.6%)	40 (0.4%)	56 (0.6%)	903 (10.0%)	239 (2.7%)	41 (0.5%)	109 (1.2%)	28 (0.3%)	53 (0.6%)	222 (2.5%)	692 (7.7%)	2,461 (27.3%)
Tackling Drugs	597	0 (0.0%)	20 (1.7%)	20 (3.4%)	0 (0.0%)	16 (2.7%)	0 (0.0%)	46 (7.7%)	0 (0.0%)	15 (2.5%)	4 (0.7%)	1 (0.2%)	1 (0.2%)	0 (0.0%)	21 (3.5%)	5 (0.8%)	8 (1.3%)	8 (1.3%)	0 (0.0%)	3 (0.5%)	16 (2.7%)	40 (6.7%)	107 (17.9%)
Justice for All	2,700	56 (2.1%)	41 (1.5%)	132 (4.9%)	41 (1.5%)	29 (1.1%)	7 (0.3%)	306 (11.3%)	7 (0.3%)	49 (1.8%)	24 (0.9%)	20 (0.7%)	9 (0.3%)	8 (0.3%)	117 (4.3%)	33 (1.2%)	33 (1.2%)	76 (2.8%)	1 (0.0%)	6 (0.2%)	81 (3.0%)	230 (8.5%)	653 (24.2%)
Respect and Responsibility	1,251	15 (1.2%)	17 (1.4%)	26 (2.1%)	33 (2.6%)	14 (1.1%)	0 (0.0%)	105 (8.4%)	1 (0.1%)	47 (3.8%)	8 (0.6%)	11 (0.9%)	4 (0.3%)	5 (0.4%)	76 (6.1%)	6 (0.5%)	6 (0.5%)	22 (1.8%)	10 (0.8%)	4 (0.3%)	106 (8.5%)	154 (12.3%)	335 (26.8%)
Building Communities	2,175	11 (0.5%)	39 (1.8%)	83 (3.8%)	109 (5.0%)	32 (1.5%)	0 (0.0%)	274 (12.6%)	9 (0.4%)	49 (2.3%)	13 (0.6%)	109 (5.0%)	28 (1.3%)	5 (0.2%)	213 (9.8%)	38 (1.7%)	93 (4.3%)	56 (2.6%)	23 (1.1%)	15 (0.7%)	92 (4.2%)	317 (14.6%)	804 (37.0%)
Protecting the Public	550	2 (0.4%)	3 (0.5%)	13 (2.0%)	13 (2.4%)	5 (0.9%)	0 (0.0%)	34 (6.2%)	2 (0.4%)	7 (1.3%)	4 (0.7%)	6 (1.1%)	0 (0.0%)	3 (0.5%)	22 (4.0%)	7 (1.3%)	2 (0.4%)	8 (1.5%)	0 (0.0%)	0 (0.0%)	10 (1.8%)	27 (4.9%)	83 (15.1%)
Subtotal	7,273	84 (1.2%)	110 (1.5%)	272 (3.7%)	196 (2.7%)	96 (1.3%)	7 (0.1%)	765 (10.5%)	19 (0.3%)	167 (2.3%)	53 (0.7%)	141 (1.9%)	48 (0.7%)	21 (0.3%)	449 (6.2%)	89 (1.2%)	142 (2.0%)	170 (2.3%)	34 (0.5%)	28 (0.4%)	305 (4.2%)	768 (10.6%)	1,982 (27.3%)
A New Deal for Transport	2,668	5 (0.2%)	109 (4.1%)	98 (3.7%)	82 (3.1%)	74 (2.8%)	14 (0.5%)	382 (14.3%)	50 (1.9%)	34 (1.3%)	18 (0.7%)	16 (0.6%)	12 (0.4%)	1 (0.0%)	131 (4.9%)	41 (1.5%)	0 (0.0%)	37 (1.4%)	1 (0.0%)	10 (0.4%)	47 (1.8%)	136 (5.1%)	649 (24.3%)
Ten Year Transport Plan	1,429	1 (0.1%)	59 (4.1%)	35 (2.4%)	25 (1.7%)	38 (2.7%)	3 (0.2%)	161 (11.3%)	29 (2.0%)	6 (0.4%)	5 (0.3%)	2 (0.1%)	4 (0.3%)	1 (0.1%)	47 (3.3%)	6 (0.4%)	0 (0.0%)	7 (0.5%)	1 (0.1%)	0 (0.0%)	3 (0.2%)	17 (1.2%)	225 (15.7%)
The Future of Transport	1,512	7 (0.5%)	58 (3.8%)	47 (3.1%)	43 (2.8%)	25 (1.7%)	5 (0.3%)	185 (12.2%)	62 (4.1%)	14 (0.9%)	17 (1.1%)	17 (1.1%)	6 (0.4%)	4 (0.3%)	116 (7.7%)	13 (0.9%)	8 (0.5%)	21 (1.4%)	0 (0.0%)	1 (0.1%)	33 (2.2%)	76 (5.0%)	377 (24.9%)
Subtotal	5,609	13 (0.2%)	226 (4.0%)	180 (3.2%)	150 (2.7%)	137 (2.4%)	22 (0.4%)	728 (13.0%)	141 (2.5%)	54 (1.0%)	36 (0.6%)	35 (0.6%)	22 (0.4%)	6 (0.1%)	294 (5.2%)	60 (1.1%)	8 (0.1%)	65 (1.2%)	2 (0.0%)	11 (0.2%)	83 (1.5%)	229 (4.1%)	1,251 (22.3%)
Quality and Choice	1,026	6 (0.6%)	9 (0.9%)	15 (1.5%)	42 (4.1%)	19 (1.9%)	0 (0.0%)	91 (8.9%)	88 (8.6%)	14 (1.4%)	0 (0.0%)	42 (4.1%)	5 (0.5%)	2 (0.2%)	151 (14.7%)	18 (1.8%)	2 (0.2%)	16 (1.6%)	3 (0.3%)	12 (1.2%)	0 (0.0%)	51 (5.0%)	293 (28.6%)
Sustainable Communities	1,170	24 (2.1%)	26 (2.2%)	18 (1.5%)	43 (3.7%)	18 (1.5%)	1 (0.1%)	130 (11.1%)	66 (5.6%)	6 (0.5%)	1 (0.1%)	12 (1.0%)	12 (1.0%)	0 (0.0%)	97 (8.3%)	52 (4.4%)	5 (0.4%)	15 (1.3%)	2 (0.2%)	4 (0.3%)	23 (2.0%)	101 (8.6%)	328 (28.0%)
Subtotal	2,196	30 (1.4%)	35 (1.6%)	33 (1.5%)	85 (3.9%)	37 (1.7%)	1 (0.0%)	221 (10.1%)	154 (7.0%)	20 (0.9%)	1 (0.0%)	54 (2.5%)	17 (0.8%)	2 (0.1%)	248 (11.3%)	70 (3.2%)	7 (0.3%)	31 (1.4%)	5 (0.2%)	16 (0.7%)	23 (1.0%)	152 (6.9%)	621 (28.3%)
Total	42,507	339 (0.8%)	1,202 (2.8%)	1,318 (3.1%)	1,369 (3.2%)	722 (1.7%)	85 (0.2%)	5,035 (11.8%)	1,306 (3.1%)	1,098 (2.6%)	491 (1.2%)	487 (1.1%)	257 (0.6%)	174 (0.4%)	3,813 (9.0%)	923 (2.2%)	363 (0.9%)	640 (1.5%)	115 (0.3%)	234 (0.6%)	978 (2.3%)	3,253 (7.7%)	12,101 (28.5%)

Percentages show keyword usage as a proportion of total text units, i.e. sentences, for each document.

Table A.2 The three narratives over time in the command papers – extended version of Table 7.5

Document	Text Units	Right (%)	Access (%)	Inform (%)	Stand (%)	Target (%)	Conven (%)	Sub (%)	Choice (%)	Indiv (%)	Pers (%)	R'pond (%)	Div (%)	Tail (%)	Sub (%)	Opp (%)	Eng (%)	Inv (%)	Emp (%)	Part (%)	Resp (%)	Sub (%)	Total (%)
First term																							
Excellence in Schools	1,349	3 (0.2%)	9 (0.7%)	43 (3.2%)	131 (9.7%)	46 (3.4%)	1 (0.1%)	233 (17.3%)	8 (0.6%)	21 (1.6%)	0 (0.0%)	4 (0.3%)	6 (0.4%)	0 (0.0%)	39 (2.9%)	28 (2.1%)	2 (0.1%)	23 (1.7%)	0 (0.0%)	4 (0.3%)	23 (1.7%)	80 (5.9%)	352 (26.1%)
The New NHS	1,486	3 (0.2%)	38 (2.6%)	33 (2.2%)	42 (2.8%)	22 (1.5%)	0 (0.0%)	138 (9.3%)	7 (0.5%)	25 (1.7%)	8 (0.5%)	19 (1.3%)	0 (0.0%)	1 (0.1%)	60 (4.0%)	13 (0.9%)	3 (0.2%)	28 (1.9%)	1 (0.1%)	7 (0.5%)	66 (4.4%)	118 (7.9%)	316 (21.3%)
New Ambitions for Our Country	1,669	19 (1.1%)	30 (1.8%)	25 (1.5%)	16 (1.0%)	5 (0.3%)	2 (0.1%)	97 (5.8%)	8 (0.5%)	48 (2.9%)	30 (1.8%)	4 (0.2%)	0 (0.0%)	11 (0.7%)	101 (6.1%)	43 (2.6%)	2 (0.1%)	2 (0.1%)	3 (0.2%)	5 (0.3%)	25 (1.5%)	55 (3.3%)	253 (15.2%)
Tackling Drugs	597	0 (0.0%)	10 (1.7%)	20 (3.4%)	0 (0.0%)	16 (2.7%)	0 (0.0%)	46 (7.7%)	0 (0.0%)	15 (2.5%)	4 (0.7%)	1 (0.2%)	1 (0.2%)	0 (0.0%)	21 (3.5%)	5 (0.8%)	8 (1.3%)	8 (1.3%)	0 (0.0%)	3 (0.5%)	16 (2.7%)	40 (6.7%)	107 (17.9%)
A New Deal for Transport	2,668	5 (0.2%)	109 (4.1%)	98 (3.7%)	82 (3.1%)	74 (2.8%)	14 (0.5%)	382 (14.3%)	50 (1.9%)	34 (1.3%)	18 (0.7%)	16 (0.6%)	12 (0.4%)	1 (0.0%)	131 (4.9%)	41 (1.5%)	0 (0.0%)	37 (1.4%)	1 (0.0%)	10 (0.4%)	47 (1.8%)	136 (5.1%)	649 (24.3%)
Modernising Social Services	1,857	15 (0.8%)	40 (2.2%)	42 (2.3%)	113 (6.1%)	23 (1.2%)	10 (0.5%)	243 (13.1%)	15 (0.8%)	60 (3.2%)	11 (0.6%)	16 (0.9%)	4 (0.2%)	4 (0.2%)	110 (5.9%)	25 (1.3%)	2 (0.1%)	26 (1.4%)	4 (0.2%)	8 (0.4%)	77 (4.1%)	142 (7.6%)	495 (26.7%)
Saving Lives	1,938	1 (0.1%)	36 (1.9%)	61 (3.1%)	51 (2.6%)	70 (3.6%)	0 (0.0%)	219 (11.3%)	4 (0.2%)	70 (3.6%)	19 (1.0%)	5 (0.3%)	6 (0.3%)	3 (0.2%)	107 (5.5%)	30 (1.5%)	4 (0.2%)	23 (1.2%)	2 (0.1%)	10 (0.5%)	39 (2.0%)	108 (5.6%)	434 (22.4%)
Quality and Choice	1,026	6 (0.6%)	9 (0.9%)	15 (1.5%)	42 (4.1%)	19 (1.9%)	0 (0.0%)	91 (8.9%)	88 (8.6%)	14 (1.4%)	0 (0.0%)	42 (4.1%)	5 (0.5%)	2 (0.2%)	151 (14.7%)	18 (1.8%)	2 (0.2%)	16 (1.6%)	3 (0.3%)	12 (1.2%)	0 (0.0%)	51 (5.0%)	293 (28.6%)
The NHS Plan	2,012	19 (0.9%)	72 (3.6%)	51 (2.5%)	92 (4.6%)	44 (2.2%)	20 (1.0%)	298 (14.8%)	28 (1.4%)	44 (2.2%)	39 (1.9%)	30 (1.5%)	4 (0.2%)	6 (0.3%)	151 (7.5%)	18 (0.9%)	4 (0.2%)	22 (1.1%)	4 (0.2%)	5 (0.2%)	19 (0.9%)	72 (3.6%)	521 (25.9%)
Ten Year Transport Plan	1,429	1 (0.1%)	59 (4.1%)	35 (2.4%)	25 (1.7%)	38 (2.7%)	3 (0.2%)	161 (11.3%)	29 (2.0%)	6 (0.4%)	5 (0.3%)	2 (0.1%)	4 (0.3%)	1 (0.1%)	47 (3.3%)	6 (0.4%)	0 (0.0%)	7 (0.5%)	1 (0.1%)	0 (0.0%)	3 (0.2%)	17 (1.2%)	225 (15.7%)
Valuing People – A New Strategy	2,023	25 (1.2%)	100 (4.9%)	58 (2.9%)	25 (1.2%)	34 (1.7%)	4 (0.2%)	246 (12.2%)	72 (3.6%)	62 (3.1%)	17 (0.8%)	13 (0.6%)	2 (0.1%)	4 (0.2%)	170 (8.4%)	65 (3.2%)	3 (0.2%)	44 (2.2%)	0 (0.0%)	21 (1.0%)	37 (1.8%)	170 (8.4%)	586 (29.0%)
Subtotal	18,054	97 (0.5%)	512 (2.8%)	481 (2.7%)	619 (3.4%)	391 (2.2%)	54 (0.3%)	2,154 (11.9%)	309 (1.7%)	399 (2.2%)	151 (0.8%)	152 (0.8%)	44 (0.2%)	33 (0.2%)	1,088 (6.0%)	292 (1.6%)	30 (0.2%)	236 (1.3%)	19 (0.1%)	85 (0.5%)	352 (1.9%)	989 (5.5%)	4,231 (23.4%)

Table A.2 The three narratives over time in the command papers – extended version of Table 7.5 – *continued*

Document	Text Units	Right (%)	Acc (%)	Inform (%)	Stand (%)	Target (%)	Conven (%)	Sub (%)	Choice (%)	Indiv (%)	Pers (%)	R'pond (%)	Div (%)	Tail (%)	Sub (%)	Opp (%)	Eng (%)	Inv (%)	Emp (%)	Part (%)	Resp (%)	Sub (%)	Total (%)
Second term																							
Schools Achieving Success	1,327	5 (0.4%)	12 (0.9%)	23 (1.7%)	119 (9.0%)	41 (3.1%)	0 (0.0%)	200 (15.1%)	15 (1.1%)	44 (3.3%)	4 (0.3%)	12 (0.9%)	29 (2.2%)	4 (0.3%)	108 (8.1%)	63 (4.7%)	4 (0.3%)	17 (1.3%)	0 (0.0%)	11 (0.8%)	30 (2.3%)	125 (9.4%)	433 (32.6%)
Justice for All	2,700	56 (2.1%)	41 (1.5%)	132 (4.9%)	41 (1.5%)	29 (1.1%)	7 (0.3%)	306 (11.3%)	7 (0.3%)	49 (1.8%)	24 (0.9%)	20 (0.7%)	9 (0.3%)	8 (0.3%)	117 (4.3%)	33 (1.2%)	33 (1.2%)	76 (2.8%)	1 (0.0%)	6 (0.2%)	81 (3.0%)	230 (8.5%)	653 (24.2%)
Future of Higher Education	1,384	4 (0.3%)	75 (5.4%)	25 (1.8%)	61 (4.4%)	5 (0.4%)	0 (0.0%)	170 (12.3%)	27 (2.0%)	39 (2.8%)	8 (0.6%)	13 (0.9%)	11 (0.8%)	2 (0.1%)	100 (7.2%)	26 (1.9%)	11 (0.8%)	15 (1.1%)	1 (0.1%)	27 (2.0%)	7 (0.5%)	87 (6.3%)	357 (25.8%)
Respect and Responsibility	1,251	15 (1.2%)	17 (1.4%)	26 (2.1%)	33 (2.6%)	14 (1.1%)	0 (0.0%)	105 (8.4%)	1 (0.1%)	47 (3.8%)	8 (0.6%)	11 (0.9%)	4 (0.3%)	5 (0.4%)	76 (6.1%)	6 (0.5%)	6 (0.5%)	22 (1.8%)	10 (0.8%)	4 (0.3%)	106 (8.5%)	154 (12.3%)	335 (26.8%)
A Five Year Strategy for Children and Learners	2,474	9 (0.4%)	40 (1.6%)	44 (1.8%)	77 (3.1%)	22 (0.9%)	1 (0.0%)	193 (7.8%)	112 (4.5%)	43 (1.7%)	60 (2.4%)	24 (1.0%)	21 (0.8%)	13 (0.5%)	273 (11.0%)	79 (3.2%)	36 (1.5%)	37 (1.5%)	2 (0.1%)	26 (1.1%)	32 (1.3%)	212 (8.6%)	678 (27.4%)
The NHS Improvement Plan	1,344	9 (0.7%)	73 (5.4%)	67 (5.0%)	48 (3.6%)	26 (1.9%)	0 (0.0%)	223 (16.6%)	109 (8.1%)	26 (1.9%)	67 (5.0%)	37 (2.8%)	16 (1.2%)	10 (0.7%)	265 (19.7%)	11 (0.8%)	12 (0.9%)	14 (1.0%)	21 (1.6%)	1 (0.1%)	21 (1.6%)	80 (6.0%)	568 (42.3%)
Choosing Health	3,365	8 (0.2%)	140 (4.2%)	204 (6.1%)	72 (2.1%)	70 (2.1%)	16 (0.5%)	510 (15.2%)	314 (9.3%)	121 (3.6%)	67 (2.0%)	33 (1.0%)	7 (0.2%)	14 (0.4%)	556 (16.5%)	131 (3.9%)	50 (1.5%)	46 (1.4%)	11 (0.3%)	25 (0.7%)	75 (2.2%)	338 (10.0%)	1,404 (41.7%)
Building Communities	2,175	11 (0.5%)	39 (1.8%)	83 (3.8%)	109 (5.0%)	32 (1.5%)	0 (0.0%)	274 (12.6%)	9 (0.4%)	49 (2.3%)	13 (0.6%)	109 (5.0%)	28 (1.3%)	5 (0.2%)	213 (9.8%)	38 (1.7%)	93 (4.3%)	56 (2.6%)	23 (1.1%)	15 (0.7%)	92 (4.2%)	317 (14.6%)	804 (37.0%)
The Future of Transport	1,512	7 (0.5%)	58 (3.8%)	47 (3.1%)	43 (2.8%)	25 (1.7%)	5 (0.3%)	185 (12.2%)	62 (4.1%)	14 (0.9%)	13 (0.9%)	17 (1.1%)	6 (0.4%)	4 (0.3%)	116 (7.7%)	13 (0.9%)	13 (0.9%)	21 (1.4%)	0 (0.0%)	1 (0.1%)	33 (2.2%)	76 (5.0%)	377 (24.9%)
Sustainable Communities	1,170	24 (2.1%)	26 (2.2%)	18 (1.5%)	43 (3.7%)	18 (1.5%)	1 (0.1%)	130 (11.1%)	66 (5.6%)	6 (0.5%)	1 (0.1%)	12 (1.0%)	12 (1.0%)	0 (0.0%)	97 (8.3%)	52 (4.4%)	5 (0.4%)	15 (1.3%)	2 (0.2%)	4 (0.3%)	23 (2.0%)	101 (8.6%)	328 (28.0%)
Opportunity and Security	1,966	56 (2.8%)	35 (1.8%)	51 (2.6%)	11 (0.6%)	21 (1.1%)	1 (0.1%)	175 (8.9%)	39 (2.0%)	75 (3.8%)	24 (1.2%)	7 (0.4%)	15 (0.8%)	33 (1.7%)	193 (9.8%)	69 (3.5%)	26 (1.3%)	10 (0.5%)	12 (0.6%)	9 (0.5%)	46 (2.3%)	172 (8.7%)	540 (27.5%)
Independence, Well-being and Choice	1,492	7 (0.5%)	52 (3.5%)	37 (2.5%)	2 (0.1%)	7 (0.5%)	0 (0.0%)	105 (7.0%)	128 (8.6%)	143 (9.6%)	21 (1.4%)	14 (0.9%)	19 (1.3%)	4 (0.3%)	329 (22.1%)	37 (2.5%)	8 (0.5%)	27 (1.8%)	9 (0.6%)	10 (0.7%)	37 (2.5%)	128 (8.6%)	562 (37.7%)
Subtotal	22,160	211 (1.0%)	608 (2.7%)	757 (3.4%)	659 (3.0%)	310 (1.4%)	31 (0.1%)	2,576 (11.6%)	889 (4.0%)	656 (3.0%)	310 (1.4%)	309 (1.4%)	177 (0.8%)	102 (0.5%)	2,443 (11.0%)	558 (2.5%)	292 (1.3%)	356 (1.6%)	92 (0.4%)	139 (0.6%)	583 (2.6%)	2,020 (9.1%)	7,039 (31.8%)

Table A.2 The three narratives over time in the command papers – extended version of Table 7.5 – *continued*

Document	Text Units	Right (%)	Acc (%)	Inform (%)	Stand (%)	Target (%)	Conven (%)	Sub (%)	Choice Indiv (%)	Pers (%)	R'pond (%)	Div (%)	Tail (%)	Sub (%)	Opp (%)	Eng (%)	Inv (%)	Emp (%)	Part (%)	Resp (%)	Sub (%)	Total (%)
Third term																						
Higher Standards; Better Schools for All	1,743	29 (1.7%)	79 (4.5%)	69 (4.0%)	78 (4.5%)	16 (0.9%)	0 (0.0%)	271 (15.5%)	106 (6.1%)	26 (1.5%)	26 (1.5%)	30 (1.7%)	36 (2.1%)	260 (14.9%)	66 (3.8%)	39 (2.2%)	40 (2.3%)	4 (0.2%)	10 (0.6%)	33 (1.9%)	192 (11.0%)	723 (41.5%)
Five Year Strategy for Protecting the Public	550	2 (0.4%)	3 (0.5%)	11 (2.0%)	13 (2.4%)	5 (0.9%)	0 (0.0%)	34 (6.2%)	7 (1.3%)	4 (0.7%)	0 (0.0%)	6 (1.1%)	3 (0.5%)	22 (4.0%)	7 (1.3%)	2 (0.4%)	8 (1.5%)	0 (0.0%)	0 (0.0%)	10 (1.8%)	27 (4.9%)	83 (15.1%)
Subtotal	2,293	31 (1.4%)	82 (3.6%)	60 (3.5%)	91 (4.0%)	21 (0.9%)	0 (0.0%)	305 (13.3%)	108 (4.7%)	30 (1.3%)	26 (1.1%)	36 (1.6%)	39 (1.7%)	282 (12.3%)	73 (3.2%)	41 (1.8%)	48 (2.1%)	4 (0.2%)	10 (0.4%)	43 (1.9%)	219 (9.6%)	806 (35.2%)
Total	42,507	339 (0.8%)	1,202 (2.8%)	1,318 (3.1%)	1,369 (3.2%)	722 (1.7%)	85 (0.2%)	5,035 (11.8%)	1,306 (3.1%)	491 (1.2%)	487 (1.1%)	257 (0.6%)	174 (0.4%)	3,813 (9.0%)	923 (2.2%)	363 (0.9%)	640 (1.5%)	115 (0.3%)	234 (0.6%)	978 (2.3%)	3,253 (7.7%)	12,101 (28.5%)

Percentages show keyword usage as a proportion of total text units, i.e. sentences, for each document.

Table A.3 The three narratives in the corporate plans – extended version of Table 8.5

Council	Text Units	Right (%)	Access (%)	Inform (%)	Stand (%)	Target (%)	Con (%)	Sub (%)	Choice (%)	Indiv (%)	Pers (%)	R'pond (%)	Diverse (%)	Tail (%)	Sub (%)	Opp (%)	Eng (%)	Inv (%)	Emp (%)	Part (%)	Resp (%)	Sub (%)	Total (%)
1. Borough, EEM, Con	399	1 (0.3%)	18 (4.5%)	19 (4.8%)	13 (3.3%)	34 (8.5%)	0 (0.0%)	85 (21.3%)	4 (1.0%)	1 (0.3%)	0 (0.0%)	1 (0.3%)	15 (3.8%)	0 (0.0%)	21 (5.3%)	8 (2.0%)	8 (2.0%)	4 (1.0%)	1 (0.3%)	3 (0.8%)	5 (1.3%)	29 (7.3%)	135 (33.8%)
2. Borough, NW, Con	493	0 (0.0%)	26 (5.3%)	41 (8.3%)	13 (2.6%)	40 (8.1%)	0 (0.0%)	120 (24.3%)	3 (0.6%)	3 (0.6%)	1 (0.2%)	5 (1.0%)	2 (0.4%)	0 (0.0%)	14 (2.8%)	3 (0.6%)	7 (1.4%)	2 (0.4%)	0 (0.0%)	3 (0.6%)	2 (0.4%)	17 (3.4%)	151 (30.6%)
3. Borough, SE, Con	384	0 (0.0%)	23 (6.0%)	8 (2.1%)	22 (5.7%)	27 (7.0%)	0 (0.0%)	80 (20.8%)	6 (1.6%)	1 (0.3%)	0 (0.0%)	1 (0.3%)	4 (1.0%)	0 (0.0%)	12 (3.1%)	9 (2.3%)	6 (1.6%)	5 (1.3%)	0 (0.0%)	6 (1.6%)	31 (8.1%)	57 (14.8%)	149 (38.8%)
4. District, WM, Lab	117	0 (0.0%)	6 (5.1%)	1 (0.9%)	2 (1.7%)	13 (11.1%)	0 (0.0%)	22 (18.8%)	0 (0.0%)	0 (0.0%)	0 (0.0%)	0 (0.0%)	2 (1.7%)	0 (0.0%)	2 (1.7%)	5 (4.3%)	0 (0.0%)	3 (2.6%)	0 (0.0%)	0 (0.0%)	3 (2.6%)	11 (9.4%)	35 (29.9%)
5. District, SW, Con	1,075	1 (0.1%)	13 (1.2%)	45 (4.2%)	17 (1.6%)	38 (3.5%)	0 (0.0%)	114 (10.6%)	4 (0.4%)	2 (0.2%)	0 (0.0%)	3 (0.3%)	4 (0.4%)	2 (0.2%)	15 (1.4%)	12 (1.1%)	19 (1.8%)	6 (0.6%)	0 (0.0%)	5 (0.5%)	6 (0.6%)	48 (4.5%)	177 (16.5%)
6. District, NW, LD	534	0 (0.0%)	14 (2.6%)	6 (1.1%)	4 (0.7%)	33 (6.2%)	0 (0.0%)	57 (10.7%)	0 (0.0%)	1 (0.2%)	0 (0.0%)	3 (0.6%)	15 (2.8%)	0 (0.0%)	19 (3.6%)	6 (1.1%)	5 (0.9%)	1 (0.2%)	1 (0.2%)	2 (0.4%)	2 (0.4%)	17 (3.2%)	93 (17.4%)
7. District, SW, NOC	1,246	2 (0.2%)	2 (0.2%)	4 (0.3%)	27 (2.2%)	6 (0.5%)	0 (0.0%)	41 (3.3%)	0 (0.0%)	0 (0.0%)	0 (0.0%)	4 (0.3%)	0 (0.0%)	0 (0.0%)	4 (0.3%)	0 (0.0%)	0 (0.0%)	4 (0.3%)	0 (0.0%)	3 (0.2%)	1 (0.1%)	8 (0.6%)	53 (4.3%)
8. District, SE, NOC	747	3 (0.4%)	18 (2.4%)	37 (5.0%)	22 (2.9%)	42 (5.6%)	0 (0.0%)	122 (16.3%)	2 (0.3%)	2 (0.3%)	0 (0.0%)	22 (2.9%)	8 (1.1%)	0 (0.0%)	34 (4.6%)	18 (2.4%)	7 (0.9%)	0 (0.0%)	3 (0.4%)	3 (0.4%)	19 (2.5%)	50 (6.7%)	206 (27.6%)
9. County, EEM, Con	1,953	1 (0.1%)	40 (2.0%)	34 (1.7%)	32 (1.6%)	46 (2.4%)	0 (0.0%)	153 (7.8%)	1 (0.1%)	2 (0.1%)	0 (0.0%)	3 (0.2%)	0 (0.0%)	0 (0.0%)	6 (0.3%)	23 (1.2%)	13 (0.7%)	3 (0.2%)	0 (0.0%)	1 (0.1%)	19 (1.0%)	59 (3.0%)	218 (11.2%)
10. County, SE, Con	383	3 (0.8%)	2 (0.5%)	15 (3.9%)	10 (2.6%)	12 (3.1%)	1 (0.3%)	43 (11.2%)	4 (1.0%)	1 (0.3%)	2 (0.5%)	3 (0.8%)	1 (0.3%)	0 (0.0%)	11 (2.9%)	12 (3.1%)	1 (0.3%)	3 (0.8%)	0 (0.0%)	2 (0.5%)	5 (1.3%)	23 (6.0%)	77 (20.1%)
11. County, WM, Lab	385	1 (0.3%)	23 (6.0%)	8 (2.1%)	1 (0.3%)	9 (2.3%)	1 (0.3%)	43 (11.2%)	11 (2.9%)	2 (0.5%)	1 (0.3%)	12 (3.1%)	7 (1.8%)	0 (0.0%)	33 (8.6%)	10 (2.6%)	6 (1.6%)	8 (2.1%)	2 (0.5%)	3 (0.8%)	3 (0.8%)	32 (8.3%)	108 (28.1%)
12. London, south, Con	1,850	1 (0.1%)	112 (6.1%)	90 (4.9%)	66 (3.6%)	138 (7.5%)	0 (0.0%)	407 (22.0%)	12 (0.6%)	14 (0.8%)	8 (0.4%)	16 (0.9%)	4 (0.2%)	2 (0.1%)	56 (3.0%)	69 (3.7%)	15 (0.8%)	39 (2.1%)	0 (0.0%)	37 (2.0%)	13 (0.7%)	173 (9.4%)	636 (34.4%)
13. London, north, Lab	443	0 (0.0%)	15 (3.4%)	28 (6.3%)	16 (3.6%)	24 (5.4%)	0 (0.0%)	83 (18.7%)	5 (1.1%)	0 (0.0%)	1 (0.2%)	1 (0.2%)	2 (0.5%)	0 (0.0%)	8 (1.8%)	8 (1.8%)	5 (1.1%)	3 (0.7%)	0 (0.0%)	2 (0.5%)	2 (0.5%)	20 (4.5%)	111 (25.1%)
14. Metropolitan, WM, Lab	647	1 (0.2%)	20 (3.1%)	25 (3.9%)	23 (3.6%)	33 (5.1%)	0 (0.0%)	102 (15.8%)	1 (0.2%)	2 (0.3%)	4 (0.6%)	13 (2.0%)	4 (0.6%)	0 (0.0%)	24 (3.7%)	17 (2.6%)	21 (3.2%)	16 (2.5%)	5 (0.8%)	11 (1.7%)	13 (2.0%)	83 (12.8%)	209 (32.3%)

Table A.3 The three narratives in the corporate plans – extended version of Table 8.5 – *continued*

Council	Text Units	Right (%)	Access (%)	Inform (%)	Stand (%)	Target (%)	Con (%)	Sub (%)	Choice (%)	Indiv (%)	Pers (%)	R'pond (%)	Diverse (%)	Tail (%)	Sub (%)	Opp (%)	Eng (%)	Inv (%)	Emp (%)	Part (%)	Resp (%)	Sub (%)	Total
15. Metropolitan, YHNE, NOC	515	0 (0.0%)	14 (2.7%)	15 (2.9%)	13 (2.5%)	34 (6.6%)	0 (0.0%)	76 (14.8%)	6 (1.2%)	0 (0.0%)	0 (0.0%)	4 (0.8%)	11 (2.1%)	0 (0.0%)	21 (4.1%)	7 (1.4%)	5 (1.0%)	6 (1.2%)	0 (0.0%)	4 (0.8%)	2 (0.4%)	24 (4.7%)	121 (23.5%)
16. Unitary, NW, Lab	1,491	3 (0.2%)	17 (1.1%)	35 (2.3%)	17 (1.1%)	90 (6.0%)	1 (0.1%)	163 (10.9%)	11 (0.7%)	2 (0.1%)	0 (0.0%)	9 (0.6%)	1 (0.1%)	0 (0.0%)	23 (1.5%)	3 (0.2%)	19 (1.3%)	9 (0.6%)	0 (0.0%)	8 (0.5%)	12 (0.8%)	51 (3.4%)	237 (15.9%)
17. Unitary, YHNE, NOC	275	0 (0.0%)	5 (1.8%)	10 (3.6%)	16 (5.8%)	23 (8.4%)	0 (0.0%)	54 (19.6%)	3 (1.1%)	1 (0.4%)	1 (0.4%)	2 (0.7%)	7 (2.5%)	0 (0.0%)	14 (5.1%)	9 (3.3%)	2 (0.7%)	6 (2.2%)	1 (0.4%)	4 (1.5%)	1 (0.4%)	23 (8.4%)	91 (33.1%)
18. Unitary, SW, Con	121	0 (0.0%)	12 (9.9%)	8 (6.6%)	9 (7.4%)	9 (7.4%)	2 (1.7%)	40 (33.1%)	6 (5.0%)	3 (2.5%)	0 (0.0%)	1 (0.8%)	1 (0.8%)	0 (0.0%)	11 (9.1%)	14 (11.6%)	1 (0.8%)	4 (3.3%)	3 (2.5%)	2 (1.7%)	0 (0.0%)	24 (19.8%)	75 (62.0%)
Total	13,058	17 (0.1%)	380 (2.9%)	429 (3.3%)	323 (2.5%)	651 (5.0%)	5 (0.0%)	1,805 (13.8%)	79 (0.6%)	37 (0.3%)	17 (0.1%)	103 (0.8%)	88 (0.7%)	4 (0.0%)	328 (2.5%)	233 (1.8%)	140 (1.1%)	122 (0.9%)	16 (0.1%)	99 (0.8%)	139 (1.1%)	749 (5.7%)	2,882 (22.1%)

Percentages show keyword usage as a proportion of total text units, i.e. sentences, for each document.

Appendix 4 – Selection of Local Authority Case Studies

To select the councils for study a list of all English councils, appended with type, region and political control, was obtained from the Office of the Deputy Prime Minister. An analysis of this data was carried out to assess the relative proportions of these variables. First this was conducted by type of council, revealing the distribution shown in Table A.4.

To obtain a balance between council types, it was decided to conduct studies in eight district and borough councils (as these represent the majority of all English councils), three counties and three unitary authorities, and two each of the London and metropolitan councils. Within the district and borough councils, a balance was obtained between rural and urban authorities.

Table A.4   Councils in England by type

Council Type	Proportion
District/Borough	61%
County	9%
London Borough	9%
Metropolitan	9%
Unitary	12%

Table A.5   Councils in England by type and political control (February 2006)

Council Type	Political control			
	Conservative	Labour	Lib. Dem.	No overall control
District/Borough	51%	11%	9%	29%
County	70%	20%	8%	3%
London Borough	31%	50%	13%	6%
Metropolitan	19%	53%	11%	17%
Unitary	26%	33%	20%	22%

Source: Office of the Deputy Prime Minister.

It was also important to obtain a balance of political control, to ensure that not all councils in the sample were controlled by the same party. The breakdown of political control within each type of council is as shown in Table A.5.

The final sample drawn for study attempted to broadly reflect the proportions above, although with a sample of 18 exact patterns could not be replicated. The sample also took into account region, selecting councils from across the six regions of England used by the then Office of the Deputy Prime Minister. The 18 councils for inclusion in the study were selected at random using Excel to generate lists of councils according to the four variables: council type, political control, region and CPA score.

Bibliography

Aberbach, J. and Rockman, B. (2002) 'Conducting and Coding Elite Interviews', *PS*, December, 673–76.

Ackerman, B. and Fishkin, J. (2004) *Deliberation Day* (New Haven: Yale University Press).

Agasoster, B. (2001) 'A framework for analysing local party policy emphases in Scotland', in Laver, M. (ed.) *Estimating the Policy Positions of Political Actors* (London: Routledge) pp. 76–89.

Aldridge, A. (2003) *Consumption* (Cambridge: Polity Press).

Alexander, D. (2002a) House of Commons, *Hansard*, 3 July, Col. 388W.

Alvarez-Rosete, A. (2005) 'Effect of diverging policy across the NHS', *British Medical Journal*, 22 October.

Appleby, J. (2006) 'Not convinced that greater patient choice improves equity of access', *Financial Times*, 1 March.

Appleby, J. and Alvarez-Rosete, A. (2005) 'Public Responses to NHS Reform,' *British Social Attitudes, the 22nd Report* (London: National Centre for Social Research).

Appleby, J., Harrison, A. and Devlin, N. (2003) *What is the Real Cost of More Patient Choice* (London: Kings Fund).

Arendt, H. (1958) *The Human Condition – part II* (Chicago: University of Chicago Press).

Aristotle (1992) *The Politics*, translated – Sinclair, T.A.; revised and represented – Saunders, T.J. (London: Penguin).

Atkinson, Tony (2005) *Atkinson Review: Final Report*. London: Palgrave Macmillan. http://www.statistics.gov.uk/about/data/methodology/specific/PublicSector/Atkinson/downloads/Atkinson_Report_Full.pdf

Audit Commission (2004) *Choice in Public Services* (London: Audit Commission).

Axtmann, R. (1996) *Liberal Democracy into the Twenty-First Century: Globalization, Integration and the Nation-State* (Manchester, Manchester University Press).

Baldock, J. (2003) 'On being a Welfare Consumer in a Consumer Society', *Social Policy and Society*, Vol. 2, No. 1, 65–71.

Bara, J. (2005) 'With a Little Help from Our Friends: Comparing British and American Party Manifestos'. Paper presented to the American Political Science Association Annual Meeting, Washington, D.C.

Bara, J. and Budge, I. (2001) 'Party Policy and Ideology: Still New Labour?', *Britain Votes 2001* (Oxford: Oxford University Press).

Barber, B. (1984) *Strong Democracy* (Berkeley, CA: University of California).

Barry, A., Osborne, T. and Rose, N. (eds) (1996) *Foucault and Political Reason: Liberalism, Neo-Liberalism and Rationalities of Government* (London: UCL Press).

Barry, N. (1990) 'Markets, Citizenship and the Welfare State: Some Critical Reflections', in Plant R. and Barry, N. (eds) *Citizenship and Rights in Thatcher's Britain: Two Views* (London: Institute of Economic Affairs).

Baudrillard, J. (1988) *Selected Writings* – Poster, M. (ed.) (Cambridge: Polity Press).

Bauman, Z. (1988) *Freedom* (Milton Keynes: Open University Press).

Bauman, Z. (1998) *Work, Consumerism and the New Poor* (Buckingham: Open University Press).

Bauman, Z. (2001) (edited by Beilharz, P.) *The Bauman Reader* (Oxford: Blackwell).

Beck, U. (1992) *Risk Society: Towards a New Modernity* (London: Sage).

Becker, G.S. (1978) *The Economic Approach to Human Behaviour* (London: University of Chicago Press).

Beetham, D. (1996) 'Theorising Democracy', in King, D. and Stoker, G. (eds) *Rethinking Local Democracy* (Basingstoke: Macmillan), pp. 28–49.

Beiner, R. (1995) 'Why Citizenship Constitutes a Theoretical Problem in the Last Decade of the Twentieth Century' in Beiner, R. (ed.) *Theorizing Citizenship* (Albany: State University of New York Press), pp. 1–28.

Bell, D. (1978) *The Cultural Contradictions of Capitalism* (New York: Basic Books), Second edition.

Benn, T. (1970) *The New Politics: A Socialist Reconnaissance* (London: Fabian Society).

Bennett, F. (2002) 'The new tax credits', in Bennett, F., Ginn, J. Grieve Smith, J., Land, H., Madeley, R., Spicker, P., West, A. (eds) *Budget 2002: A Catalyst Response* (London: Catalyst Forum), pp. 30–37.

Benney, M. and Hughes, E.C. (1984) 'Of Sociology and the Interview', in Blumler, M. (ed.) *Sociological Research Methods: an Introduction* (Basingstoke: Macmillan).

Bentley, T. (2007) 'Learning to let go: The potential of a self-creating society', in Hassan, G. (ed.) *After Blair: Politics after the New Labour decade* (London: Lawrence and Wishart), pp. 94–106.

Berelson, B. (1952) *Content Analysis in Communication Research* (New York: Hafner Publishing Company).

Bevan, A. (1952) *In Place of Fear* (London: William Heinemann).

Bevir, M. (2005) *New Labour: A Critique* (London: Routledge).

Bevir, M. and O'Brien, D. (2003) 'From Idealism to Communitarianism: the Inheritance and Legacy of John Macmurray', *History of Political Thought*, Vol. 24, No. 2, 305–29.

Bevir, M. and Rhodes, R.A.W. (2003) *Interpreting British Governance* (London: Routledge).

Bevir, M. and Rhodes, R.A.W. (2004) 'Interpretation as Method, Explanation and Critique: A Reply'; 'The Interpretive Approach in Political Science: a Symposium', *British Journal of Politics and International Relations*, Vol. 6, No. 2, 156–61.

Bevir, M. and Rhodes, R. (2006) 'Interpretive Approaches to British Government and Politics', *British Politics*, Vol. 1, No. 1, 84–112.

Birch, R.C. (1974) *The Shaping of the Welfare State* (Harlow: Longman).

Blackmore, M. (1997) 'Complaints Within Constraints: A Critical Review and Analysis of the Citizen's Charter Complaints Task Force', *Public Policy and Administration*, Vol. 12, No. 3, 28–41.

Blair, T. (1995) Mais lecture, 22 May.

Blair, T. (1996) *New Britain: My Vision of a Young Country* (London: Fourth Estate).

Blair, T. (1999) Speech to the National Council of Voluntary Organisations Annual Conference, http://www.ncvo-vol.org.uk/press/speeches/index.asp?id=2481

Blair, T. (2002) *The Courage of Our Convictions: why reform of the public services is the route to social justice* (London: Fabian Society).

Blair, T. (2003) Speech to the Fabian Society, 17 June.

Blair, T. and Schröder, G. (1999) *The Way Forward for Europe's Social Democrats.* http://www.socialdemocrats.org/blairandschroeder6-8-99.html

Blyth, M. (1997) 'Moving the political middle: redefining the boundaries of state action', *Political Quarterly*, Vol. 68, 231–40.

Blunden, F. (2006) 'Choice needs to be carefully managed', *Financial Times*, 24 February.

Boaden, N., Goldsmith, M., Hampton, W. and Stringer, P. (1982) *Public Participation in Local Services* (Harlow: Longman).

Bourdieu, P. (1984) *Distinction: A Social Critique of the Judgement of Taste*, translated – R. Nice (London: Routledge and Kegan Paul).

Brenner, M. (1985) 'Intensive Interviewing', in Brenner, M., Brown, J. and Canter, D. (eds) *The Research Interview: Uses and Approaches* (London: Academic Press), pp. 147–62.

Brereton, M. and Temple, M. (1999) 'The New Public Service Ethos: An Ethical Environment for Governance', *Public Administration*, 77, 3, 455–74.

Brown, G. (2003) 'State and Market: Towards a Public Interest Test', *Political Quarterly*, Vol. 74, No. 3 – edited version of a speech delivered to the Social Market Foundation, Cass Business School, 3 February 2003.

Brown, Gordon (2006) Speech to the Fabian Society, 14 January, http://www.hm-treasury.gov.uk/newsroom_and_speeches/press/2006/press_03_06.cfm

Brudney, J.L. (1984) 'Local Coproduction of Services and the Analysis of Municipal Productivity', *Urban Affairs Quarterly*, Vol. 19, No. 4, 465–84.

Brudney. J.L. and England, R.E. (1983) 'Towards a Definition of the Coproduction Concept', *Public Administration Review*, Vol. 43, No. 1, 59–65.

Buchanan, J. *et al* (1978) *The Economics of Politics* (London: The Institute of Economic Affairs Readings; 18).

Budge, I., Klingemann, H., Volkens, A., Bara, J. and Tanenbaum, E. (eds) (2001) *Mapping Policy Preferences: Estimates for Parties, Electors and Governments 1945–1998* (Oxford: Oxford University Press).

Burns, D., Hambleton, R. and Hoggett, P. (1994) *The Politics of Decentralisation* (Basingstoke: Macmillan).

Butcher, T. (1997) 'The Citizen's Charter: creating a customer-oriented civil service', Barberis, P. (ed.) *The Civil Service in an Era of Change* (Aldershot: Dartmouth), pp. 54–68.

Butler, R. (1994) 'Reinventing Government: A Symposium', *Public Administration*, Vol. 72, No. 2, 263–70.

Cabinet Office (1991) *The Citizen's Charter: Raising the Standard*, Cmnd 1599 (London: HMSO).

Cabinet Office (1993) *Open Government*, Cmnd 2290 (London: HMSO).

Cairncross, L., Clapham, D. and Goodlad, R. (1997) *Housing Management, Consumers and Citizens* (London: Routledge).

Cairney, P. (2002) 'New Public Management and the Thatcher Healthcare Legacy: enough of the theory, what about the implementation?', *British Journal of Politics and International Relations*, Vol. 4, No. 3, 375–98.

Campbell, C. (1989) *The Romantic Ethic and the Spirit of Modern Consumerism* (Oxford: Blackwell).

Campbell, C. (2004) 'I Shop therefore I Know that I Am: The Metaphysical Basis of Modern Consumerism', in Ekström, Karin M. and Brembeck, Helene (eds) *Elusive Consumption* (New York: Berg), pp. 27–44.

Campbell, M. (2006) Speech to the Spring Conference of the Liberal Democrats, 5 March, http://www.libdems.org.uk/conference/speech-to-the-spring-conference-2006-by-sir-menzies-campbell-mp-leader-of-the-liberal-democrats-.html

Caney, S. (2001) 'International Distributive Justice', *Political Studies*, Vol. 49, No. 5, 974–97.

Carens, J. (1995) 'Aliens and Citizens: The Case for Open Borders', in Beiner, R. (ed.) *Theorizing Citizenship* (Albany: State University of New York Press), pp. 229–55.

Carter, Neil (1991) 'Learning to Measure Performance: the Use of Indicators in Organisations', *Public Administration*, Vol. 69, No. 1, 85–101.

Catalyst/Public World (2006) *Academy Schools: Case Unproven* (London: NASUWT).

Centre for Management and Policy Studies (CMPS) (2001) 'Engaging the Citizen', 6 March. Online. Available http: http://www.cpms.gov.uk/engaging.asp

Chandler, J. (1996) 'Citizens and Customer Care', in Chandler, J. (ed.) (1996) *The Citizen's Charter* (Aldershot: Dartmouth), pp. 40–54.

Christie, L. (1994) 'Viewpoint: Next Steps – A Union Critique', in Norman Flynn (ed.) *Public Finance Foundation Reader: Change in the Civil Service* (London: CIPFA), pp. 45–8.

Clarke, J. (1999) 'Coming to terms with culture', in H. Dean and R. Woods (eds) *Social Policy Review 11* (Luton: Social Policy Association).

Clarke, J. (2004) 'Dissolving the Public Realm? The Logics and Limits of Neo-Liberalism', *Journal of Social Policy*, Vol. 33, No. 1, 27–48.

Clarke, J. (2005) 'The people's choice? New Labour and public service reform', *Renewal*, Vol. 13, No. 4, 52–8.

Clarke, J. (forthcoming) 'Consumerism and the remaking of state-citizen relationships', in McDonald, C. and Marston, G. (eds) *Reframing Social Policy: A Governmental Approach* (London: Edward Elgar).

Clarke, J. and Newman, J. (1997) *The Managerial State* (London: Sage).

Clarke, J. and Newman, J. (2004) 'Governing in the modern world?', in R. Johnson and D.L. Steinberg (eds) *Labour's Passive Revolution* (London: Lawrence and Wishart), pp. 53–65.

Clarke, J., Cochrane, A. and Smart, C. (1987) *Ideologies of Welfare: from Dreams to Disillusion* (London: Hutchinson).

Clarke, J., Gerwirtz S. and McLaughlin, E. (2000) 'Reinventing the Welfare State', *New Managerialism, New Welfare* (London: the Open University Press in association with Sage Publications).

Coats, D. (2007) 'Hard Labour? The future of work and the role of public policy', in Hassan, G. (ed.) *After Blair: Politics after the New Labour Decade* (London: Lawrence and Wishart).

Cohen, J. and Rogers, J. (1995) 'Secondary Associations and Democratic Governance', in Cohen, J. and Rogers, J. (eds) *Associations and Democracy* (London: Verso).

Coleman, S. (1999) 'Cutting out the middle man: from virtual representation to direct deliberation', in Hague, B. and Loader, B. (eds) *Digital Democracy: Discourse and Decision-Making in the Information Age* (London: Routledge).

Communities and Local Government (CLG) (2006) *Strong and Prosperous Communities – The Local Government White Paper*, Cmnd 6939 (London: The Stationery Office).

Connelly, J. (1993) *Citizens, Charters and Consumers* (Southampton: Southampton Institute of Higher Education).

Conservative Party (1987) *The Next Moves Forward* – Election Manifesto, part 2 (London: Conservative Central Office).

Constant, B. (1988) 'The Liberty of the Ancients Compared with that of the Moderns', in Constant, B. *Political Writings* (Cambridge: Cambridge University Press).

Cooper, C. and Hawtin, M. (1997) 'Introduction', in Cooper, C. and Hawtin, M. (eds) *Resident Involvement in Community Action* (Coventry: Chartered Institute of Housing).

Coote, A. and Lenaghan, J. (1997) *Citizen's Juries: Theory into Practice* (London: IPPR).

Corrigan, P., Jones, T., Lloyd, J. and Young, J. (1988) 'Citizen Gains', *Marxism Today*, August, 18–21.

Corry, D. (1998) 'The Role of the Public Sector and Public Expenditure', in Franklin. J. (ed.) *Social Policy and Social Justice: the IPPR Reader* (Cambridge: Polity Press), pp. 73–101.

Cottam, H. and Leadbeater, C. (2004) *Health: Co-creating Services* (London: Design Council).

Cowell, A. (2006) 'Memo from Britain: Tory Introduces Himself to a Skeptical Lot: His Party', *New York Times*, 4 October.

Crouch, C. (2001) 'Citizenship and Markets in Recent British Education Policy', in Crouch, C., Eder, K., and Tambini, D. (eds) *Citizenship, Markets and the State* (Oxford: Oxford University Press), pp. 111–33.

Crouch, C. (2003) *Commercialisation or Citizenship: Education Policy and the Future of Public Services* (London: Fabian Society).

Crouch, C. (2007) 'New Labour and the problem of democracy', in Hassan, G. (ed.) *After Blair: Politics after the New Labour Decade* (London: Lawrence and Wishart).

Crouch, C., Eder, K. and Tambini, D. (2001) 'Introduction', in Crouch, C., Eder, K. and Tambini, D. (eds) *Citizenship, Markets and the State* (Oxford: Oxford University Press), pp. 1–19.

Crowther Hunt, N. and Kellner, P. (1980) *The Civil Servants: An Enquiry into Britain's Ruling Class* (London: Macdonald).

Crozier, M., Huntington, S. and Watanuki, J. (1975) *The Crisis of Democracy* (New York: New York University Press).

Cullum, Philip (2004) Speech to the Catalyst conference, 27 November.

Dagger, R. (1997) *Civic Virtues, Citizenship, and Republican Liberalism* (New York: Oxford University Press).

Daly, G., Mooney, G., Davis, H. and Poole, L. (2004) 'Whatever Happened to Stock Transfer? A Comparative Study of Birmingham and Glasgow councils' attempts to privatize their council housing stock', Paper for the Transforming

Social Housing Conference, Sheffield, April. http://www.york.ac.uk/inst/chp/hsa/spring04/papers.htm

Davies, J. (2001) *Partnerships and Regimes: the politics of urban regeneration in the UK* (Aldershot: Ashgate).

Davies, P. (2001) 'Spies as Informants: Triangulation and the Interpretation of Elite Interview Data in the Study of the Intelligence and Security Services', *Politics*, Vol. 21, No. 1, pp. 73–80.

Davies, W. (2006) 'Beyond communitarianism and consumerism', *Renewal*, Vol. 14, No. 1, 66–72.

Deakin, N. (1994) 'Accentuating the Apostrophe: the Citizen's Charter', *Policy Studies*, Vol. 15, No. 3, 48–58.

Dean, H. (1999) 'Citizenship', in Powell, M. (ed.) *New Labour, New Welfare State?* (Bristol: Policy Press), pp. 213–34.

Department of Education and Science (1986) *A New Choice of School* (London: DES).

Department for Education and Skills (DfES) (1997) *Excellence in Schools*, Cmnd, 3681 (London: HMSO).

Department for Education and Skills (DfES) (2001) *Schools Achieving Success*, Cmnd 5230 (London: HMSO).

Department for Education and Skills (DfES) (2003) *Future of Higher Education*, Cmnd 5735 (London: HMSO).

Department for Education and Skills (DfES) (2004) *A Five Year Strategy for Children and Learners* (London: DfES).

Department for Education and Skills (DfES) (2005) *Higher Standards; Better Schools for All*, Cmnd 6677 (London: HMSO).

Department of the Environment (1986) *Paying for Local Government*, Cmnd 9714 (London: HMSO).

Department of the Environment, Transport and the Regions (DETR) (1998) *Modern Local Government: In Touch with the People*, Cmnd 4014 (London: Stationery Office).

Department of the Environment, Transport and the Regions (DETR) (1998a) *A New Deal for Transport: Better for Everyone*, Cmnd 3950 (London: HMSO).

Department of the Environment, Transport and the Regions (DETR) (2000a) *Quality and Choice: A Decent Home for All* (London: DETR).

Department of the Environment Transport and the Regions (DETR) (2000a) *The Housing Green Paper: 'Quality and Choice: A Decent Home For All'* (London: HMSO).

Department of the Environment, Transport and the Regions (DETR) (2000b) *Ten Year Transport Plan* (London: DETR).

Department of Health (DoH) (1998a) *The New NHS: Modern and Dependable*, Cmnd 3809 (London: HMSO).

Department of Health (DoH) (1998b) *Modernising Social Services*, Cmnd 1469 (London: HMSO).

Department of Health (DoH) (1999) *Saving Lives: Our Healthier Nation*, Cmnd 1523 (London: HMSO).

Department of Health (DoH) (2000) *The NHS Plan: A Plan for Investment, A Plan for Reform*, Cmnd 4814-I (London: HMSO).

Department of Health (DoH) (2001) *Valuing People: A New Strategy for Learning Disability for the 21st Century*, Cmnd 5086 (London: The Stationery Office)

Department of Health (DoH) (2004a) *Choosing Health: Making Healthier Choices Easier*, Cmnd 6374 (London: HMSO).

Department of Health (DoH) (2004b) *The NHS Improvement Plan: Putting People at the Heart of Public Services*, Cmnd 6268 (London: the Department of Health).

Department of Health (DoH) (2005a) *Commissioning a Patient-Led NHS* (London: DoH), 28 July.

Department of Health (DoH) (2005b) *Independence, Well-being and Choice: Our Vision for the Future of Social Care for Adults in England*, Cmnd 6415 (London: HMSO).

Department of Social Security (DSS) (1998) *New Ambitions for Our Country: A New Contract for Welfare*, Cmnd 3805 (London: HMSO).

Department of Transport, Local Government and the Regions (DTLR) (2001) *Strong Local Leadership, Quality Public Services*, Cmnd 5327 (London: Stationery Office).

Department for Transport (2004) *The Future of Transport* (London: Department for Transport).

Department of Work and Pensions (DWP) (2005) *Opportunity and Security throughout Life* (London: DWP).

Dicey, A.V. (1962) *Lectures on the Relationship between Law and Public Opinion in England During the Nineteenth Century* (London, Macmillan). Second edition. Originally published 1914.

Donovan, N., Brown, J. and Bellulo, L. (2001) *Satisfaction with Public Services: A Discussion Paper* (London: Performance and Innovation Unit) http://www.strategy.gov.uk/ downloads/files/satisfaction.pdf

Dorey, P. (2005) (ed.) *Developments in British Public Policy* (London: Sage).

Dowding, K. (2004) 'Interpretation, Truth and Investigation: Comments on Bevir and Rhodes', *British Journal of Politics and International Relations*, Vol. 6, No. 2, 136–42.

Downs, A. (1985) *An Economic Theory of Democracy* (New York: Harpers and Row).

Driver, S. and Martell, L. (1998) *New Labour: Politics after Thatcherism* (Malden, Mass: Polity Press).

Durden, P. (2001) 'Housing Policy', in Savage, S.P. and Atkinson, R. (eds) *Public Policy under Blair* (Basingstoke: Palgrave), pp. 139–54.

Dwyer, P. (1998) 'Conditional citizens? Welfare rights and responsibilities in the late 1990s', *Critical Social Policy*, Vol. 18, No. 4, 493–518.

Economist (2004) 'Choosing to Choose', 7 April.

Eddington, R. (2006) The Eddington Transport Study (London: H.M. Treasury).

Elcock, H. (1996) 'What Price Citizenship? Public Management and the Citizen's Charter?', in Chandler, J. (ed.) *The Citizen's Charter* (Aldershot: Dartmouth), pp. 24–39.

Elkin, S. (1987) *City and Regime in the American Republic* (Chicago: University of Chicago Press).

Elster, J. (1997) 'The Market and the Forum: Three Varieties of Political Theory', in Goodin, R.E. and Pettit, P. (ed.) *Contemporary Political Philosophy: An Anthology* (Oxford: Blackwell), pp. 128–42.

Emmerson, C., Frayne, C. and Love, S. (2004) *A Survey of Public Spending in the UK* (London: Institute of Fiscal Studies), http://www.ifs.org.uk/bns/bn43.pdf

Erridge, Andrew (2003) 'Contracting for Public Services: competition and part-nership', in Bovaird, Tony and Elke Loffler (eds) *Public Management and Governance* (London: Routledge), 89–100.

Esping-Anderson, G. (1990) *The Three Worlds of Welfare Capitalism* (Cambridge: Polity Press).

Etzioni, A. (1994) *Guardian*, 24 July.

Etzioni, A. (2004) *The Post Affluent Society*, Review of Social Economy, Vol. 62, No. 3, 407–20.

Fairclough, N. (2000) *New Labour: New Language* (London: Routledge).

Faulks, K. (1998) *Citizenship in Modern Britain* (Edinburgh: Edinburgh University Press).

Ferlie, E., Ashburner, L., Fitzgerald, L. and Pettigrew, A. (1996) *The New Public Management in Action* (Oxford: Oxford University Press).

Finlayson, A. (2003a) *Making Sense of New Labour* (London: Lawrence and Wishart).

Finlayson, A. (2003b) 'Public choice theory – enemy of democracy', *Soundings*, Issue 24, 25–40.

Finlayson, A. (2004) 'Meaning and Politics: Assessing Bevir and Rhodes', in The Interpretive Approach in Political Science: a Symposium, *British Journal of Politics and International Relations*, Vol. 6, No. 2, 149–56.

Finlayson, A. (2007) 'Making Labour safe: globalisation and the aftermath of the social democratic retreat', in Hassan, G. (ed.) *After Blair: Politics after the New Labour Decade* (London: Lawrence and Wishart).

Fischer, F. (2003) *Reframing Public Policy: Discursive Politics and Deliberative Practices* (Oxford: Oxford University Press).

Fishkin, J. (1991) *Democracy and Deliberation* (New Haven: Yale University Press).

Fiske, J. (1989) *Understanding Popular Culture* (London: Unwin Hyman).

Flynn, N. (1997) *Public Sector Management* (London: Prentice Hall). Second edition.

Foucault, M. (1986) *The Foucault Reader* (London: Penguin).

Fraser, D. (2000) 'The Post-war Consensus: A Debate not Long Enough?', *Parliamentary Affairs*, Vol. 53, No. 2, 347–62.

Frazer, E. (1999) *The Problems of Communitarian Politics: Unity and Conflict* (Oxford: Oxford University Press).

Freeden, M. (1996) *Ideologies and Political Theory: A Conceptual Approach* (Oxford: Oxford University Press).

Freeden, M. (1999) 'The Ideology of New Labour', *Political Quarterly*, Vol. 70, No. 1, 42–51.

Frew, C. (2006) 'Direct Payments for Social Care: The management of power and risk'. Presented at the Association of American Geographers Annual Conference, Chicago, 10 March.

Friedman, M. (1962) *Capitalism and Freedom* (Chicago: University of Chicago Press).

Friedman, M. and Friedman, R. (1980) *Free to Choose: A Personal Statement* (Harmondsworth: Penguin).

Fry, G.K. (1979) *The Growth of Government: The Development of Ideas about the Role of the State and the Machinery and Functions of Government in Britain since 1780* (London: Frank Cass).

Fung, A. and Olin Wright, E. (2003) 'Thinking about Empowered Participatory Governance', in Fung, A. and Olin Wright, E. (eds) *Deepening Democracy: Institutional Innovations in Empowered Participatory Governance* (London: Verso), pp. 3–42.

Gabriel, Y. and Lang, T. (1995) *The Unmanageable Consumer* (London: Sage).

Gamble, A. (2007) 'New Labour and Old Debates', in G. Hassan (ed.) *After Blair: Politics After the New Labour Decade*, London: Lawrence and Wishart, pp. 26–36.

Gershon, Sir Peter (2004) *Releasing Resources to the Front Line: Independent Review of Public Sector Efficiency.* London: HMSO. http://www.hm-treasury.gov.uk/media/B2C/11/efficiency_review120704.pdf

Giddens, A. (1994) *Beyond Left and Right: the Future of Radical Politics* (Cambridge: Polity Press).

Giddens, A. (1991) *Modernity and Self-Identity: Self and Society in the Late Modern Age* (Cambridge: Polity).

Giddens, A. (1998) *The Third Way* (Cambridge: Polity Press).

Goldthorpe, J.H., Lockwood, D., Bechhofer, F. and Platt, J. (1969) *The Affluent Worker in the Class Structure* (Cambridge: Cambridge University Press).

Goss, S. (2005) 'The reform of public services reform', *Renewal*, Vol. 13, No. 2/3, 41–8.

Goss, S. (2007) 'Re-imagining the public realm', in Hassan, G. (ed.) *After Blair: Politics after the New Labour decade* (London: Lawrence and Wishart), pp. 107–19.

Gould, P. (1998) *The Unfinished Revolution* (London: Little Brown).

Gower Davies, J. (1974) *The Evangelistic Bureaucrat* (London: Tavistock).

Gray, A. and Jenkins, B. (1995) 'From Public Administration to Public Management: Reassessing a Revolution?', *Public Administration*, Vol. 73, No. 1, 75–99.

Gray, A. and Jenkins, B. with Flynn, A. and Rutherford, B. (1991) 'The management of change in Whitehall: the experience of the FMI', *Public Administration*, Vol. 69, No. 1, 41–60.

Greener, I. (2005) 'The Role of the Patient in Healthcare Reform: Customer, Consumer or Creator?', in Dawson, Sandra and Sausman, Charlotte (eds) *Future Health Organisations and Systems* (Basingstoke: Palgrave), pp. 227–45.

Greenleaf, W.H. (1983/2003) *The British Political Tradition: Vol 1 – The Rise of Collectivism* (London: Routledge).

Grieve Smith, J. (2002) 'Public finances and the macroeconomic picture', in Bennett, F., Ginn, J. Grieve Smith, J., Land, H., Madeley, R., Spicker, P., West, A. (eds) *Budget 2002: A Catalyst Response* (London: Catalyst Forum), pp. 7–13.

Griffiths, R. (1983) *NHS Management Inquiry: Report to the Secretary of State for Social Services* (London, Department of Health and Social Security).

Gyford, J. (1991) *Citizens, Consumers and Councils: Local Government and the Public* (London: Macmillan).

Habermas, J. (1994) 'Citizenship and National Identity', in Van Steenbergen, B. (ed.) *The Condition of Citizenship* (London: Sage) pp. 20–35.

Habermas, J. (1976) *Legitimation Crisis* (London: Heinemann).

Habermas, J. (1995) 'Citizenship and National Identity: Some Reflections on the Future of Europe', in Beiner, R. (ed.) *Theorizing Citizenship* (Albany: State University of New York Press), pp. 255–82.

Hall, S. (1979) 'The Great Moving Right Show', *Marxism Today*, January, 14–20.

Hall, S. (1988) *The Hard Road to Renewal: Thatcherism and the Crisis of the Left* (London: Verso).

Hall, S. (2003) 'New Labour's Double Shuffle', *Soundings*, Issue 24, 10–24.

Hall, S. and Jacques, M. (eds) (1989) *New Times* (London: Lawrence and Wishart).

Halpern, D., Bates, C., Beales, G. and Heathfield, A. (2004), *Personal Responsibility and Changing Behaviour* (London: Strategy Unit) http://www.pm.gov.uk/files/pdf/pr.pdf

Harding, A. (2000) 'Regime formation in Manchester and Edinburgh', in Stoker, Gerry (ed.) *The New Politics of British Local Governance* (Basingstoke: Macmillan), pp. 54–71.

Harms, J. and Kellner, D. (1998) 'Towards a Critical Theory of Advertising', *Illuminations*. Online. Available http: http://www.gseis.ucla.edu/faculty/kellner/Illumina%20Folder/kell6.htm

Harris, J. (1996) '"Contract" and "Citizenship"', in Marquand, D. and Seldon, A. (eds) *The Ideas that Shaped Post-War Britain* (London: Fontana) pp. 122–38.

Hart, J.T. (2006) *The Political Economy of Health Care: A Clinical Perspective* (London: the Policy Press).

Harvey, D. (1989) *The Condition of Postmodernity: An Enquiry into the Origins of Cultural Change* (Oxford: Basil Blackwell).

Hay, C. (1999) *The Political Economy of New Labour* (Manchester: Manchester University Press).

Hay, C. (2003) 'How to study the Labour Party: contextual, analytical and theoretical issues', in Callaghan, J., Fielding, S. and Ludlam, S. (eds) *Interpreting the Labour Party: Approaches to Labour politics and history* (Manchester: Manchester University Press), pp. 182–96.

Hay, C. (2004) 'Taking Ideas Seriously' in Explanatory Political Analysis, The Interpretive Approach in Political Science: a Symposium, *British Journal of Politics and International Relations*, Vol. 6, No. 2, 142–9.

Hayek, F. (1944) *The Road to Serfdom* (London: Routledge & Kegan Paul).

Heater, D. (1990) *Citizenship: The Civic Ideal in World History, Politics and Education* (Harlow: Longman).

Hencke, D. (2005) 'Public-private deal's £37m windfall profit', *The Guardian*, 10 February.

Hennessy, P. (1990) *Whitehall* (London: Fontana Press).

Hetherington, P. (2004) 'Bevan's Baby', *The Guardian*, 14 July.

Hewitt, P. (2005) Speech to NHS Confederation, 17 June.

Hill, M. (2005) *The Public Policy Process* (London: Pearson Longman).

Hills, J. (ed.) (1990) *The State of Welfare* (Oxford: Oxford University Press).

Hilton, M. (2003) *Consumerism in Twentieth-Century Britain: The Search for a Historical Movement* (Cambridge: Cambridge University Press).

Hindmoor, A. (2005) 'Public Policy: Targets and Choice', *Parliamentary Affairs*, Vol. 58, No. 2, 272–86.

Hirschman, A.O. (1970) *Exit, Voice and Loyalty* (Cambridge, Massachusetts: Harvard University Press).

Hirschman, A.O. (1982) *Shifting Involvements: Private Interest and Public Action* (Oxford: Basil Blackwell).

Hirst, P. (1994) *Associative Democracy: New Forms of Economic and Social Governance* (Cambridge: Polity Press).

HMSO (2002) *Homelessness Act 2002* (London: HMSO)

HM Treasury (1980) *The Government's Expenditure Plans 1980–81 to 1983–84*, Cmnd 7841 (London: HMSO)

HM Treasury (2003) *Public Services: Meeting the Productivity Challenge* (London: HMSO), April.

Hoare, S. (2002) 'Not good at sums', *The Guardian*, 26 November.

Home Office (1998) *Tackling Drugs to Build a Better Britain*, Cmnd 3945 (London: HMSO).

Home Office (2002) *Justice for All*, Cmnd 5563 (London: HMSO)

Home Office (2003) *Respect and Responsibility: Taking a Stand Against Anti-Social Behaviour*, Cmnd 5778 (London: HMSO).

Home Office (2004) *Building Communities, Beating Crime – A better policy service for the 21st Century*, Cmnd 6360 (London: HMSO).

Home Office (2006) *A Five Year Plan for Protecting the Public and Reducing Reoffending* (London: Home Office).

Hogg, S. and Hill, J. (1995) *Too Close to Call* (London: Little, Brown).

Hoggett, P. (1987) 'A Farewell to Mass Production? Decentralisation as an Emergent Private and Public Sector Paradigm', in Hoggett, P. and Hambleton, R. (eds) *Decentralisation and Democracy*, Occasional paper 28 (University of Bristol: School for Advanced Urban Studies).

Hoggett, P. (2001) 'Agency, Rationality and Social Policy', *Journal of Social Policy*, Vol. 30, No. 1, 37–56.

Hood, C. (1986) *Administrative Analysis* (Hemel Hempstead: Harvester Wheatsheaf).

Hood, C. (1991) 'A Public Management for All Seasons', *Public Administration*, Vol. 69, No. 1, 3–19.

Hood, C., Peters, G. and Wollmann, H. (1996) 'Sixteen Ways to Consumerise Public Services: Pick 'n' Mix or Painful Trade-Offs?', *Public Money and Management*, Oct–Dec, 44–50.

Horkheimer, M. and Adorno, T. (1973) *Dialectic of Enlightenment* (London: Allen Lane).

Hunt, T. (2004) *Building Jerusalem: The Rise and Fall of the Victorian City* (London: Weidenfeld and Nicholson).

Hupe, P. (1993) 'The politics of implementation: individual, organizational and political co-production in social services delivery', in Hill, M. (ed.) *New Agendas in the Study of the Policy Process* (London: Harvester Wheatsheaf), pp. 130–51.

Hutton, John (2005) 'Public Service Reform: the Key to Social Justice', Speech to the Social Market Foundation, 25 August, http://www.smf.co.uk/modules.php?op=modload&name=News&file=article&sid=105&mode=thread&order=0&thold=0

Ignatieff, M. (1995) 'The Myth of Citizenship' in Beiner, R. (ed.) *Theorizing Citizenship* (Albany: State University of New York Press), pp. 53–77.

Jeffrey, C. (2004) 'Devolution: What Difference has it Made?', Interim Findings of the Devolution and Constitutional Change Programme, March, http://www.devolution.ac.uk/pdfdata/Interim_Findings_04.pdf

Jenson, J. and Phillips, S. (2001) 'Redesigning the Canadian Citizenship Regime: Remaking the Institutions of Representation', in Crouch, C., Eder, K. and Tambini, D. (eds) *Citizenship, Markets and the State* (Oxford: Oxford University Press) pp. 69–89.

Jessop, B. (1994) 'Towards a post-Fordist welfare state', in Burrows, R. and Loader, B. (eds) *Towards a Post-Fordist Welfare State?* (London: Routledge), pp. 13–37.

Johnson, N. (2001) 'The Personal Social Services', in Stephen P. Savage and Rob Atkinson (eds) *Public Policy Under Blair* (Basingstoke: Palgrave), pp. 174–91.

Jones, B. and Batchelor, L (1993) *The Sustaining Hand: Community Leadership and Corporate Power* (Lawrence: University of Kansas Press).

Jordan, B. (1989) *The Common Good: Citizenship, Morality and Self-Interest* (Oxford: Blackwell).

Jordan, A. and Richardson, J. (1987) *Government and Pressure Groups in Britain* (Oxford: Clarendon Press).

Katz, D., Gutek, B., Kahn, R. and Barton, E. (1975) *Bureaucratic Encounters: A Pilot Study in the Evaluation of Government Services* (Ann Arbor, MI: Institution for Social Research, the University of Michigan).

Keating, M. (2005) 'Policy convergence and divergence in Scotland under devolution', in Adams, J. and Robinson, P. (eds) *Devolution in Practice: Public Policy Differentiation within the UK* (London: IPPR).

Kelly, J. (2003) 'The Audit Commission: Guiding, Steering and Regulating Local Government', *Public Administration*, Vol. 81, No. 3, 459–76.

Kemp, P. (1994) 'Can the Civil Service Adapt to Managing by Contract?', in Norman Flynn (ed.) *Public Finance Foundation Reader: Change in the Civil Service* (London: CIPFA), pp. 57–62.

Kilfoyle, P. (1997) House of Commons, *Hansard*, Col. 471, 25 November.

King, A. (1975) 'Overload: Problems of Governing in the 1970s', *Political Studies*, Vol. 23, 284–96.

King, D. (1987) *The New Right: Politics, Markets and Citizenship* (Basingstoke: Macmillan).

King, D. (1999) *In the Name of Liberalism: Illiberal Social Policy in the United States and Britain* (Oxford: Oxford University Press).

Kitzinger, J. (1994) 'The methodology of Focus Groups: the importance of interaction between research participants', *Sociology of Health and Illness*, Vol. 16, No. 1, 103–21.

Klein, R. (2001) *The New Politics of the NHS* (Harlow: Prentice Hall). Fourth edition.

Kymlicka, W. (2001) *Politics in the Vernacular: Nationalism, Multiculturalism and Citizenship* (Oxford: Oxford University Press).

Kymlicka, W. (2002) *Contemporary Political Philosophy: An Introduction* (Oxford: Oxford University Press).

Kymlicka, W. and Norman, W. (1995) 'Return of the Citizen: A Survey of Recent Work on Citizenship Theory', in Beiner, R. (ed.) *Theorizing Citizenship* (Albany: State University of New York Press), pp. 283–322.

Labour Party (1989) *Meet the Challenge, Make the Change* (London: Labour Party).

Labour Party (1992) *Citizen's Charter: Labour's better deal for consumers and citizens* (London: Labour Party).

Labour Party (1997) *New Labour: Because Britain Deserves Better* (London: Labour Party).

Labour Party (2005) *Britain: Forward not Back* (London: Labour Party).

Lawson, N. (2005) 'Choice must not define what it means to be modern', *Guardian*, 2 September.

Leadbeater, C. (1988) 'Power to the People', *Marxism Today*, October.

Leadbeater, C. (2004) *Personalisation through Participation* (London: Demos)

Le Grand, J. (2003) 'The Least Worst Way to Improve Public Services: The Case of Competition', *Renewal*, Vol. 11, No. 2, 29–33.

Le Grand, J. (2006a) 'The Blair Legacy? Choice and Competition in Public Services', Public Lecture, London School of Economics, 21 February.

Le Grand, J. (2006b) 'Why is Which? Helping critics of the less well-off?', *Financial Times*, 28 February.

Le Grand, J. and Bartlett, W. (1993) 'Introduction', in Le Grand, J. and Bartlett, W. (eds) *Quasi-Markets and Social Policy* (Basingstoke: Macmillan).

Lent, A. and Arend, N. (2004) *Making Choices: How can Choice Improve Local Public Services* (London: New Local Government Network).

Letwin, Oliver (2005) 'With Cameron we can win', *Daily Telegraph*, 3 July.

Levine, D. (1981) *Economic Theory Volume 2* (London: Routledge and Kegan Paul).

Levitas, R. (2000) 'Community, Utopia and New Labour', *Local Economy*, Vol. 15, No. 3, 188–97.

Levitas, R. (2005) *The Inclusive Society: Social Exclusion and New Labour* (Basingstoke: Palgrave), Second edition.

Lewis, N. (1993) 'The Citizen's Charter and Next Steps: A New Way of Governing?', *Political Quarterly*, Vol. 64, 316–26.

Lewis, N. and Birkinshaw, P. (1993) *When Citizens Complain* (Buckingham: Open University Press).

Leys, C. (2003) *Market-Driven Politics: Neoliberal Democracy and the Public Interest* (London: Verso).

Lipsky, M. (1980) *Street Level Bureaucracy* (London: Russell Sage).

Lister, R. (1990) *The Exclusive Society* (London: Child Poverty Action Group).

Lister, R. (2000) 'To RIO via the third way: Labour's "welfare" reform agenda', *Renewal*, Vol. 8, No. 4, 9–20.

Lister, R. (2002) 'Towards a new welfare settlement', in C. Hay (ed.) *British Politics Today* (Cambridge: Polity Press).

Lister, R. (2003) 'Investing in the Citizen-workers of the Future: Transformations in Citizenship and the State under New Labour', *Social Policy and Administration*, Vol. 37, No. 5, 427–43.

London Edinburgh Weekend Return Group (1979) *In and Against the State* (London: Pluto Press).

Loughlin, M. and Scott, C. (1997) 'The regulatory state', in Dunleavy, P., Gamble A., Holliday, I. and Peele, G. (eds) *Developments in British Politics 5* (Basingstoke: Macmillan).

Low, E. (2000) 'The Concept of Citizenship in Twentieth-Century Britain: Analysing Contexts of Development', in Catterall, P., Kaiser, W. and Walton-Jordan, U. (eds) *Reforming the Constitution: Debates in Twentieth-Century Britain* (London: Frank Cass) pp. 179–200.

Lowndes, V., Pratchett, L. and Stoker, G. (2001) 'Trends in Public Participation: Part 2 – Citizens' Perspectives', *Public Administration*, Vol. 79, No. 2, 445–55.

Ludlam, S. and Smith, M. (2004) (eds) *Governing as New Labour: Policy and Politics under Blair* (Basingstoke: Palgrave).

Lupton, D. (1995) *The Imperative of Health* (London: Sage).

Lusk, P. (1997) 'Tenants Choice and tenant management: who owns and who controls social housing?', in Cooper, C. and Hawtin, M. (eds) *Resident Involvement in Community Action* (Coventry: Chartered Institute of Housing), pp. 65–79.

Lyons, M. (2004) *Well Placed to Deliver? Shaping the Pattern of Government Service* (London: H.M. Treasury).

Macmurray, J. (1949) *Conditions of Freedom* (London: Faber and Faber).

Mandelson, P. and Liddle, R. (1996) *The Blair Revolution: Can New Labour Deliver?* (London: Faber and Faber).

Marcuse, H. (1964) *One Dimensional Man: studies in the ideology of advanced industrial society* (London: Routledge and Kegan Paul).

Marquand, D. (2004) *Decline of the Public* (Cambridge: Polity Press).

Marshall, T.H. (1992) 'Citizenship and Social Class', in Marshall, T.H. and Bottomore, T. *Citizenship and Social Class* (London: Pluto Press). Originally published in 1950.

Martin, B. (2001) *Privatisation of municipal services: Potential, limitations and challenges for the social partners*, International Labour Office Working Paper.

Mattinson, D. and Trayner, G. (2004) 'Public Trust: Delivery has to be seen to be believed', *Progress*, March/April, http://www.progressives.org.uk/magazine/Default.asp?action=magazine&articleid=630

McIvor, M. (2005) 'New Labour, neo-liberalism and social democracy', *Soundings*, Issue 31, 78–87.

Milburn, A. (2006) 'New Labour: A New Agenda for the Next Decade', *Progress Online: The Sovereignty Debates*, 14 September, http://progressonline.org.uk/Magazine/article.asp?a=1385

Miles, S. (1998) *Consumerism as a Way of Life* (London: Sage).

Miliband, E. (2005) 'Digging Labour up by the grass-roots', *Fabian Review*, Autumn, http://www.fabian-society.org.uk/documents/ViewADocument.asp?ID=113&CatID=52

Miliband, D. (2006) 'Putting people in control', Speech to the National Council of Voluntary Organisations, 21 February, http://www.labour.org.uk/index.php?id=news2005&ux_news%5Bid%5D=milibandncvo&cHash=3c0a11dcf0

Mill, J.S. (1963) 'Considerations on Representative Government', in *Collected Works*, Vol. 19 (London: Routledge and Kegan Paul) pp. 371–577.

Mill, J.S. (1966) *Representative Government* (Oxford: Oxford University Press).

Miller, D. (1995) 'Citizenship and Pluralism', *Political Studies*, Vol. 43, No. 3, 432–50.

Miller, D. (2000) *Citizenship and National Identity* (Oxford: Polity Press).

Miller, C. and Stirling, S. (2004) *Co-production in Children's Services* (London: Office of Public Management).

Morrell, K. (2006) 'Policy as Narrative: New Labour's Reform of the National Health Service', *Public Administration*, Vol. 84, No. 2, 367–85.

MORI (2001) 'Hanging in the balance: public support for the fire strike, http://www.morimrc.ie/mrr/2002/c021115.shtml

MORI (2002) 'Local Elections: Why no one gives a monkeys', http://www.mori.com/mrr/2002/c020503.shtml

MORI, 2004, 'Attitudes to Public Service Reform', 6 July.

MORI, 2006 'Improving Public Services, http://www.ipsos-mori.com/polls/trends/mdi-public-services.shtml

Morton, J. (1991) 'The 1890 Act and its aftermath – the era of the "model dwellings"', in Lowe, S. and Hughes, D. (eds) *A New Century of Social Housing* (Leicester: Leicester University Press) pp. 12–32.

Moss, G. and O'Loughlin, B. (2005) 'New Labour's Information Age Policy Programme: an Ideology Analysis', *Journal of Political Ideologies*, Vol. 10, No. 2, 165–83.

Mulgan, G. (1991) 'Power to the Public', *Marxism Today*, May, 14–19.

Murray, C. (1984) *Losing Ground: American Social Policy 1950–1980* (New York: Basic Books).

Murray, R. (1989) 'Fordism and Post-Fordism', in Hall, S. and Jacques, M. (eds) *New Times: The Changing Face of Politics in the 1990s* (London: Lawrence and Wishart), pp. 38–53.

Musgrave, R. (1959) *The Theory of Public Finance* (London: McGraw Hill).

Musgrave, R. and Musgrave, P. (1980) *Public Finance in Theory and Practice* (London: McGraw-Hill Kogakusha). Third edition.

National Consumer Council (NCC) (2003) 'Expectations of Public Services', http://www.ncc.org.uk/publicservices/consumer_concerns_2003.pdf

National Consumer Council (NCC) (2005) *A Playlist for Public Services*, http://www.ncc.org.uk/publicservices/playlist.pdf

National Consumer Council/Unison/Catalyst (2006) *Shared Solutions* (London: Unison).

Needham, C. (2003) *Citizen-Consumers: New Labour's Marketplace Democracy* (London: Catalyst).

Needham, C. (2004) 'Citizen-Consumers: the Government-Citizen Relationship in England, 1997–2003', Unpublished D.Phil thesis.

Needham, C. (2005) 'Brand Leaders: Clinton, Blair and the Limitations of the Permanent Campaign', *Political Studies*, Vol. 53, No. 2, 343–61.

Neuendorf, Kimberly, A. (2002) *The Content Analysis Handbook* (Thousand Oaks, Ca: Sage).

Newman, J. (2001) *Modernising Governance* (London: Sage).

Newman, J. (2006) 'A Politics of "the Public"', *Soundings*, Issue 32, 162–76.

Niskanen, W. (1971) *Bureaucracy and Representative Government* (Chicago: Aldine, Atherton).

Norris, P. (2001) 'New Labour and public opinion: the Third way as centrism', in S. White (ed.) *New Labour: The Progressive Future?* (Basingstoke: Palgrave, 2001).

Nozick, R. (1974) *Anarchy, State and Utopia* (Oxford: Basil Blackwell).

O'Connor, J. (1973) *The Fiscal Crisis of the State* (London: St James Press).

Office of the Deputy Prime Minister (ODPM) (2003) *National Procurement Strategy for Local Government* (London: ODPM). http://www.odpm.gov.uk/stellent/groups/odpm_localgov/documents/downloadable/odpm_locgov_024923.pdf

Office of the Deputy Prime Minister (ODPM) (2005) *Improving Delivery of Mainstream Services in Deprived Areas – the Role of Community Involvement*, Research Report 16 (London: ODPM).

Office of the Deputy Prime Minister (ODPM) (2005a) *Sustainable Communities: Homes for All* (London: ODPM).

Olson, M. (1971) *The Logic of Collective Action: Public Goods and the Theory of Groups* (Cambridge, Mass: Harvard University Press). Originally published 1965.

Orr, K. (2005) 'Interpreting Narratives of Local Government Change under the Conservatives and New Labour', *British Journal of Politics and International Relations*, Vol. 7, No. 3, 371–85.

Osborne, D. and Gaebler, T. (1992) *Reinventing Government: How the Entrepreneurial Spirit is Transforming the Public Sector* (New York: Plume).

Ostrom, V. (1989) *The Intellectual Crisis in American Public Administration* (London: University of Alabama Press). Second edition.

Ostrom, E. (1996) 'Crossing the Great Divide: Coproduction, Synergy, and Development', *World Development*, Vol. 24, No. 6, 1073–87.

Ostrom, V., Bish, R. and Ostrom, E. (1988) *Local Government in the Unites States* (San Francisco, California: Institute for Contemporary Studies).

Painter, C. (1999) 'Public Service Reform from Thatcher to Blair: A Third Way', *Parliamentary Affairs*, Vol. 52, No. 1, 94–112.

Panitch, L. and Leys, C. (2001) *The End of Parliamentary Socialism: From New Left to New Labour* (London: Verso). Second edition.

Parliamentary Ombudsman (2005) *Tax Credits: Putting Things Right* (London: The Stationery Office). http://www.ombudsman.org.uk/improving_services/special_reports/pca/taxcredits05/

Parks, R.B., Baker, P.C., Kiser, L., Oakerson, R., Ostrom, E., Ostrom, V., Percy, S.L., Vandivort, M.B., Whitaker, G.P. and Wilson, R. (1981) 'Consumers as Coproducers of Public Services: Some Economic and Institutional Considerations', *Policy Studies Journal*, Vol. 9, No. 7, 1001–11.

Parry, G. (1991) 'Conclusion: Paths to Citizenship', in Vogel, U. and Moran, M. (eds) *The Frontiers of Citizenship* (London: Macmillan) pp. 166–201.

Pattie, C. (2001) 'New Labour and the electorate', in Ludlam, S. and Smith, M. (eds) *New Labour in Government* (Basingstoke: Macmillan).

Percy, S.L. (1984) 'Citizen Participation in the Coproduction of Urban Services', *Urban Affairs Quarterly*, Vol. 19, No. 4, 431–46.

Peston, R. (2006) *Brown's Britain* (London: Short Books).

Peters, T. and Waterman, R. (1985) *In Search of Excellence: Lessons from America's Best-Run Companies* (London: HarperCollins). Originally published 1982.

Pirie, M. (2001) *Citizens and Consumers* (London: Adam Smith Institute). www.adamsmith.org.uk/cissues/citizens.htm

Plant, R. (2003) 'A Public Service Ethic and Political Accountability', *Parliamentary Affairs*, Vol. 56, No. 4, 560–79.

Pocock, J. (1995) 'The Ideal of Citizenship Since Classical Times', in Beiner, R. (ed.) *Theorizing Citizenship* (Albany: State University of New York Press) pp. 1–28.

Poister, Theodore, H. and Henry, Gary, T. (1994) 'Citizen Ratings of Public and Private Service Quality: A Comparative Perspective', *Public Administration Review*, Vol. 54, No. 2, 155–60.

Polanyi, K. (1957) *The Great Transformation: the political and economic origins of our time* (Beacon Hill, Boston: Beacon Press).

Pollitt, C. (1993) *Managerialism and the Public Services* (Oxford: Blackwell).

Pollitt, C. (1994) 'The Citizen's Charter: a preliminary analysis', *Public Money and Management*, Vol. 14, No. 2, 9–14.

Pollitt, C. (2003) *The Essential Public Manager* (Milton Keynes: Open University Press).

Pollock, A. (2002) *What's good about the NHS: and why it matters who provides the service* (London: Unison). http://www.keepournhspublic.com/pdf/whyweneed theNHS.pdf

Pollock, A., with Leys, C., Rowland, D. and Gnani, S. (2004), *NHS Plc* (London: Verso).

Potter, J. (1988) 'Consumerism and the Public Sector', *Public Administration*, Vol. 66, No. 2, 149–64.

Pottier, A. (2005) 'Delivering Efficiency in Local Services', presentation to the Association for Public Service Excellence conference 'Securing Efficiencies in Local Government Services', Huddersfield, UK, July.

Powell, M. (ed.) (1999) *New Labour, New Welfare State?* (Bristol: Policy Press).

Powell, M. (2000) 'Something old, something new, something borrowed, something blue: the jackdaw politics of New Labour', *Renewal*, Vol. 8, No. 4, 21–31.

Power, M. (1994) *The Audit Explosion* (London: Demos).

Prabhakar, R. (2004) 'New Labour and the Reform of Public Services', in Ludlam, S. and Smith, M.J. (eds) *Governing as New Labour: Policy and Politics under Blair*, Palgrave.

Pressman, J. and Wildavsky, A. (1973) *Implementation: how great expectations in Washington are dashed in Oakland* (Berkeley, Ca: University of California Press).

Prior, D., Stewart, J. and Walsh, K. (1995) *Citizenship: Rights, Community and Participation* (London: Pitman).

Public Administration Select Committee (PASC) (2000) *Innovations in Citizen Participation in Government*, Sixth Report, 2000–01. Minutes of Evidence, 12 April 2000.

Rawls, J. (1993) *Political Liberalism* (New York: Columbia University Press).

Ray, Leonard (2001) 'A natural sentences approach to the computer coding of party manifestos', in Laver, M. (ed.) *Estimating the Policy Positions of Political Actors* (London: Routledge) pp. 149–61.

Rees, A.M. (1996) 'T.H. Marshall and the Progress of Citizenship', in Bulmer, M. and Rees, A.M. (eds) *Citizenship Today: The Contemporary Relevance of T.H. Marshall* (London: University College, London Press), pp. 1–24.

Reid, J. (2005) 'Social Democratic Politics in an Age of Consumerism', Brough Lecture, Paisley University, 28 January.

Rhodes, R. (1987) 'Developing the public service orientation', *Local Government Studies*, May/June, 63–73.

Rhodes, R. (1994) 'The Hollowing out of the State', *Political Quarterly*, Vol. 65, No. 2, 138–55.

Rhodes, R. (1997) *Understanding Governance: Policy Networks, Governance, Reflexivity and Accountability* (Milton Keynes: Open University Press).

Ridley, N. (1988) *The Local Right: Enabling not Providing* (London: Centre for Policy Studies).

Robson, W. (1943) *Social Security* (London: Allen and Unwin).

Rose, N. (1999) *Powers of Freedom: Reframing Political Thought* (Cambridge: Cambridge University Press).

Rouse, J. and Smith, G. (1999) 'Accountability' in Powell, M. (ed.) *New Labour, New Welfare State?* (Bristol: Policy Press), pp. 235–56.

Rousseau, J. (1973) *The Social Contract* (London: Everyman).

Rowland, D., Price, D. and Pollock, A. (2004) 'Implications of the draft European Union services directive for health care', *The Lancet*, Vol. 364, No. 9441, 1 October.

Rustin, M. (2004) 'Is there a future for social democracy?', *Soundings*, Issue 28.

Sabatier, P.A. (1991) 'Two Decades of Implementation Research: From Control to Guidance and Learning', in Kaufmann, F-X. (ed.) *The Public Sector: Challenge for Coordination and Learning* (New York/Berlin: Walter de Gruyter), pp. 257–70.

Sachdev, S. (2004) *Paying the Cost? Public Private Partnerships and the Public Service Workforce* (London: Catalyst Forum).

Samuelson, P. (1954) 'The Pure Theory of Public Expenditure', *Review of Economics and Statistics*, Vol. 36, 387–9 – reproduced in Stiglitz, J. (ed.) (1966) *The Collected Scientific Papers of Paul A. Samuelson, Volume 2* (London: MIT Press).

Sandel, M. (1984) 'Morality and the Liberal Ideal', *New Republic*, 7 May, 15–17.

Savage, S. and Atkinson, R. (2001) (eds) *Public Policy under Blair* (Basingstoke: Palgrave).

Savas, E. (1987) *Privatization: the Key to Better Government* (Chatham, New Jersey: Chatham House).

Schumpeter, J. (1976) *Capitalism, Socialism and Democracy* (London: Allen and Unwin). Fifth edition. Originally published 1943.

Seldon, A. (1977) *Charge* (London: Temple Smith).

Seldon, A. and Kavanagh, D. (eds) (2005) *The Blair Effect, 2001–5* (Cambridge: Cambridge University Press).

Shaw, I. and Aldridge, A. (2003) 'Consumerism, Health and Social Order', *Social Policy and Society*, Vol. 2, No. 1, 35–43.

Silverman, D. (1998a) 'Analysing conversation', in Seale, C. (ed.) *Researching Society and Culture* (London: Sage) pp. 261–74.

Smith, A. (2006) 'Increase in tuition fees inevitable, university head warns', *Education Guardian*, 4 October.

Smith, M. (2004) 'Conclusion: Defining New Labour', in Ludlam, S. and Smith, M. (eds) *Governing as New Labour* (Basingstoke: Palgrave), pp. 211–25.

Smith, G. and Wales, C. (2000) 'Citizens' Juries and Deliberative Democracy', *Political Studies*, Vol. 48, No. 1, 51–65.

Spencer, H. (1969) *The Man versus the State* (Harmondsworth: Penguin 1969).

Steele, J. and Corrigan, P. (2001) *What Makes a Public Service Public?* (London: Public Management Foundation).

Stewart, J. (1994) 'The Rebuilding of Public Accountability', in Norman Flynn (ed.) *Public Finance Foundation Reader: Change in the Civil Service* (London: CIPFA), pp. 75–9.

Stewart, J. (1997) *More Innovations in Democratic Practice* (Birmingham: School of Public Policy).

Stewart, J. and Clarke, M. (1987) 'The Public Service Orientation: Issues and Dilemmas', *Public Administration*, Vol. 65, No. 2, 161–77.

Stewart, J., Kendall, E. and Coote, A. (1994) *Citizens' Juries* (London: Institute of Public Policy Research).

Stoker, G. (1988) *The Politics of Local Government* (Basingstoke: Macmillan).

Stoker, G. (1989) 'Creating a Local Government for a Post-Fordist Society: the Thatcherite Project?', in Stewart, J. and Stoker, G. (eds) *The Future of Local Government* (Basingstoke: Macmillan), pp. 141–70.

Stoker, G. (1995) 'Regime Theory and Urban Politics', in Judge, D., Stoker, G. and Wolman, H. (eds) *Theories of Urban Politics* (London: Sage), pp. 54–71.

Stoker, G. and Mossberger, K. (1994) 'Urban regime theory in comparative perspective', *Environment and Planning C: Government and Policy*, Vol. 12, 195–212.

Stone, C. (1989) *Regime Politics: Governing Atlanta, 1946–1988* (Lawrence, Kansas: University Press of Kansas).

Strategy Unit (2006) *Strategic Priorities for the UK: The Policy Review* (London: Cabinet Office), November.

Sullivan, H. (2001) 'Modernisation, Democratisation and Community Governance', *Local Government Studies*, Vol. 27, No. 3, 1–24.

Tawney, R.H. (1931) *Equality* (London: Allen and Unwin).

Taylor, C. (1986) 'Alternative Futures: Legitimacy, Identity and Alienation in Late Twentieth Century Canada', in Cairns, A. and Williams, C. (eds) *Constitutionalism, Citizenship and Society in Canada* (Toronto: University of Toronto Press).

Taylor, C. (1989) 'The Liberal-Communitarian Debate', in Rosenblum, N. (ed.) *Liberalism and the Moral Life* (Cambridge, Mass: Harvard University Press).

Taylor, I. (1999) 'Raising the Expectation Interest: New Labour and the Citizen's Charter', *Public Policy and Administration*, Vol. 14, No. 4, 197–206.

Taylor, M. (2001) 'High Noon for the Centre Left', round table discussion with Alibhai-Brown, Y., D. Ancona, M., Barnett, A. and Nairn, T., *Open Democracy*, May, http://www.opendemocracy.net/content/articles/PDF/343.pdf

Templeton, S-K. (2003) 'Health Minister Chisholm: NHS treats "patients" not "consumers"', *Sunday Herald*, 28 September.

Thatcher, M. (1995) *The Path to Power* (London: HarperCollins).

Thomson, P. (1994) in Flynn, N. (ed.), *Public Finance Foundation Reader: Change in the Civil Service* (London: CIPFA), pp. 33–40.

Titmuss, R. (1968) *Commitment to Welfare* (London: Allen and Unwin).

Tocqueville, A. (1994) *Democracy in America* (London: Everyman).

Toynbee, P. (2006) 'Labour has one serious candidate – but it also seems to have a death wish', *The Guardian*, 29 September.

Travers, T. and Esposito L. (2003) *The Decline and Fall of Local Democracy: A History of Local Government Finance*, London: Policy Exchange.

Travis, A. (2003) 'Public backs private – with no strings attached', *The Guardian*, 1 October.

Trentmann, F. (2004) 'Beyond Consumerism: New Historical Perspectives on Consumption', *Journal of Contemporary History*, Vol. 39, No. 3, 373–401.

Trentmann, F. (2006) 'The Modern Genealogy of the Consumer', in Brewer, J. and Trentmann, F. (eds) *Consuming Cultures, Global Perspectives: Historical Trajectories, Transnational Exchanges* (Oxford: Berg).

Turner, B. (1994) 'Postmodern Culture/Modern Citizens', in Van Steenbergen, B. (ed.) *The Condition of Citizenship* (London: Sage), pp. 153–68.

Tyson, S. (1994) 'Turning Civil Servants into Managers', in Norman Flynn (ed.) *Public Finance Foundation Reader: Change in the Civil Service* (London: CIPFA), pp. 63–8.

Ungerson, C. (2004) 'Whose Empowerment and Independence? A Cross-National Perspective on "Cash for Care" Schemes', *Ageing and Society*, Vol. 24, 189–212.

Unison (2006) *Positively Public: Survey Results*, http://www.unison.org.uk/acrobat/B2239.pdf

Van Gunsteren, H. (1994) 'Four Conceptions of Citizenship', in Van Steenbergen, B. (ed.) *The Condition of Citizenship* (London: Sage) pp. 36–48.

Van Steenbergen, B. (1994) 'The Condition of Citizenship: An Introduction', in Van Steenbergen, B. (ed.) *The Condition of Citizenship* (London: Sage).

Veblen, T. (1970) *The Theory of the Leisure Class* (London: Unwin). Originally published 1925.

Vine, J. (2005) Interview with David Cameron, *BBC Politics Show*, 13 March, http://news.bbc.co.uk/1/hi/programmes/politics_show/4331969.stm

Volkens, A. (2001) 'Manifesto research since 1979: From reliability to validity', in Laver, M. (ed.) *Estimating the Policy Positions of Political Actors* (London: Routledge) pp. 33–49.

Wainwright, H. (1981) 'Conclusion', in Rowbotham, S., Segal, L. and Wainwright, H. (eds) *Beyond the Fragments: Feminism and the Making of Socialism* (London: Merlin).

Wainwright, H. (1994) *Arguments for a New Left: Answering the Free-Market Right* (Oxford: Blackwell).

Waldegrave, W. (1993) *The Reality of Reform and Accountability in Today's Public Service* (London: Public Finance Foundation).

Waldegrave, W. (1994) 'The Reality of Reform and Accountability in Today's Public Service', in Norman Flynn (ed.) *Public Finance Foundation Reader: Change in the Civil Service* (London: CIPFA) pp. 81–8.

Walker, D. (2004) 'Surplus to Requirement', *Society Guardian*, 3 March.

Walsh, K. (1994) 'Marketing and Public Sector Management', *European Journal of Marketing*, Vol. 28, No. 3, 63–71.

Walshe, K. (2003) 'Foundation hospitals: a new direction for NHS reform?', *Journal of the Royal Society of Medicine*, Vol. 96, March, 106–10.

Walzer, M. (1989) 'Citizenship', in Ball, T., Farr, F. and Hanson, R. (eds) *Political Innovation and Conceptual Change* (Cambridge: Cambridge University Press) pp. 211–19.

Walzer, M. (1995) 'The Civil Society Argument', in Beiner, R. (ed.) *Theorizing Citizenship* (Albany: State University of New York Press) pp. 153–74.

Wanless, D. (2002) *Securing Our Future Health: Taking a Long-Term View: Final Report* (London: Department of Health).

Warde, A. (1994) 'Consumers, consumption and post-Fordism', in Burrows, R. and Loader, B. (eds) *Towards a Post-Fordist Welfare State?* (London: Routledge), pp. 223–38.

Waugh, P. (2003) 'Milburn and Clarke take on Brown over Reforms', *The Independent*, 12 January.

Webb, E.J., Campbell, D.T., Schwartz, R.D. and Sechrest, L. (1996) *Unobtrusive Measures: Nonreactive Research in the Social Sciences* (Chicago: Rand McNally).

Webb, S. and Webb, B. (1920) *A Constitution For the Socialist Commonwealth of Great Britain* (London: Longmans, Green and Co).

Weber, R. (1990) *Basic Content Analysis* (London: Sage).

Whitfield, D. (2006) *New Labour's Attack on Public Services* (Nottingham: Spokesman Books).

Whitty, G., Edwards, T. and Gerwitz, S. (1993) *Specialisation and Choice in Urban Education* (London: Routledge).

Wikström, S. (1996) 'The customer as co-producer', *European Journal of Marketing*, Vol. 30, No. 4, 6–19.

Wilkinson, S. (1998) 'Focus Groups in Feminist Research: Power, Interaction and the Co-Construction of Meaning', *Women's Studies International Forum*, Vol. 21, No. 1, 111–25.

Williams, R. (1988) *Keywords: a vocabulary of culture and society* (London: Fontana). Second edition.

Wintour, P. (2003) 'Ministers push Blairite agenda', *The Guardian*, 12 February.

Wright, T. (1990) *Citizens and Subjects* (London: Routledge).

Young, M. (1949) *Small Man: Big World: A Discussion of Socialist Democracy* (London: Labour Party).

Zuboff, S. and Maxmin, J. (2003) *The Support Economy: Why Corporations are Failing Individuals and the Next Episode of Capitalism* (London: Allen Lane).

Index